Dublin

Since 1922

Dublin
Since 1922

Tim Carey

HACHETTE
BOOKS
IRELAND

First published in 2016 by Hachette Books Ireland

A CIP catalogue record for this title is available from the British Library.

ISBN 978 1 47362 002 5

Book design and typesetting by Anú Design
Printed and bound in Germany by Mohn Media

Hachette Books Ireland's policy is to use papers that are natural, renewable and recyclable and made from wood grown in sustainable forests. The logging and manufacturing processes are expected to conform to the environmental regulations of the country of origin.

Hachette Books Ireland
8 Castlecourt Centre
Castleknock
Dublin 15, Ireland

A division of Hachette UK Ltd
Carmelite House, Victoria Embankment,
London EC4Y 0DZ
www.hachettebooksireland.ie

@tim_carey1
www.timcarey.ie

To Sinead, Jennifer and Aaron

Children gathering shells, Sandymount Strand, 1969.

Contents

1922

A Capital Once Again

[page 1]

1923–1929

Consolidation

[page 39]

1930–1939

Housing, the Church and Traffic

[page 75]

1940–1949

From War to Republic

[page 115]

1950–1963

A Conservative City with a Rebellious Streak

[page 151]

1964–1979

Lurching towards Modernity

[page 187]

1980–1993

A Time of Shadows and Light

[page 223]

1994–2008

Celtic Tiger Capital

[page 261]

Endnotes
[page 297]

Acknowledgements
[page 307]

Permissions Acknowledgements
[page 308]

1922

A Capital Once Again

Monday, 16 January 1922

A crowd assembles at Palace Street, off Dame Street, to watch history unfold.

At the end of this short street where the less than exalted premises of the Mercantile Permanent Building Society, the Sick and Indigent Room Keepers' Society and the Dublin branch of the United Kingdom's Temperance and General Life Office is situated, is a simple archway with a plain wrought iron gate. It is an underwhelming entrance to what has been the very seat of British rule in Ireland since the twelfth century.

With views blocked by centuries of accretions on the surrounding streets, the Castle is almost invisible to the city's passing life. But being out of sight has not meant being out of mind. Because the Castle's presence has permeated the city and extended to every town, village and country road. Most importantly, though, it has been to the forefront of the thoughts of anyone who had dared to plan, scheme or conspire to end the union between Ireland and Britain.

Until today.

Today there is no Union Jack on the flagstaff, and the entrance to the citadel is less fearsome than it has been of late. Its military guard has been removed, and to

Throughout the city there are signs of peace. Here, Auxiliaries bid farewell at Dublin Castle prior to their evacuation.

those who have gathered the bastion appears to be only defended by members of the unarmed Dublin Metropolitan Police (DMP) – though few are foolish enough to believe that should things get out of hand, sterner defences will not be readily available.

Immediately beyond the gate is the Castle's Lower Yard. Today, bar the remains of one of the Castle's medieval towers, it presents a genteel renaissance edifice. In short, the Castle bears almost no resemblance to a castle.

In the Lower Yard are the administrative offices of various government departments, Reformatory Schools, Public Works, Paymaster General, Chief Commissioner of the DMP. Beyond is the Upper Yard with the illustrious offices of what have been the leading figures of British rule since the Acts of Union. There are also the State Apartments and St Patrick's Hall, the centrepiece of what had been until recently the Castle's annual social season. With the start of European hostilities in 1914, the Castle's banquets and dances, with their attendant pomp and ceremony, were suspended as being inappropriate at a time of mass slaughter. When less conventional hostilities broke out in Ireland these occasions, so closely associated with British rule, were deemed inadvisable on security grounds.

Today is cold as steel, as grey as a military blanket. Above the Castle it appears to some as though flurries of snow have arrived with the arctic air. But instead of flakes settling on the ground they are flecks of ash thrown by fires burning behind the Castle walls – remnants of papers and files the departing administration do not want to bring with them, but that they do not want to leave in the hands of the country's new leaders either.

In advance of today's formalities, armoured cars, Crossley Tenders, charabancs and military lorries have been busy to-ing and fro-ing across Dublin. Barbed wire has been re-coiled onto wooden rolls and sandbags removed from in front of public buildings while Sinn Féin prisoners have been released from Mountjoy Prison, on the North Circular Road, to the cheers of tricolour-waving supporters. Because the War of Independence is over.

The evacuation of members of the hated Auxiliary Police – the paramilitary division of the Royal Irish Constabulary – is already underway.

On Friday the first 60 'Auxies' marched the mile from Beggars Bush Barracks on the south side of the city to Westland Row train station. Passing out of the barracks with rifles slung over shoulders they sang with gusto, 'We Are the Boys of the RIC'. When one called, 'Are we downhearted?' the emphatic reply of 'No!' echoed against the area's red-brick buildings.

As they crossed Mount Street Bridge, youngsters taunted them. 'Up the Rebels,' they shouted. But instead of menace came the good-natured retort of 'Up King George.' Then their mood became melancholic as they broke into a rendition of the

Great War music hall song 'Pack Up Your Troubles in Your Old Kit Bag, and Smile, Smile, Smile'.

Earlier this morning, the crowd that had gathered at the Castle's gate to get a glimpse of the end of British Rule; the beginnings of a new Irish State, was small – the Dame Street traffic passed by relatively unimpeded – but it has been growing. Some think their mood was curiously muted, almost placid. But for those who have witnessed events in the city in recent years, this is understandable: people can become inured to excitement, to history. But there is also something that might be gleaned from their expressions. Uncertainty. Because, though today might be one of celebration, the question on everyone's mind is: what is going to happen next? In the five weeks since the 'Anglo-Irish Treaty' was signed in London on 6 December, talk in the city has been all about dominion status, stepping stones, betrayal of the Republic, an oath to the king, partitioning of Ireland, freedom to achieve freedom. The Treaty was adopted on 7 January by Dáil Éireann in a lecture theatre in University College Dublin at Earlsfort Terrace by a vote of 64 to 57. But that, everyone knew, was not the end of the matter. Those who opposed the Treaty walked out behind their leader Éamon de Valera. When Michael Collins shouted 'Deserters all!' his denunciations were met with calls of 'Up the Republic!' and 'Oath-breakers and cowards!' No one is too sure about what is going to come from all that.

The day before yesterday the new 'Irish Free State Provisional Government' met at the Mansion House, the residence of Dublin's Lord Mayor. Once they ratified the Treaty, the country's new leaders had their photograph taken in the House's garden. 'It may become historic,' one of today's newspapers comments, as though there might be some doubt about the matter.

Instead of going straight to the Castle to demand entry and take the keys to power, the Provisional Government politely sent the Castle a copy of the minutes of their meeting and arrangements were put in place for what is billed as the transfer of power on Monday, 16 January.

Today.

Unimpeded by barriers, the crowd mills about on Palace Street. The cold and tedium is broken with mocking cheers for the periodic comings and goings of dispatch riders, tradesmen and messengers who are ushered through by police. Wider paths are cleared for cars, some of which are laden with boxes, furniture and provisions – the beginning of the exodus – with others containing the stiff figures of high-ranking Crown servants going about the serious business of withdrawing from a country.

As it approaches one o'clock, word gets round – probably circulated by one of the many journalists in attendance whose job it is to know these things – that the Lord

Michael Collins, marked with an 'X', leaves Dublin Castle after the symbolic meeting with Lord French.

Lieutenant, the physical embodiment of the union between Britain and Ireland, and members of the Provisional Government will arrive at 1.30 p.m.

Now there is serious activity.

The police move the crowd back to Dame Street.

Soon, volleys of cheers are heard as three motor cabs drive down Dame Street in the direction of the Castle. In them are Michael Collins and the seven other members of the Irish Provisional Government.

Though Arthur Griffith, Michael Hayes, William Cosgrave and Joseph McGrath were born in Dublin, none of them know it better than the Corkman Collins.

During the conflict this Corkman made the streets of Dublin his own: its geography was delineated by the location of the safe houses he used to escape the clutches of the crown's forces. It was in Dublin that his 'Squad' took on the Castle's network of spies and informers and won what many regard as the key battle of the War of Independence. Crucially, Collins turned the historic tables by infiltrating Dublin Castle with his own spies. This is an irony he must surely be savouring as the cabs turn off Dame Street, go down Palace Street and pass through the arch to the Upper Yard where officials crowd overlooking windows to watch the arrival of Ireland's new leaders.

Pursued by a posse of cameramen, the Provisional Government step from the cabs and enter Dublin Castle. A minute later – procedural etiquette to the very end – Lord French arrives.

The press is not admitted to the State Room for the occasion, but through the windows, Collins, recently the most wanted man in Ireland, is seen at the head of

6

the table with the Lord Lieutenant. The mood is relaxed. Collins is buoyant..

After half an hour the new government leaves, with Collins pushing some of his colleagues back into a cab so he can get away from the photographers as quickly as possible.

And that is it.

In the words of one journalist, after seven centuries of British rule, Dublin Castle 'was quietly handed over to eight gentlemen in three taxi-cabs'.

Dublin, once again, is a capital city.

❖ ❖ ❖ ❖ ❖ ❖ ❖ ❖ ❖ ❖ ❖

Friday, 20 January 1922

The exodus of the 47,000 British troops who have been stationed in Ireland begins.

Steamers of various lines are moored along the quays and special military trains are scheduled from the remaining garrison towns. The first train is from the Curragh and carries 200 soldiers and four officers of the Duke of Wellington regiment. With their ammunition, baggage, mules and equipment, they board the Slieve Gallion for Holyhead en route to Tidworth in Wiltshire.

For three nights, members of the Dublin Council of Unemployed have occupied the Rotunda, protesting at the high level of unemployment in the city. They claim there are 30,000 Dubliners out of work. They flew a red flag from a window and issued a manifesto asking 'Do the citizens of Dublin want highway robbery to be the order of the day?' However, their action has not been popular. On Friday night an angry crowd gathered outside and attacked the Rotunda. They were stopped, but a young man managed to climb up the building and remove the red flag. Tonight, Saturday, 21 January, another large, hostile crowd has gathered. Shortly before midnight, to avoid a confrontation, the unemployed leave under the protection of Volunteers and the DMP.

Meanwhile one of the most important and popular parts of Dublin's entertainment calendar, the traditional pantomime season, is coming to an end. Tonight in the Empire Theatre, almost directly opposite the gate of Dublin Castle on Dame Street, there is the last performance of *Babes in the Wood*, with 'New Songs! Jokes! Dances!', while the Queen's Theatre on Great Brunswick Street has *Jack and Jill* and the Gaiety, the Grand Dame of them all, has Aladdin – 'A Huge Success' – for two more weeks.

Although the evacuation is a sign of peace, the scenes along the Liffey are soon reminiscent of the days of the 1914 mobilisation, with the quays jammed with horses, men and instruments of war. Poignantly, at the same time that this activity takes place, a consignment of gravestones is loaded onto a steamer that will bring them to France to mark the final resting places of some of the tens of thousands of Irishmen recently killed on French soil.

When the Slieve Gallion loosens its moorings at 12.45 p.m. the only witnesses are bored railwaymen and dockers and newsreel cameramen – the soldiers' countenance briefly lifts for the cameramen, but when they stop filming, their cheers and smiles recede.

❖ ❖ ❖ ❖ ❖ ❖ ❖ ❖ ❖ ❖ ❖

Tuesday, 31 January 1922

In uniforms made by the Irish Co-operative Society, the first 46 members of the new National Army of Ireland assemble in the Phoenix Park. Their meeting point is the equestrian statue of Viscount Gough, former Commander-in-Chief of India, under the shadow of the oversized obelisk that is the Duke of Wellington monument – it is difficult to find a place in this city that has not some association with the British Empire.

Attired in dark green trousers, jackets and caps, polished leather boots and leggings, the soldiers brandish new rifles with gleaming bayonets. At the appointed time, they march behind a kilt band and parade down the quays. Passing the Royal Barracks, Tommies playing football on the green run to the railings to watch what for them, so used to military displays in the Empire, must seem a less than impressive procession. But on this day, size is in no proportion to symbolism.

All traffic stops for the new army. When they cross the river at Grattan's Bridge the streets are thronged. Members of the Provisional Government standing on the steps of City Hall, where they have set up their temporary offices, review the troops. When the soldiers turn 'eyes right' in salute there is a sudden outburst of cheering from the huge crowd.

The soldiers then continue on their way down Dame Street, Nassau Street, Merrion Square and Mount Street to Beggars Bush to hoist the Irish flag over what is now the headquarters of the new Irish Army.

Thursday, 2 February 1922

At 7 a.m. a 33-year-old small 'birdlike' woman with 'the energy of a thoroughbred racehorse' and a heart to match waits anxiously on a platform at Paris's Gare de Lyon train station for the arrival of the Dijon express. But she is not there to meet a person, she is waiting for a book. A book that is set in Dublin on a single day in 16 June 1904.

The woman is Sylvia Beach. Born in Baltimore, USA, in 1887, her father's vocation as a Presbyterian pastor brought her to Paris at the age of 14. While he ministered to the religious needs of American students, she explored and fell in love with the city. After three years, Pastor Beach was transferred to Princeton where his congregation included former president of the United States Grover Cleveland and future president Woodrow Wilson.

In 1917, Sylvia Beach came back to Paris with her sister, before working for a period as a Red Cross volunteer in Belgrade, distributing pyjamas and bath towels. She returned to Paris once again in 1919.

Beach then sought to fulfil her long-held ambition of owning a bookshop. Initially, she had thought of opening a French one in New York, but then decided to try an American one in Paris. On 19 November 1919, Beach's Shakespeare and Company, English Language Bookshop and Lending Library opened its doors on rue Dupuytren.

Shakespeare and Company quickly became the haunt of newly arrived Americans and the Paris literary community, including André Gide, Gertrude Stein and Ezra Pound. Life for Beach would no doubt have been more than satisfactory had it continued in this vein, but it took a remarkable turn in the summer of 1920 when she met a man whom she had worshipped. It was Dubliner James Joyce, whose book of short stories *Dubliners* and autobiographical work *Portrait of the Artist as a Young Man* recounting his youth in Dublin, made him famous in literary circles.

Joyce had come to Paris from Trieste where he had lived since 1904 to write the final chapters of a novel he had been working on for seven years – lately he had been devoting up to 17 hours a day to it and estimated that he

Bookshop owner Sylvia Beach and writer James Joyce in Paris where she has just published his novel set in Dublin on 16 June 1904: *Ulysses*.

had spent 20,000 hours labouring towards its completion. It had come to the stage where he could think of little else and wished to be free of it – 'I am very tired of it and so is everybody else,' he wrote in one letter – and longed to sleep for six months, to read any book that was not his own. But still he obsessed and wrote to people in Dublin asking them to check small details for him. Was it possible for a person of average physique to climb over the railings of an Eccles Street house and lower himself to two or three feet from the ground? Was it true that the Grand Canal near Clanbrassil Street had frozen over in 1893?

When they met, Beach's first words to the writer were of undisguised admiration: 'Is this the great James Joyce?' She shook his limp, almost boneless hand and looked into his deep blue eyes in which she saw 'a light of genius'. When Joyce spoke, his voice was 'pitched like a tenor's'. She thought he could have passed for an English gentleman except for his pronunciations of certain words which betrayed his city of birth and upbringing.

After joining her lending library, Joyce became a regular at Shakespeare and Company (which had since moved a short distance to rue de l'Odéon). One day when in the shop, he told the American about the difficulties he was having getting his book published. He feared he would never see it printed. Given the circumstances, his concerns were quite reasonable.

After five chapters had appeared in instalments in an English magazine, *The Egoist*, it was pulled when some subscribers complained about its sordid contents. Serialisation in America was cut short by legal proceedings. The most eagerly awaited literary novel of the twentieth century was in danger of never making it between covers.

Hearing about the almost insurmountable difficulties, Beach, without hesitation, asked the writer if he would let Shakespeare and Company publish his book. Joyce accepted immediately. In a moment the bookseller became a publisher.

It is a responsibility she has taken very seriously. And it is why she is here at the Gare de Lyon waiting on the Dijon train.

Beach has engaged a Dijon printer named Darantier to supply 1,000 copies – 100 of which would be on Holland handmade paper and signed by the author which will sell for the ridiculously high price of 350 francs. The book is being sold by private subscription and advance sales are, thankfully, healthy – such is its appeal to the world's literary community that the most convenient way she has found to organise the subscriptions received so far is by country of origin.

If Joyce's life has been taken over by his book, so too has the American's. She has matched the author's efforts and supported him financially to the point of endangering the very survival of her bookshop. Darantier too has not been found wanting. Apart from the unforeseen difficulty of sourcing the exact shade of blue required for the cover – that of the Greek flag – Joyce has made countless late changes to the text. Now, finally, Beach and Darantier have done everything possible to ensure that the first copy arrives in Paris today. Because today is James Joyce's birthday and the author, who has waited so long, wants his book published on 2 February.

Last night Darantier gave a parcel to the train's guard for delivery to a woman who will be at the platform in Paris.

With her heart 'going like the locomotive', the train from Dijon comes slowly to a halt. When she sees 'the conductor getting off, holding a parcel and looking around for someone' she identifies herself, takes the books, gets into a cab and delivers to James Joyce his own copy of *Ulysses*.

It is clear to all in the literary world that *Ulysses* will reinvent the novel. But the book set in Dublin on the day he met his wife in Finn's Hotel, Lincoln Place goes largely un-remarked upon in his native city. Indeed, if one scours the papers of the city in which the book is set, the city of the author's birth, one would not find a mention that *Ulysses* has even been published.

❖ ❖ ❖ ❖ ❖ ❖ ❖ ❖ ❖ ❖ ❖

Sunday, 12 February 1922

O'Connell Street is the scene of numerous political demonstrations. Such is their frequency, that the tram company and shops on the city's main street complain about the disruption to commerce. Rosamund Jacob, a novelist who moved to Dublin from Waterford in 1920, writes in her diary about an anti-Treaty demonstration she attended on O'Connell Street earlier in the day:

> I made my way to the heart of the biggest crowd at the Parnell monument platform and heard de Valera, Mrs Pearse and Count Plunkett there. The latter was bad, Mrs P middling – not very audible of course, de Valera much as usual. He had a good reception, but there wasn't much enthusiasm after that. Tremendously in earnest and good in spots, but not very exhilarating. I wormed my way out after half an hour or so and got down to the next platform, and there was Madame de M[arkievicz] roaring away, and a fearful squash going on the side walk, some men apparently out to kill. When Madame was over a little blonde [sic] thing

In advance of the national holiday, the first of the city's red pillar letter boxes is painted green on Tuesday, 14 March. It is on Dame Street, opposite the Lower Yard of Dublin Castle.

The first national festival in an independent Ireland is being celebrated in spring-like weather. While the religious aspect of St Patrick's Day is observed in its usual fervour, the day is also marked by the revival of the Irish language in church sermons, prayers and hymns – Irish Language Fund collectors are doing great business – and by children wearing national costumes.

like a young German began to make the best speech I had yet heard – and it was [Liam] Mellows. He talked plain, restrained, forcible stuff about the necessity above all of honesty and sincerity in politics – meaning what you say and saying what you mean, not swearing you'll only take a republic one year and climbing down the next – better than that but can't remember it.

❖ ❖ ❖ ❖ ❖ ❖ ❖ ❖ ❖ ❖ ❖

Wednesday, 22 March 1922

As the capital of Ireland, Dublin is, by definition, the seat of government. But at the moment there are two bodies that are claiming to be the legitimate government of the country.

The Dáil, which has both pro- and anti-Treaty members and which meets in the National University lecture theatre at Earlsfort Terrace, has no power. The Provisional Government, made up of pro-Treaty members of the Dáil under the chairmanship of Michael Collins, is based a few hundred yards away in the magnificent new Government Buildings at Merrion Street. In theory it is subordinate to the Dáil but that is not the way things are working in practice. The Provisional Government is taking on the mantle of real authority.

But in Dublin, for the moment at any rate, the military situation is clearer than in other parts. Whereas outside the capital, barracks being vacated by the British are divided between pro- and anti-Treaty forces, in Dublin the situation is more straightforward. All the barracks that the British have left are in government hands.

Friday, 14 April 1922

Tonight the military situation in Dublin is about to become much more complicated as a group of armed men with a renewed sense of purpose, who are intent on an objective and who are fed up with a policy they refer to as 'drift', walk down a footpath on the north side of the River Liffey and approach the Four Courts. An architectural masterpiece built in the last decades of the eighteenth century, it is the centre of the country's judicial system and, since the destruction of the GPO in 1916 by British shelling and the burning of the Custom House by Irish Volunteers during the War of Independence, easily the finest intact building in the city. With its huge dome set in relief against the night sky, some of the men give others a bunt up over the railings. Shortly afterwards the police guard are sent on their way and the Four Courts is entirely in the hands of Republicans opposed to the Treaty.

A little later cars and motor lorries arrive with a woefully inadequate supply of sandbags and barbed wire to barricade the buildings. To fortify the scores of windows, various legal tomes are pressed into service against the state.

Following a busy night, Ernie O'Malley, the Four Courts garrison's Director of Organisation, sits down on a roof and watches the light of the rising sun glint off the Liffey, illuminate the cathedrals of Christchurch and St Patrick and reach down into the mysterious workings of the Guinness Brewery.

Now, in addition to the two competing governments, there are three armed groups in the city: what remains of the British garrison, the National Army, and these republicans in the Four Courts.

❖ ❖ ❖ ❖ ❖ ❖ ❖ ❖ ❖ ❖

Monday, 24 April 1922

The city has come to a standstill. There are no postal services, telephones or public transport. All shops, restaurants, theatres, picture houses, banks and pubs are closed and the stock exchange, even the city's golf courses, are deserted to show people's opposition to the growth of militarism in the metropolis. Because since the taking of the Four Courts, a person has hardly been able to walk down a street without having to be wary of military cars carrying men with guns at the ready or being held up and searched for weapons. City nights are now punctuated with the crackle of gunfire and the explosion of bombs.

Although organised by the Labour Party and the Trade Union Congress, all classes are taking part in the strike. They want the men at Beggars Bush Barracks and the Four Courts to declare that they will not take up arms against each other. But at the end of the 15-hour strike, few are confident that this show of public concern has had any effect whatsoever.

❖ ❖ ❖ ❖ ❖ ❖ ❖ ❖ ❖ ❖

Saturday, 29 April 1922

A conference called by Archbishop Byrne and the Lord Mayor takes place in the Mansion House with a vague but laudable objective: 'That something should be done in the way of peace'. Michael Collins and Arthur Griffith, Éamon de Valera and Cathal Brugha as well as three labour representatives discuss the political situation. But after three hours, the conference breaks up without agreement. Things are now even worse than before, because a little bit of hope has been extinguished.

❖ ❖ ❖ ❖ ❖ ❖ ❖ ❖ ❖ ❖

Monday, 22 May 1922

At last! After a number of failed efforts, there appears to be a formula for peace. At the Sinn Féin Árd Fheis a 'Conciliation Committee' reaches a compromise between the pro- and anti-Treaty sides. An election pact is agreed between Collins and de Valera. Under this pact, a coalition of all sitting Sinn Féin TDs' names will go on the ballot paper in the upcoming general election against an opposition of independents, Labour and the Farmers' Party.

The Dublin hurling team defeats Cork in the 1920 All-Ireland final at Croke Park on Sunday, 14 May – the match was supposed to have taken place in August 1920 but had to be postponed because of the military situation. It is Dublin's third hurling All-Ireland victory. However, none of the players who represent the capital were born in it, but had come from the country and made Dublin their home.

Friday, 16 June 1922

Today is election day. According to the agreement that was reached, the election is not supposed to be about passing judgment on the Treaty. However, it is not working out that way.

The Coalition candidates are identified on the ballot paper according to their position on the Treaty – pro-Treaty candidates are listed as 'Coalition Treaty', those opposed 'Coalition Republican'. More than six months after the Treaty was signed, the people are given their first chance to demonstrate what they think of it and they are going to take it.

In addition, yesterday Michael Collins, in a speech he made in Cork, broke the pact by calling on people to vote for whoever they wanted. Many of today's newspapers advise the same thing.

There are 210,000 people eligible to vote in Dublin. By the end of a remarkably peaceful day – the only disturbance takes place when Republicans break into the counting station at Trinity College but quickly withdraw – almost 65 per cent of the electorate have voted.

Dublin is a disaster for the republicans and a resounding victory for the government. While nationally, 78 per cent vote for pro-Treaty candidates, in Dublin the figure is 88 per cent.

Today is not only election day. Because 16 June is also the anniversary of the day on which Joyce set *Ulysses*, of which there is still no mention in Dublin's press. But the small number of Dubliners who subscribed and received their copies may read the book, in homage, on this day. Some may even decide to visit places that are featured.

❖ ❖ ❖ ❖ ❖ ❖ ❖ ❖ ❖ ❖ ❖

Monday, 26 June 1922

More than two months after the occupation of the Four Courts and ten days after the election, National Army soldiers from Beggars Bush take up covering positions while an armoured car trains its machine gun on the entrance to Harry Ferguson's car dealership on Lower Baggot Street. Inside, members of the Four Courts garrison, under Commandant Leo Henderson, are commandeering 15 cars to send to Ulster to support the IRA there. Until now, such activities have been overlooked by the

National Army troops arrive at a Baggot Street car dealership where Republican troops have been trying to commandeer cars. Calm is restored when all are released except for Commandant Leo Henderson, who is brought to Mountjoy Prison.

Provisional Government, because it was for the North and the two sides had agreed objectives there. But things have changed.

And it is not only due to the outcome of the election.

Last Thursday, Sir Henry Wilson, one of the highest ranking British officers during the Great War and, until recently, security advisor to the Northern Irish government, was assassinated in London. The British government believe that men in the Four Courts ordered his killing, though this is far from certain and they flatly deny any involvement. The immediate reaction of British Prime Minister Lloyd George was to ask General Macready, commander of the British forces in Ireland, to prepare to attack the Four Courts. But yesterday the order was rescinded, to Macready's great relief (he thought of no better way of uniting the Irish factions than for the British to get involved). Instead Lloyd George wrote to Michael Collins demanding that the Provisional Government take action or he would regard the Treaty as having been violated.

So today, it looks as if there will be confrontation at the Baggot Street car dealership. However, when all the Republicans are let go, except for Commandant Henderson who is detained and brought to Mountjoy Prison, calm is restored.

But only for a time.

The Four Courts Republicans are incensed at Henderson's arrest and are bent on retaliation.

A few hours later, they abduct a senior member of the National Army, General

'Ginger' O'Connell, at Leeson Street Bridge while he walks his fiancée home from the theatre. When he is brought to the Four Courts, Ernie O'Malley telephones Portobello Barracks and asks to speak to National Army Chief of Staff, Eoin O'Duffy.

After a delay O'Duffy comes on the line. 'Hello.'

'Hello, this is O'Malley, Director of Organisation, speaking.'

'Hello, Mr O'Malley. What do you want?'

'I have to tell you that Mr O'Connell, your Assistant Chief, is now in custody.'

'What?'

O'Malley repeats the information before continuing, 'He will be released in exchange for Commandant-General Henderson whom you have now in prison.'

'Is that all?'

'Yes, Mr O'Duffy. Goodnight.'

'Goodnight, Mr O'Malley.'

The two then hang up.

❖ ❖ ❖ ❖ ❖ ❖ ❖ ❖ ❖ ❖ ❖

Tuesday, 27 June 1922

The Provisional Government decides that the armed group in the Four Courts will no longer be tolerated.

At 3 p.m., two columns of troops, two armed cars and a number of armour-plated lorries leave Beggars Bush Barracks. By evening, troops in battle dress patrol the streets, stop people, carry out searches. Hundreds of soldiers surround the Four Courts.

Inside the judicial buildings, 180 Republicans dig trenches, barricade doors, clean weapons. Members of Cumann na mBan, the women's Republican organisation, set up a field hospital in anticipation of casualties. The men in the Four Courts know they are in a trap.

❖ ❖ ❖ ❖ ❖ ❖ ❖ ❖ ❖ ❖ ❖

Wednesday, 28 June 1922

At 3.40 a.m., a National Army soldier approaches the Four Courts' main gate and hands in a note. It is an ultimatum demanding that the garrison leave and give up their weapons.

There is no reply.

At 4.10 a.m., soldiers of the National Army open fire with rifles. Shortly afterwards, the city is woken by the booms and reverberations of two shells exploding against the eighteenth-century walls. To one observer it seems that Hell had been 'let loose in a city in which an hour before the only sound was that of pattering raindrops'.

The British have loaned two 18-pound field guns and supplied ten shells for each.

For the next few hours, there is intermittent shelling, machine gun and rifle fire. At 8 a.m. it dies down. An hour later, sporadic firing resumes, though nothing decisive. At 2.30 p.m., two shells smash into the front of the Four Courts sending a huge cloud of dust and smoke across the river, briefly obscuring the view of onlookers who have assembled downstream.

The Four Courts is not the only building under attack. A building on Parnell Square, also occupied by Republicans, is under fire. Having been pummelled by an armoured car and grenades, the Rebels soon leave, torching the building as they go.

From 11 a.m., firing breaks out in various parts of the city as Republican snipers try to divert attention away from the Four Courts and impede the movement of government troops. There is almost continuous firing on Aungier, Wexford, Camden and Clanbrassil Streets which are on the main route into town from Portobello Barracks. Other areas of conflict include O'Connell Street, Capel Street, Dominick Street, Parnell Square, Gardiner Place, North Great George's Street, High Street, Smithfield and St Stephen's Green.

By the afternoon, the city is closed down, the streets almost deserted. Republicans have taken over Barry's, Moran's and Hughes' Hotels on Gardiner Street but government troops' attention is still concentrated at the Four Courts.

At the Four Courts it is apparent that the two pieces of artillery and the minimal ration of shells will be insufficient. The government hoped that the mere fact of

National Army troops fire on the Four Courts Republican garrison with artillery supplied by the British.

People crowd along the quay walls to watch the fighting at the Four Courts. It is an entertaining but dangerous pastime.

shelling would lead to an early surrender, but the Republican troops show no signs of considering that course of action.

Emmet Dalton, National Army Director of Military Operations, goes to General Macready to ask for more ammunition and field guns. Initially, Macready is reluctant to help. For one thing, he is far from confident that the Irish government will not suddenly join forces with the Four Courts men and attack the remaining British garrison with any ammunition he might supply. In addition, he cannot understand why Dalton will not just order his men to storm the buildings. After all, he commands more than enough troops to bring the whole matter to a speedy conclusion. But Dalton explains that his men won't put their lives at unnecessary risk; they prefer to shell from a safe distance rather than fight at close quarters. He even fears that if they don't get more firepower, his soldiers will walk away. In the end Macready relents, but gives over only shrapnel shells – without high explosives these will make little impression on the structure, but will allow the semblance of a barrage to be kept up.

As the first day of fighting comes to an end, architect James Gandon's masterpiece is badly pockmarked from shelling and rifle and machine gun fire, but structurally sound. The Republicans issue a defiant statement: 'All well at the Four Courts. The efforts to make British subjects out of Irish Republicans by force of arms continues to fail.'

It is now apparent that this is the start of a civil war that will be fought out between two military groups. Because there is no rallying to either cause by Dubliners. No mobs roam the streets. Whoever their sympathies may lie with, and the vast majority are with the government, they do not join the fighting. People are either staying close to home waiting for it to end or enjoying the spectacle of war as if they are patrons at an open-air theatre. But just because they have not joined in the affray does not mean they do not suffer casualties. Sadly, far from it.

Ten people, who had started today with no wish to fight or die for Ireland, Republic or otherwise, are now lying cold in the city morgues. The first civilian fatality was Mary Kelly, Chancery Place, who died of shock shortly after the Four Courts shelling began. The first direct military casualty was James Hurley of 35 Chancery Lane, shot while passing a Republican ambush at 9.15 a.m. near O'Connell Street. Others among the deceased are William Doyle, porter in the Ormond Hotel, shot in the back of the head – when he was brought to Jervis Street Hospital 'he was ghastly pale, and was gasping out his last when a nun brought holy water, a blessed candle and a crucifix, and those present knelt and prayed'. The oldest is 79-year-old James Shine, killed by a stray bullet on his way home from seven o'clock mass; the youngest, 12-year-old Patrick Joseph Cosgrove, another innocent victim caught in the crossfire.

❖ ❖ ❖ ❖ ❖ ❖ ❖ ❖ ❖ ❖ ❖

Thursday, 29 June 1922

General Macready relents and supplies the Irish Army with two more field guns and hundreds of explosive shells.

The extra firepower soon takes its toll. The thick walls are smashed through. With cavities allowing direct shots into the building, the Four Courts central hall is becoming a ruin.

A short time later, the eastern part of the Four Courts is breached by the National Army – the attack takes the lives of three of its soldiers.

Meanwhile, skirmishes are taking place all over the city centre. Republicans, under the command of Oscar Traynor, occupy buildings in the O'Connell Street, Parnell Square and Gardiner Street areas although the military purpose of this, apart from diversion, is far from clear – they are really just more traps.

The occupation of these buildings might show the Republicans' military naiveté, but this is matched by certain actions of the National Army. Earlier in the day, British forces were nearly drawn into the battle when an artilleryman was trying to pick off a sniper in the Four Courts' dome with his field gun. The shells passed through the dome as if it wasn't there and landed across the city at British military HQ in Kilmainham, causing considerable alarm.

Friday, 30 June 1922

At 1 a.m., the shelling starts again. Depriving the enemy of sleep is the cheapest of weapons. The guns at Winetavern Street, Lower Bridge Street and Hammond Lane soon blow away the front and south-west gates of the Four Courts.

Outgunned and hemmed in, the Republicans' position is becoming untenable.

At 10.30 a.m., the Winetavern Street gun moves up the quays to fire shells into the central block. Then at 11 a.m., a fire starts. Soon there are many. Surrender can only be a matter of time.

At 12.30 p.m. the fire brigade arrives to battle the blazes. At its head is Captain Myers who requests a ceasefire – his men cannot be expected to work amid flying bullets and exploding shells. At first, the National Army is reluctant to give up the advantages gained in battle – Ireland is more important than saving the Four Courts, Captain Myers is told. However, a short time later, all shooting stops and the firemen enter what is now a building gripped by flames.

Wreckage is strewn across the floors, and makeshift barricades hamper progress. The firemen's mood is not helped when they are told that the Republicans have laid a number of mines – one explodes when they break through a door – and that four tonnes of explosives are stored in one building and two more in another. The place might go up at any minute.

Meanwhile, shooting starts again in scores of locations around the city as Republicans try to divert attention from the doomed garrison.

Back at the Four Courts, just as Myers goes outside to connect a hose to a water supply, a huge blast knocks him off his feet. Four tonnes of explosives stored in the basement of the record tower have gone off. Some 50 soldiers, five Republicans and three of Myers' men are injured but miraculously no one is killed. What glass had been left in

Firing continues on the Four Courts.

As the siege of the Four Courts is being brought to an end a huge blast occurs when explosives stored by the Republicans in the basement of the Record Tower go off.

windows in the immediate area is gone now. Such was the force of the blast that buildings shook and windows shattered as far away as O'Connell Street and Grafton Street.

The greatest casualty of the explosion is the country's historical records. Because in the dense column of smoke and soot mushrooming into the Dublin sky are the swirling fragments of countless papers that had been stored in the Public Records Office. A state just born is now without much of its past.

The blast causes a stunned silence in the city but after a few minutes, as the cloud from the Four Courts drifts across town, shelling resumes.

By 2.30 p.m. all defiance is over.

At 3.30 p.m., despite the efforts of Captain Myers and his men, the Four Courts' fire is out of control. Shortly afterwards, Republicans wave a white towel of surrender tied to a broomstick.

Meanwhile, for miles around, the city is being littered with remnants of probate orders, divorce papers, legal reports, census returns, Chancery rolls and other recent contents of the Records Office.

The Provisional Government, jubilant at the course of events, sends a telegram to every post office in the country announcing that the Four Courts has surrendered. In expectation that Republicans holed up in and around O'Connell Street will give up their positions, a letter of thanks is issued to the National Army.

Saturday, 1 July 1922

Government optimism has proven premature. The hundreds of Republicans who have taken over various buildings around the city show no signs of dispersing. Rather, they are reinforcing positions, barricading windows and doors with anything they find and breaking through party walls to allow movement between buildings.

However, for a time, the city is relatively quiet and, apart from the occupied buildings, life almost returns to normal. In this lull government soldiers rest, reorganise, rearm, and set up barricades at key junctions with commandeered vehicles, carts, and even bathtubs.

The people of the city take a breather but peace is short-lived, as later in the day fighting breaks out in many areas.

In the evening, the brunt of the government attacks is borne by the Talbot Street area. Again, civilians are in the thick of it. A little girl from 9 Thomas Court has her face blown away, while 24-year-old Michael Lynn of Talbot House is mortally wounded by a bullet in his side while he stands at a window.

Among the Republicans is C.S. Andrews who, along with 20 others, has taken up position on the top floor of the Dublin Tramways Office at the corner of O'Connell Street and North Earl Street. From his window he covers O'Connell Bridge and Westmoreland Street. Coming under attack from the Ballast Office, he returns fire with his Lee Enfield. As he does so, he is amazed as a crowd stands opposite the Ballast Office as though they are witnessing a motor accident. Once in a while, a person walks down O'Connell Street, seemingly oblivious to the sights and sounds of war. It is a wonder the civilian death toll is not even higher.

Later in the evening, an armoured car pulls up at the corner of Henry Street and fires belt after belt of machine gun bullets into the Tramways building.

❖ ❖ ❖ ❖ ❖ ❖ ❖ ❖ ❖ ❖

Sunday, 2 July 1922

Assorted bric-a-brac barricade the windows and doors of various buildings, pavements are littered with glass and debris, tramway standards are bent and mangled, their wires hanging limp. As a government military cordon closes in around O'Connell Street, Marlborough Street and Gardiner Street, the Republicans appear to have no plan except to hold out as best they can and, when their positions become untenable, to escape.

As the fighting continues, the National Army are becoming more experienced. They take up positions against a sniper like seasoned troops – lying flat on the ground when in the open and advancing from cover to cover while under fire.

In this most cautious of conflicts, an unusual show of daring is displayed by two members of the National Army who make a foray into the danger zone. Under covering fire, they work their way across O'Connell Street to Tyler's Shoe Shop, which has a strong force of Republicans, and throw several grenades in through the windows. Then they do the same to Hickey's Fabric Store before returning to safety.

The west side of O'Connell Street is being cleared of Republicans while the Tramways Office is the first major stronghold on the east side to be attacked when it is silenced by guns in Arnotts' tower, the Metropole Hotel and Elverys.

❖ ❖ ❖ ❖ ❖ ❖ ❖ ❖ ❖ ❖ ❖

Monday, 3 July 1922

The night is lit up by fire spitting from the machine guns and the red flames of exploding grenades. At 1 a.m., an armoured car takes up position outside the Metropole Cinema. Another pulls up to the corner of Talbot Street. A third shelters behind Nelson's Pillar. Supported by machine guns in Arnotts' tower and Elverys, the cars open fire for thirty minutes. Special attention is paid to the Hammam and Gresham hotels and the Tramways Office where the Republicans, lying under the windowsills to avoid the hail of fire, recite the Rosary. The attack ends when the armoured cars run out of ammunition.

Apart from the activity of snipers, this is an engagement that typifies the fighting. In a conflict where the two sides rarely come face to face, small numbers of heavily armed soldiers of the National Army make forays into the danger zone where there is usually a larger, but significantly less well-armed, force concealed in buildings.

During the night, a brief halt is called to allow the wounded to be taken from the Hammam. From inside, inveterate fighter Cathal Brugha sends a message to his attackers. Once the wounded are removed, he will signal with two gunshots that they can attack again; he invites them to 'do their worst'.

At 3 a.m., the National Army has nearly completed the encirclement of O'Connell Street. The number of Republicans steadily declines – some escape through back lanes while the captured are brought to Mountjoy. The success of the government assaults leads Captain Dalton of the National Army to conclude that the Republicans will surrender 'at any moment'.

By dawn, the Republican area is further reduced to a block bounded by the east side of Upper O'Connell Street, North Earl Street and Findlater Place – the main Republican strongholds are Hickey's, Boyer's and Nagle's shops on North Earl Street and, on O'Connell Street, the Tramway Offices and the Hammam and Gresham hotels.

For most in the city, the fighting is an inconvenience. But for those living in the tenements east of O'Connell Street, it is more serious than that. They have had no idea when a grenade, shell or sniper's bullet would find them. Without their breadwinners able to work, they are completely reliant on charity supplied by the St Vincent de Paul, who have set up a base at Buckingham Street – their own building on O'Connell Street being in the thick of battle. Unsurprisingly, many

After the fall of the Four Courts, the battle for control of buildings held by Republican in O'Connell Street and the surrounding area starts.

Artillery at the corner of Henry Street and O'Connell Street, with the base of Nelson's Pillar in view, takes aim at buildings held by Republicans.

of the civilian dead are now coming from this area. Some are killed in their own homes or going about the business of survival, while others described in the press as having the 'insatiable and utterly futile curiosity of the inveterate sensation-seeking street lounger' have also perished. Among the latest is that of a young girl, Kate Dowling, shot through the heart as she stood with a group of gazers at the corner of Marlborough Street.

In the evening, a message is sent to those Republicans still in the Hammam Hotel warning of another attack if they do not surrender. Two hours later, a note is returned by Brugha which reads, 'Not damned likely.'

At 9 p.m., the 18-pounder at the Henry Street corner opens fire again.

❖ ❖ ❖ ❖ ❖ ❖ ❖ ❖ ❖ ❖ ❖

Tuesday, 4 July 1922

At 2 a.m., what the government hopes will be the final attack commences.

The end is just a matter of time. Snipers still scattered on rooftops wait for opportunities to get away while 'lead is spattering round the bell of St Thomas's Church; a machine gun cackles its derisive laugh in Parnell St, and a very odd rifle grenade booms a solitary report'. Sometime after 6 a.m., the 30 men who had taken over St Thomas's Church surrender. At the same time, another group in the Hammam comes out with their hands raised.

With the last Republicans still holding out, another bombardment of the east side of O'Connell Street is planned.

At 8 p.m., bullets rip into the Gresham. An hour later, the artillery at Henry Street

An armoured car outside the block of buildings held by Republicans on O'Connell Street as the first fire breaks out.

opens up while a solitary soldier behind the Parnell monument flings grenades. At 10.15 p.m., the 18-pounder takes a 45-minute break before starting again.

❖ ❖ ❖ ❖ ❖ ❖ ❖ ❖ ❖ ❖ ❖

Wednesday, 5 July 1922

The 18-pounder has been firing through the night and has inflicted impressive damage, smashing several holes through the block of buildings between Cathedral Street and Findlater Place. From one splintered window the tattered, scorched remains of a tricolour flag hangs limp.

At 8 a.m. the shelling stops.

Three hours later, another heavy bombardment commences, reducing the entrance of the Hammam to a gaping hole. At 11.30 a.m., an armoured lorry approaches and soldiers throw in a dozen grenades.

When three National Army soldiers try to break down the door of the Gresham two defiant shots rip through the door, forcing their retreat.

Then a relentless attack by armoured cars is directed against the hotel – when one car's machine gun barrel overheats it pulls away only to be replaced by another.

Shortly before midday soldiers enter the Hammam and the Gresham hotels and set them on fire. The progress of the flames can be followed by the thud and crackle of exploding mines and ammunition.

Meanwhile, the death toll of the innocent has continued to rise. Some of the latest victims are on North Great George's Street, struck by bullets flying through gaps blown in the O'Connell Street buildings. Among them are 31-year-old Leo Walpole, a former soldier, shot in the liver while making tea for his elderly mother in number 23, and James Clarke, shot in the head in number 30.

Fires rage in various buildings when Captain Myers and his men arrive. Some are beyond saving – as they arrive the front wall of the Hammam Hotel crashes down, sending a blinding cloud of dust, smoke and ash across the thoroughfare.

But the fire brigade are no longer concerned about individual buildings. They are trying to rescue the city.

By 2.30 p.m., the east side of Upper O'Connell Street is an inferno with nearly every building ablaze. The firemen are particularly anxious to put out a fire in Thwaites Mineral Water factory on O'Connell Street because it could spread to the vaults of Gilbeys Wine & Spirit Merchants. Extending as far as the Rotunda, the underground stores are packed with thousands upon thousands of bottles of potent whiskey. If they are added to the inferno, Saturday's Four Courts explosion will seem a mere firework display. Visiting the scene, the Lord Mayor sums up the situation: 'If the whiskey vaults go, I fear for the city.' However, the fire brigade manages to stop the flames just yards from the high-proof bottles.

Another potentially disastrous fire in a corporation paint and wood depot is also extinguished in the nick of time.

Some of the devastation of Upper O'Connell Street.

The Four Courts, once one of the most iconic buildings in Dublin is left in ruins. People wonder if it will ever be rebuilt.

Then, to all intents and purposes, the final scene in the battle for Dublin is played out at the rear of the Granville Hotel. At around 7 p.m. a white flag is waved and 20 strained and wan Republicans surrender. When the prisoners are brought to a garage at the rear of the Granville, one realises they are not all there. 'Where's Brugha?' he shouts. 'God help us, he's burned.'

But minutes later, Cathal Brugha, pale-faced, tired and stained with smoke and gunpowder, leaps through the flames from the Granville with gun in hand. To calls to surrender he replies hoarsely, 'No!'. Then a single shot is fired and a bullet smashes through his femur, tearing an artery. A neat circle of blood appears on the front of his leg, while in the back there is a gaping exit wound four inches in diameter. When he is put on a stretcher, he lies on his back, motionless.

With that it is over.

After nine days' fighting 16 National Army and 12 Republicans are dead. However, the total military dead is exceeded by civilians, 33 of whom have lost their lives.

As this night comes to an end, 28-year-old *Irish Times* journalist Bertie Smyllie, writing under the pen name 'Nichevo' (Russian for 'who cares'), leaves a near-deserted O'Connell Street. When he arrives at his D'Olier Street desk, he sits down and writes:

> Over the burning buildings, the sky is lit up in lurid splendour. The gaunt
> figure of Nelson surmounts the scene, a grim-looking silhouette against

clouds of rose-tinted smoke which are being belched out of the inferno, while nearer at hand, the cloaked form of Daniel O'Connell stands, a stately sentinel over the night.

Greedy flames are eating the heart of Sackville [O'Connell] street. Clerys, Eason's, Elverys, and the other creatures of Easter week are bathed in the glare of their elders' destruction; the old Post Office, mindful of its own ordeal not so very long ago, seems to be cowering fearfully in the background. Hose pipes swish their violent tongues of water at the raging cataract, but the angry crackle of bursting masonry makes mockery of their efforts. The red-shirted men, who are working like heroes, are toiling in vain. The block of buildings is doomed. And what a loss it is to Dublin! How many pages of history have been written in the Gresham Hotel? Post Office, Customs House, Four Courts, and Gresham – one by one the old landmarks of our city are going from us. Is there no limit to the greed of destruction?

❖ ❖ ❖ ❖ ❖ ❖ ❖ ❖ ❖ ❖ ❖

Thursday, 6 July 1922

The most significant single loss to the architectural fabric of the city is the Four Courts – it is doubtful if it will ever be rebuilt. But Upper O'Connell Street is a scene of total devastation with 22 buildings destroyed by shelling and fire. The entire block between Findlater Place and Cathedral Street is laid waste. The Gresham, Hammam, Granville, Edinburgh Temperance and Crown hotels are destroyed. So too are buildings previously occupied by William Moore, photographic artist, bog

At 2 p.m. on Wednesday, 9 August commerce overcomes political adversity when the newly restored Clerys shop, 'The Shopping Centre of Ireland', on Lower O'Connell Street, spared in the fighting, re-opens for the first time after its destruction in the 1916 Rising. There is no official ceremony – just a blessing from Rev. Flanagan of the Pro-Cathedral – because now is not the time for gala occasions.

Soon large crowds 'admire the gorgeous display in the elaborately dressed windows'. Among the numerous messages of congratulations is a telegram received from Gordon Selfridge in London and a white leather horseshoe from the owners of Brown Thomas and Company, Clerys' southside competitors.

oak carver and picture frame maker, the Oxford Cigar Saloon and Billiard Rooms, the Hibernian Bible Society, Miss McDonagh's dressmakers, the Catholic Truth Society, and the Society of St Vincent de Paul, among others. But it is not only those that have been at the centre of the fighting that bear the marks of ten days of conflict. Scores of other buildings have had their exteriors scarred by bullets and bombs, their internal walls smashed through, their windows ripped out, their doors demolished. The city's glaziers will be busy for months.

In response to a call from the Provisional Government for new recruits to the National Army to take the fighting to other parts of the country, long queues of men form at Brunswick Street, Kilmainham and Swords police stations, the King's Inns, Portobello Barracks and Amiens Street Railway Station. Although the fight will continue outside of Dublin, with the symbol of power, the seat of government, the main port and the centre of communications in the hands of the government, there is only one way that this conflict will end.

The badly damaged Tramways building is pulled down.

Monday, 28 August 1922

Dublin has become a city of tragic funerals – civilians, National Army soldiers and Republicans all killed for the cause of Ireland. Two of the largest have been those of Cathal Brugha the week after the fighting – the cortege paused amid the ruins of O'Connell Street where Brugha was shot – and last week that of Arthur Griffith – the President of the Dáil who died from cerebral haemorrhage.

But today is different. Nothing like it has been seen in the city since the 1891 funeral of parliamentarian Charles Stewart Parnell. Because today is the funeral of Michael Collins.

Although he was from Cork and had been killed in Cork, Collins' last wish was that he be buried in Dublin by the men of the Dublin Brigade who fought for him during the War of Independence and Civil War.

After requiem high mass, the remains of the lost leader are placed on a gun carriage

In the months after the fighting, thousands of compensation claims are lodged with the city's authorities. They now exceed £3 million. The most poignant applications are from those who have put a price on a lost relation. Among these are Mrs Walpole, 23 North Great George's Street, who requests £1,500 for the death of her son; Kate Clarke of 2 Lower Gloucester Street, who asks for £500 for the death of her nephew; John Dowling from Goldenbridge argues that his dead daughter is worth £600; and James White of Benburb Street asks for £1,500 for the death of his son.

But human life in the city is cheap because the largest sums are demanded for destroyed property. The Law Society claims £300,000 for the destruction of the Four Courts, S.R. Armstrong of Oakley Road, Ranelagh, who owned 11, 12 and 13 Upper O'Connell Street, wants £100,000, and R.M. Gray and Walter Archibald are looking for £100,000 for 17, 18 and 19 Upper O'Connell Street.

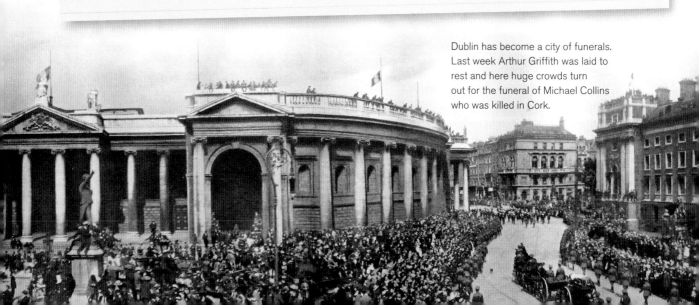

Dublin has become a city of funerals. Last week Arthur Griffith was laid to rest and here huge crowds turn out for the funeral of Michael Collins who was killed in Cork.

drawn by six horses led by the Dublin Brigade, marching with arms reversed. A band plays the funeral dirge. The procession route, lined by crowds six to eight deep, goes from Marlborough Street to Talbot Street, across Butt Bridge, down Great Brunswick Street, Merrion Square, St Stephen's Green, Grafton Street, College Green, Westmoreland Street, O'Connell Bridge and finally on to Glasnevin. It takes an hour and a half for the procession to pass any given point – when the gun carriage reaches Glasnevin, the end just crosses O'Connell Bridge.

❖ ❖ ❖ ❖ ❖ ❖ ❖ ❖ ❖ ❖

Friday, 17 November 1922

Since July, the main fighting between national troops and Republicans has taken place outside Dublin. But that does not mean the city has been at peace. There have been almost constant attacks in and around the capital which have killed nearly 100 more people – the latest victims are two national soldiers killed on Dalkey's Ulverton Road.

One government response to this continued guerilla activity is the passing of the Public Safety Act which sanctions state executions.

This morning the act claims its first victims in Kilmainham Gaol.

James Fisher, employed in Ruddel's cigarette factory on James's Street, Richard Twohig, employed at the Inchicore railway works, John Gaffney of 3 Usher Street and Peter Cassidy of 7 Usher Street, both of whom were electricians with Dublin Corporation, were tried by court martial in Wellington Barracks and sentenced to death for taking part in an attack on national troops.

At dawn, the four are brought to the entrance of the prison's Stonebreakers' Yard, where the leaders of the 1916 Rising were executed, and shot by members of the National Army.

❖ ❖ ❖ ❖ ❖ ❖ ❖ ❖ ❖ ❖

Thursday, 7 December 1922

As TDs Sean Hales and Pádraic Ó Máille leave a hotel on Ormond Quay after lunch to go to Dáil Éireann, two gunmen approach and open fire. Both TDs are shot, Ó'Máille mortally so. His assassination is revenge by Republicans for the government's execution policy.

❖ ❖ ❖ ❖ ❖ ❖ ❖ ❖ ❖ ❖ ❖

Friday, 8 December 1922

Retribution continues in the city as the cabinet decides on a reprisal for Ó'Máille's assassination. Four leading Republicans – Liam Mellowes, Rory O'Connor, Richard Barrett and Joe McKelvey – who have been detained in Mountjoy Prison since the surrender of the Four Courts garrison in July, and who could therefore have had no connection with the assassination of Ó'Máille, are taken from their cells and shot.

❖ ❖ ❖ ❖ ❖ ❖ ❖ ❖ ❖ ❖ ❖

Friday, 15 December 1922

Politics might be occupying the minds of some people but the thoughts of others are beginning to turn to civic matters.

There is a new international movement towards 'town planning'. In Dublin, the Civics Institute has been to the forefront of promoting good planning rather than having the city shaped little by little, day by day, by 'greed and carelessness'. According to the report, 'Dublin today presents a similar spectacle to Paris prior to the operations of Napoleon III and Haussmann: it is a city of magnificent possibilities …'

Among the changes proposed in Patrick Abercrombie's winning plan for a competition held by the Civics Institute is a new national theatre at the top of O'Connell Street.

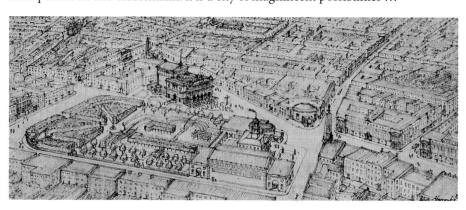

Abercrombie calls for the replacement of the 'ignoble' pedestrian 'Metal Bridge' over the Liffey with one that can take automobiles.

In 1914, the Civics Institute held an international competition calling for professionals to formulate a plan for a new Dublin. Because with the passing of the Home Rule bill it was believed that Dublin would soon become a capital once again. And the new capital should be one that is properly planned.

The competition had a first prize of £500, sponsored by the Lord Lieutenant, and was adjudicated over by Patrick Geddes, pioneering town planner from Edinburgh; Dublin Corporation's Architect C. J. McCarthy; and John Nolen, landscape architect from Cambridge, Massachusetts. But the Home Rule bill was shelved at the outbreak of the Great War, and following the 1916 Rising leaving much of Lower O'Connell Street was in ruins. In October 1916, the Civics Institute announced that the competition had been won by a group led by Patrick Abercrombie, then Professor of Civic Design at Liverpool University. However, the Institute did not want to publish the winning entry until the political situation had settled. Six years later, they decide that the time has finally come to let the public see the winning entry.

Abercrombie and his colleagues want to transform Dublin. The most pressing issue to be addressed is that of housing. Conditions in the city have even deteriorated since the 1913 Housing Commission of Inquiry described the slums of Dublin as some of the worst in Europe. Abercrombie's solution is for suitable housing for 64,000 people in Cabra, Crumlin and Drumcondra, all of which are just a 10- to 12-minute tram journey from the city centre and employment. A further residential area is proposed for land to be reclaimed from Dublin Bay at Clontarf, but this is for private developers to build on.

Housing might be the most pressing issue, but it is proposals for the redevelopment of the city centre that grab most public attention.

In Abercrombie's Dublin, a person walking down the quays would encounter a city transformed. There is a new bridge over the Liffey at the Custom House. The Loop Line Bridge is gone, with trains running through a tunnel underneath the Liffey.

O'Connell Street would be transformed from a thoroughfare jammed with traffic to one where just a single tram line would run. It would become a place to stroll, along a formal monumental route from a new national theatre and auditorium built at Rutland Square, past various historical memorials to Parnell, Nelson, Daniel O'Connell, William Smith O'Brien and Thomas Davis, to what will be the new parliament buildings at College Green.

The plan calls for the removal of the 'ignoble' pedestrian Metal Bridge that crosses the Liffey between Merchant's Arch and Liffey Street. Opened in 1816, there was a toll of first a halfpenny and then a penny to cross it, but in 1919 it was made free. The Metal Bridge would be demolished for a modern one that would carry vehicular traffic and ease traffic congestion at College Green.

At the top of Capel Street, which Abercrombie regards, because of its proportions, as possibly the finest street in the city, there would be a new catholic cathedral at a site certainly more fitting than its current one tucked away off O'Connell Street. Behind the cathedral, there would be a 500-foot cenotaph, at the base of which would be a pantheon of famous historical figures and, at the top, a statue of St Patrick.

The Four Courts would become Dublin's new central area, where the various routes entering the city would converge in a 'great traffic circus'. There would also

be an underground station with trains connecting to Broadstone, Amiens Street, Westland Row, Harcourt Street and Kingsbridge stations.

Part of this stroll would be along a new tree-lined mall to the Phoenix Park.

The Abercrombie plan gives an idea of how Dublin could develop if the principles of good town planning were followed. However, before any work is done, the members of the Institute decide today that a full 'civic survey' of the city should be carried out. So, at least for the time being, good planning for Dublin is shelved pending the collection of this information.

General Macready salutes his troops leaving the Phoenix Park on the last day of the British evacuation of the Free State.

Sunday, 17 December 1922

It is fitting that as a tumultuous year comes to an end, Dublin bids a final farewell to the remaining British garrison. After handing over their Phoenix Park headquarters to the National Army, the Leicesters, Worcesters, Wiltshires and Border regiments march down the Liffey to waiting ships.

At the docks, the crowd break through police cordons and surround the soldiers. But it is all good-humoured as the soldiers shout 'Up Dublin!' and 'Up the Free State!' While these soldiers sail from Dublin Port, General Macready, the last Irish military commander, departs from the ceremonial port of Dún Laoghaire aboard the HMS Dragon. After a seventeen-gun salute, the Dragon joins the other naval ships in Dublin Bay and, as darkness falls, they steam in convoy out of Irish territorial waters.

A final farewell from the last of the British garrison to leave Ireland's capital.

1923–1929

Consolidation

Monday, 29 January 1923

Parts of Dublin city still resemble a war zone. Since July's fighting, there has been no progress in the reconstruction of the destroyed parts of O'Connell Street, the Custom House and Four Courts remain shells, while the building that languishes longest is perhaps the most iconic of them all, the General Post Office (GPO) on O'Connell Street.

The GPO is in virtually the same state it was after it was shelled by British forces in April 1916. For nearly seven years, postal services have operated from buildings scattered around the city centre. But, finally, the Postmaster General has revealed plans for its reconstruction.

The Postmaster General is in no doubt that the building should remain the city's central post office, a role it occupied from 1818 until the Easter Rising. Located in the middle of the busiest shopping area of the city, with its passing traffic and demand for parcel services, it is also at the heart of the city's transport network. The GPO has been so central to Dublin that milestones along the routes out of the city are measured in distances to the GPO. Its association with the Easter Rising and the foundation of the Irish State is another compelling reason. For the Postmaster General, there is no more suitable site.

However, there are others who do not see it this way.

The Greater Dublin Reconstruction Movement (GDRM), founded last year with

Jack B. Yeats painting of The Liffey Swim (1923). Started in 1920, by 1923 it is the biggest free event in the city. On the evening of Monday 20 August, thousands line the walls of the river between Guinness Wharf and Butt Bridge to watch 34 swimmers compete for the Irish Independent Challenge Cup.

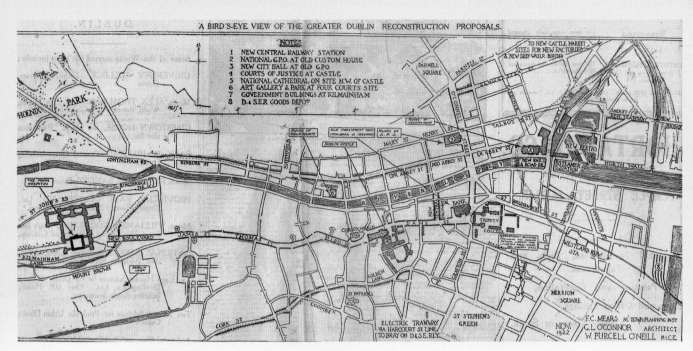

NOTES
1 NEW CENTRAL RAILWAY STATION
2 NATIONAL G.P.O. AT OLD CUSTOM HOUSE
3 NEW CITY HALL AT OLD G.P.O.
4 COURTS OF JUSTICE AT CASTLE
5 NATIONAL CATHEDRAL ON SITE N.W. OF CASTLE
6 ART GALLERY & PARK AT FOUR COURTS SITE
7 GOVERNMENT BUILDINGS AT KILMAINHAM
8 D. & S.E.R. GOODS DEPOT

The Greater Dublin Reconstruction Movement proposes a processional route from Trinity College to new 'government buildings' at the Royal Hospital, passing new courts of justice and catholic cathedral on the site of Dublin Castle. The destroyed Four Courts would be replaced by an art gallery and, most controversially, the GPO would be moved to the Customs House, with the O'Connell Street building becoming the headquarters for Dublin Corporation, whose staff and functions are scattered around the city.

the aim of promoting good planning for the new capital, believes that Abercrombie's report is out of date. So they have put forward a new vision for Dublin.

Among their proposals is a new 'highway' starting at O'Connell Street, cutting through Westmoreland Street, Dame Street and Thomas Street and finishing at the Royal Hospital, Kilmainham, where the Dáil, temporarily housed at Leinster House, the home of the Royal Dublin Society, would sit. Their plan also includes a new central railway station at Amiens Street, a courts of justice building at Dublin Castle, a new cathedral at the top of Dame Street, and an art gallery and park on the site of the Four Courts, the remains of which will be demolished.

Possibly their most controversial proposal is that the GPO should move to the Custom House where it would be convenient for foreign post, although inconvenient for the majority of Dubliners. The original GPO building would then become Dublin Corporation's new City Hall.

The debate is heated, and with arguments raging, the government orders the Postmaster General to cease all preparatory work at the O'Connell Street building until a final decision on its use is reached.

The city is parched. The Vartry Reservoir in Roundwood, County Wicklow, which opened in 1868 to serve the city with a capacity of 11.3 billion litres of water, has become inadequate. On Wednesday, 20 June 1923, an extension opens, providing an additional 5.6 billion litres to slake Dublin's thirst.

Saturday, 20 October 1923

An exhibition by the Society of Dublin Painters at the St Stephen's Green gallery features ten artists. The number of painters might be small but the exhibition has a huge range of styles on display and shows painters of a younger generation. Among these are Mainie Jellett, who has returned from Paris.

One of her paintings is the first in the 'Cubist' style to be exhibited in Ireland. It is not to everyone's taste though. As one reviewer writes, 'I fear I did not seem in the least to understand her paintings. They are in squares, odd shapes and clashing colours. They may, to the man who understands the most up to date, modern art, mean something; but to me they presented an insoluble puzzle.' Another review calls her art 'sub-human'. It seems that although Dublin is now a European capital it is not yet quite ready for the latest artistic trends.

Mainie Jellet's 'Decoration' (1923) is the first 'Cubist' painting exhibited in Ireland.

Sligo-born poet William Butler Yeats is sitting in his Merrion Square home on Wednesday, 14 November 1923 when the telephone rings. On the other end is Bertie Smyllie of *The Irish Times*. Smyllie has news.

Yeats is being awarded the 1923 Nobel Prize for Literature. According to the Nobel Committee, he has been chosen 'for his always inspired poetry, which in a highly artistic form gives expression to the spirit of a whole nation'. Yeats is acutely aware of what the award will mean for Ireland, how it will put the new nation on the world's cultural map. But despite the lofty citation, the poet has more mundane concerns. 'How much is it worth, Smyllie?' he asks. 'How much is it worth?' Because, for one thing, the house needs new carpets.

Monday, 14 April 1924

As part of a general change in policy throughout much of Europe after the Great War, it has become accepted that public bodies should take a leading role in housing the poor. Today, Dublin Corporation completes the first houses in its initial venture, at the Fairbrothers Field development between the Liberties and South Circular Road.

These five-roomed homes are undoubtedly an improvement in circumstances for their occupiers. But when the scheme is finished, there will be a total of just 350 built. That is going to make no impression in a city where one-third of the population lives in tenements. More, much more, is required.

❖ ❖ ❖ ❖ ❖ ❖ ❖ ❖ ❖ ❖

Monday, 5 May 1924

The city streets have names that make some people uncomfortable. Because, apart from the rare exception such as Tara Street, which is named after the Meath hill where the High Kings of Ireland were crowned, and Lord Edward Street, named after the revolutionary leader who died in 1798, they bear the names of earls, lords, viceroys, viscounts and other figures of the former British ascendancy. Such is the association between the streets of the city and the British past, there were even calls that Dublin should not be the capital of a new Ireland. It was too British.

In a first flush of patriotism, a number of name changes are made. Richmond Bridge, named after the Duke of Richmond, Lord Lieutenant of Ireland, becomes O'Donovan Rossa Bridge, after the fenian; the pedestrian Wellington Bridge, named after the duke – although better known as the Metal Bridge – becomes the Liffey Bridge; Sackville Street becomes O'Connell Street, after Daniel O'Connell; Denzille Street becomes Fenian Street; Great Brunswick Street becomes Pearse Street (Patrick Pearse was born in number 27); Queen's Square becomes Pearse Square; and Rutland Square, named after the Duke of Rutland, is renamed Parnell Square, after Charles Stewart Parnell.

But the desire to change the names proves limited as many proposals are not approved. Some because they are arbitrary and some because people have no wish to simply erase the past. Beresford Place, named after the Rt. Hon. John Beresford who was responsible for bringing Gandon to Ireland in the eighteenth century, does not become Connolly Place after James Connolly, the executed 1916 leader; D'Olier

An unusually quiet scene at College Green in 1924.

Street, named after the Wide Streets Commissioner, does not become Smith O'Brien Street, after the leader of the Young Ireland Movement in 1848; Baggot Street Lower does not become Sheare's Place, after the brothers executed after the 1798 Rebellion; Capel Street, Bolton Street and part of Lower Dorset Street, named after the family of a Lord Lieutenant, the Earl of Bolton and the first Duke of Dorset, respectively, is not changed to Silken Thomas Street after the man who rebelled against King Henry VIII; George's Street is not named after Cahir Mór, ancestor of the Kings of Leinster; and the residents of Fitzwilliam Square have successfully resisted attempts by the 'Blessed Oliver Plunkett Memorial Association' to have their elegant square renamed after the executed seventeenth-century archbishop.

Following an investigation into the poor management of the city, the Dáil dissolves Dublin Corporation on Tuesday, 20 May 1924. Power is taken from the councillors, who have previously directly run the city, and invested in three commissioners appointed by the Dáil. This is part of a nationwide review of local authority management, but the situation in Dublin is seen as particularly important 'as at the present time the efficient administration of the city, as the capital of the Free State, has become a question of national interest'.

Thursday, 10 July 1924

Two years after the end of the Civil War and eight years after the Easter Rising, there is still no progress at the GPO. But it is not the only site lying idle. Although the owners of buildings damaged or destroyed in 1922 have received their compensation,

few are using it to rebuild. The capital's main street is littered with derelict sites still piled with rubble from when their buildings were destroyed either during the fighting or pulled down afterwards. But neither Dublin Corporation nor the government are willing to continue to stand by while O'Connell Street remains in such a state. Today the Dublin Reconstruction (Emergency Provisions) Act 1924 comes into effect. It is the first instance of town planning control in the city since the Wide Streets Commissioners of the eighteenth century.

According to the act, all plans for the reconstruction of buildings or redevelopment of sites on O'Connell Street must be lodged with the corporation for approval by the City Architect Horace O'Rourke. If he believes that the proposals in their scale, design or materials 'would be injurious to the amenity of the street', he may request that they be resubmitted. The corporation is also given the power to compulsorily purchase sites that lie vacant or where, after two years, progress has stopped. Because Dublin, indeed Ireland, needs its main street back.

❖ ❖ ❖ ❖ ❖ ❖ ❖ ❖ ❖ ❖ ❖

Saturday, 2 August 1924

Bunting, plants and flowers decorate the city's streets for the first major international event to be held in Ireland since the end of the fighting. The Tailteann Games, the 'Irish race' Olympics, is opening. Based on the ancient Celtic festival that was once held at Tailt, County Meath, they are being held in Dublin because it is the only place in Ireland with the venues, accommodation, transport and population to host such an event.

International competitors at the Tailteann Games swimming competition held at the pond in the Zoological Gardens.

The opening ceremony is taking place at Croke Park where a mock castle, round tower and other ancient Gaelic symbols tempt visitors, dignitaries and athletes to imagine they are not in a modern European city but have travelled back to a golden era of Irish history.

With the Paris Olympics just over, many newly crowned Olympians have come to Dublin, including the famous American high jumper Harold Osborn and the Australians Richmond Eve (high diver) and Andrew Charlton (swimmer).

At 3 p.m., the opening ceremony, 'one of the finest things ever witnessed in the city', starts. At one end of the ground, a 500-strong choir sings a welcome to the athletes and spectators. Overhead an aeroplane display takes place. From the grounds of Clonliffe College, there is an Irish Army artillery salvo, while sirens from ships in Dublin Bay compete with the pealing of bells throughout the city.

For two weeks, Dublin will be taken over by the games and their cultural events. Athletics, weight-throwing, jumping, cycling and shinty will be at Croke Park. But there is also chess in Trinity College, billiards in the Catholic Club, boxing at Portobello Barracks and the La Scala Opera House, handball at Ballymun and Clondalkin, arts and crafts at the RDS Showgrounds, motor cycle racing in the Phoenix Park, tennis at the Fitzwilliam Club, golf at Royal Dublin, and swimming, diving and water polo at the pond in the Zoological Gardens.

Tuesday, 7 October 1924

Until now, the capital has not had a permanent seat of government. After the 1922 election, Michael Collins had asked the Royal Dublin Society if the state could use its premises at Leinster House until the government could find proper accommodation of its own. It would just be for a few months, they were told.

Today the society and its members must be ruing their generosity.

At first everyone thought that the new parliament would be in the Bank of Ireland on College Green. It had seemed the logical choice. The bank had originally housed the former eighteenth-century Irish parliament. However, it is ruled out due to the prohibitive cost of providing the bank with alternative accommodation. No matter how important the seat of state power might be, the state has little money to spend on it.

Alternatives included the Royal Hospital, Kilmainham, Dublin Castle or the construction of an entirely new building. The Royal Hospital was out because it would cost £450,000 to convert it into a two-house legislature. Politicians also did not like the idea of being exiled to the outskirts of the city. Dublin Castle was discounted because it would be accommodating the law courts until the still-derelict Four Courts was one day restored. And the construction of a new parliament building at a cost £2 million was deemed too expensive.

So today, the Royal Dublin Society is punished for its initial generosity because Leinster House is going to be the permanent home of the Irish parliament. Many of the society's members are not pleased. Founded in 1731 with the mission of improving the poor economic condition of the country by promoting agriculture, arts, industry and science through the dissemination of new ideas and knowledge, it moved to the Duke of Leinster's House, the finest townhouse in the city, in 1815. The

A children's party in Dublin in the 1920s.

The Irish flag flies over the statue of Queen Victoria as Leinster House, the headquarters of the Royal Dublin Society, is made the permanent home of Dail Eireann in 1924.

RDS has made a magnificent contribution to the city and was instrumental in the founding of the National Galley, National Museum, Natural History Museum and the National Library, all of which are located around Leinster House.

The society will be compensated with a huge cash lump sum and it will also have a new building constructed at its showgrounds in Ballsbridge. However, many fear that their society, once so important to the city, will no longer be central to Dublin.

Now at Leinster House, political discourse will replace intellectual ferment.

The most awkward part of this arrangement is that the members of the Dáil will conduct the business of governing an independent Ireland under the watchful gaze of a huge statue of Queen Victoria.

❖ ❖ ❖ ❖ ❖ ❖ ❖ ❖ ❖ ❖ ❖

Tuesday, 11 November 1924

On the sixth anniversary of the end of the Great War, the city's past remains contested.

The Legion of Irish ex-servicemen of the British Army is erecting a temporary celtic memorial cross in College Green to mark Armistice Day. President Cosgrave was invited to lay a wreath in memory of the tens of thousands of the Irish Great

Huge crowds attend the Armistice Day commemoration at College Green in 1924.

War dead. However, Cosgrave thought it would be 'hypocritical' for him to attend a British Army commemoration when, at the time of the Great War, he had been imprisoned by the British. At a government cabinet meeting, it was decided that the 'time was not ripe for the Government to publicly associate itself with functions of this nature' and the Legion was asked to withdraw the invitation.

Such is the size of the crowd this morning that by 10 a.m. it is impossible to get closer to College Green than Grafton Street or Fleet Street. As 11 a.m. approaches, floral wreaths are passed over people's heads and laid at the base of the monument. Then the crowd becomes utterly silent, except for the crying of some women and girls who lost loved ones in the war. After the last post is sounded, many in the crowd sing 'God Save the King'.

✣ ✣ ✣ ✣ ✣ ✣ ✣ ✣ ✣ ✣ ✣

Friday, 9 January 1925

The new capital continues to take shape in the aftermath of war as the Minister for Finance finally decides that the General Post Office will stay as a post office – Dublin Corporation will have to wait for a headquarters.

However, there will also be shops because, despite the city's poverty, there is no shortage of people spending money. Opposite the GPO there is Clerys, the self-styled 'national shopping centre' to which people from all over the country travel. Around the corner is Henry Street, the city's main shopping thoroughfare.

And as part of the GPO's restoration, there will be Ireland's first glass-covered shopping arcade linking Henry Street and Prince's Street.

❖ ❖ ❖ ❖ ❖ ❖ ❖ ❖ ❖ ❖ ❖

Thursday Night, Friday Morning, 12-13 March 1925

For two years, Frank Duff and his Legion of Mary have been trying to close down the brothels in Monto, the city's red-light district. The area known as 'Monto', after Montgomery Street, the original name of Foley Street, is where brothel-keepers and their prostitutes, many of whom are young country women who have 'got into trouble', have operated almost unhindered. Duff's main concern is that 'the spectacle of open vice' in Monto draws men in and corrupts them. Through constant calls to houses of ill-repute and marches through the area, he has managed to reduce the number of working girls to a few dozen – many have entered the Harcourt Street Hostel for fallen women. Tonight is the last push as scores of gardaí arrive into the locale around Foley Street, to the north-east of O'Connell Street. During tonight's raid, over 120 people are arrested. Though only two are going to be charged – Molly Butler and Elizabeth McKenna for being brother-keepers – the raid is the death knell for Monto. But no one believes it means the end of prostitution.

To mark St Patrick's Day, the government puts on a military parade. Troops including members of the Infantry, the Armoured Car Corps, Artillery, Military Police, Signal Corps and the Army School of Music assemble at Arbour Hill Barracks. They then march along the north quays, across Grattan Bridge, down Parliament Street and Dame Street to College Green where they salute the dignitaries before returning to Arbour Hill.

The Dublin Metropolitan Police, in existence since 1836 and for decades the only separate police force in the country, independent of the RIC, is disbanded on Friday, 3 April. Its 1,200 members are now part of the Garda Síochána, although for a time they will still wear the uniform of the DMP.

Despite its Munster roots and the fact that the number of people who play gaelic games in the city is less than elsewhere, the Gaelic Athletic Association's Annual Congress on Sunday, 12 April officially decides that in future the All-Ireland finals will take place in Dublin.

Monday, 27 April 1925

In the *Irish Independent* a man from the country writes about a day out in Dublin, a city he has not been to for some years. When he gets to O'Connell Street, the first thing he notices is how evident the destruction on O'Connell Street remains – despite last year's law, O'Connell Street still has gaping holes and 'ugly fissures'. But then, suddenly, there are signs of modernity, efficiency, even pomposity as new temples of commerce present themselves.

On entering one of these a man in coat-tails approaches and asks him, 'What department, please?'

It is as though he has entered a fairy palace. From a balcony, 'music, soft sinuous music, is streaming down to my ears. It beats gently, recurring until my senses swoon.' Fantastically, overhead 'droops a tree in full bloom' while the world's merchandise is laid out 'row after row, methodical and attractive'. Everywhere there is a 'phantasmagoria of colour'.

Grace Plunkett's cover of the progamme of *The Dublin Revue*. Started last year by John McDonagh, this year's review at the Olympia again stars 26-year-old Jimmy O'Dea.

After a time he is surprised again by the man in coat-tails who, with hands apart, smiles and asks, 'Department, please?' In a panic he replies, 'Gloves' and shortly afterwards finds himself buying, for no apparent reason, a pair of ladies' gloves.

The visitor believes that everything one could want during life's progress can be found under this roof. 'A baby's gown to start and a coffin to finish with, and yet, in between what careful consideration is given to all the sartorial details of one's passing years.' The young can get a football or corduroy knickers, a mature man a suit of plus-fours and a set of golf sticks. And in the later years, he could get a walking stick, a pipe, soothing tobacco and all the medicines he might need.

When he leaves, the man looks above the door to see the name of the fairyland: 'Clerys' the sign reads.

On Friday, 1 May 1925, a large group of curious onlookers gather as the city's first 'telephone kiosk' or 'public telephone on the street' is being erected at College Green, behind the Henry Grattan statue.

Saturday, 6 June 1925

Just how desperate the poor are to leave the city's overcrowded tenements is shown by the avalanche of applications received by Dublin Corporation for the first phase of a housing scheme at Marino. The Marino scheme, made possible by a government

Thousands of Dubliners apply for the first major working-class housing scheme built by Dublin Corporation, located in the north side suburb of Marino. It is a world away from the tenements.

The shutting down of the Monto district has not ended prostitution in the city. On 9 June, Lily O'Neill, also known as 'Honour Bright', a 26-year-old prostitute from Newmarket Street, is found dead on Ticknock Mountain. She had been shot through the heart and left lung. Dr Patrick Purcell from Blessington and Leopold J. Dillon from Dunlavin were seen with her at St Stephen's Green. Both are tried for her murder. But at the end of the trial, the jury takes just three minutes to acquit them.

grant, is intended to be a model suburb based on the best town planning principles. Designed by Frederick Hicks, the Marino estate is being built in the new 'garden city' style where people will live in airy, healthy surroundings in houses with living rooms, parlours, three bedrooms, sculleries, larders, bathrooms, WCs, coal cellars and gas heating. In contrast to where the occupants will come from, there is a rigid geometry to Marino's design with two large circular greens, radiating roads and T-shaped cul-de-sacs.

Some 4,400 people have applied for the first 248 houses. But these houses are not for everyone. Priority will be given to households with eight or more people and they will only be for what is being described as the 'aristocracy' of the city's working classes, as they are being sold for £400 and require a £25 deposit, putting them well beyond the means of the most needy.

❖ ❖ ❖ ❖ ❖ ❖ ❖ ❖ ❖ ❖ ❖

Monday, 22 June 1925

Tonight, London entertainment comes to Dublin as 200 people attend the city's first 'cabaret' in the Mansion House's Round Room. The show is being put on by the proprietors of the New Princes' Hotel and Restaurant, Paddington, London with the night's music provided by the New Princes' Toronto Orchestra, one of the finest dance bands in the world, Hal Swaine and the New Princes' Saxophone Five, and Dublin's own Adelaide Orpheus Band.

The evening commences with dancing, followed by supper and then the cabaret. Among the dancers are American Hazel Shelley, 'The Wonder Dancer' and the great Italo-French performer Mademoiselle Terpsichore whose graceful and rhythmic movement is both acrobatic and clearly exhausting. The night is such a success that cabarets will surely become a favourite form of Dublin evening entertainment.

Despite the inclusion of the Adelaide Orpheus Band, the Irish Dance Musicians

Union, led by its President Mr Verso Napper, is picketing the cabaret. They are objecting for many reasons, including the importation of a 'Turk' to mix 'cock-tail drinks', but most importantly, because the dancing at the cabaret is not being conducted 'along proper lines'. Napper and his union are anxious to raise dancing from what they regard as the lowly state, with sexual undertones, to which it has been recently declining.

✦ ✦ ✦ ✦ ✦ ✦ ✦ ✦ ✦ ✦

Monday, 6 July 1925

One of the most pressing issues facing the people who manage the city, but also those who live and work in it, is how it is going to cope with the new mode of transport.

The motor car is taking over and it is becoming a major problem.

Since 1914, the number of Buicks, Peugeots, Lanchesters, Napiers, Renaults, Rolls Royces and other vehicles in the city has doubled to more than 11,000. But it is not only their numbers, it is also that they are being used more and more frequently by their owners going about their daily business.

In addition to the private car, there has been the appearance of the public taxi. More than 70 taxis are now working the streets. What is regarded as the inevitable

A 1920s scene of O'Connell Bridge as the city's streets are being increasingly taken over by the automobile.

disappearance of the traditional Dublin horse-drawn jarvey is lamented in an *Irish Independent* article on Tuesday, 25 March 1925:

> No longer will the visitor cheerfully submit himself to the stiff exactions by a gentleman with an engaging and fluent tongue. No longer will the sights of Áth Cliath be pointed out with a proud, if perhaps grimy, forefinger, while a Dublin brogue whispers in his ear of the greatness of Ireland's capital. No longer will questions, both economic and political, be decided for him with an amazing finality … The loquacity of our jarvey was undamable, and his flow of ideas extraordinary. He could discuss any subject with his fare, with an ease befitting a professor. Yet his knowledge was not book-lore. He learnt his lessons from the book of everyday life …

Added to the automobile and taxi is the advent of another new mode of public transport, the motorised omnibus or 'bus', which makes its first appearance today. (The first route travelled is between O'Connell Bridge and Killester).

Just how much these changes are affecting the city's traffic is shown by two surveys.

In one, the movements of traffic were measured between 4.30 p.m. and 6.30 p.m. at various points in the city. College Green is confirmed as the busiest intersection with 5,552 motor vehicle passing in two hours, Nassau Street is the second with 3,983, followed by the junction of George's Street and Dame Street with 3,341. The congestion is even worse than these figures suggest because they do not include either trams or the city's thousands of cyclists.

Another traffic survey that was carried out on the main trunk roads, replicating previous ones carried out in 1911 and 1913, shows how dramatic the changes have been in little more than a decade.

At Donnybrook, on the Dublin–Bray road, the daily number of motor cars has increased from 255 to 1,019, the number of lorries from 1 to 206 and buses from none to 43. The only decline is in the number of horse-drawn vehicles, down from 758 to 202. At Drumcondra, on the Dublin–Balbriggan road, there is a similar pattern, with motor cars increasing from 69 to 334, lorries from 2 to 127 and omnibuses from none to 31, while horse-drawn traffic is down from 465 to 197.

Apart from congestion, the car is causing other problems.

One is safety.

In 1924, 32 people were killed by cars. Until recently, the only legislation governing road behaviour was the Dublin Traffic Act of 1875, which the automobile has rendered obsolete. Motorists drive in a devil-may-care manner – their attitude is exemplified by Phibsborough's Michael Holland who, when fined £5 for driving in a reckless manner after he crashed into a lamp standard on Westmoreland Street, defended himself by saying that it was not his fault, he would not have crashed into the lamp standard if it was not there.

But it is not just those behind the wheel who behave irresponsibly. Pedestrians seem to believe that everyone else is somehow responsible for their safety, while the city's cyclists recognise no law whatsoever.

In January, new traffic rules came into effect which stipulate that all traffic, even cyclists, shall stay on the left-hand-side of the road and that recognised signals will be used for various road manoeuvres.

A final problem caused by the fast-moving, rubber-wheeled vehicles is that they are destroying the roads. Until now, Dublin's city roads have been made of cobblestones or water-based macadam. Both had well-serviced, slow-moving wheels and iron-shod horses' hoofs, but under the weight and speed of cars, the water-based macadam surfaces are disintegrating, often within a year of being laid, while the city's cobbles, though more durable, are uncomfortable for drivers, and the noise of cars on cobbles can be almost deafening. On Middle Abbey Street, the noisiest in the city, the din makes normal conversation in premises such as the *Irish Independent* and Eason's almost impossible.

So wholesale changes are taking place to the city's road surfaces. The old surfaces and cobblestones are being ripped up and the roads relaid with tar asphalt, estimated to have a ten-year life span and guaranteed to reduce noise.

❖ ❖ ❖ ❖ ❖ ❖ ❖ ❖ ❖ ❖

Friday, 20 November 1925

Just before 7 a.m., armed men hold up two gardaí on duty outside the Masterpiece Cinema on Talbot Street. Then a car comes from the direction of Nelson's Pillar and stops. The driver gets out, throws a brown parcel into the picture house and takes cover. Seconds later, a massive explosion destroys half the front of the building, damaging neighbouring premises.

The motive for the attack is clear. The cinema has been showing, to large houses, the movie *Ypres: The Agony and Glory of the Immortal Salient*. It is a dramatic re-enactment of one of the bloodiest battles of the Great War and one in which many Irishmen fought and died. But there are some who obviously do not want Dubliners to learn about the Great War, or even indeed remember it.

Tuesday, 15 December 1925

The Civic Survey that was called for as part of the new plan for Dublin has been completed.

The findings of the survey highlight, once again, the seriousness of the housing situation. The overcrowded slums remain Dublin's defining characteristic. Housing in the city is more than a 'question', more than a 'problem', it is a 'tragedy'. In some areas 23 per cent of people live in one-room accommodation. According to the survey though, the 'evil of tenements' occupies much talk, but people tend to 'devote nine-tenths of their words to the horrors, and only one-tenth to constructive suggestions'. Exacerbating the problem has been the trend – part cause, part consequence – of 'the steady migration of almost every citizen of substance from the central areas to the suburbs'. As the wealthy left their fine houses, mainly on the north side of the city, they usually subdivided and rented them to 'large numbers of agricultural labourers and others of unskilled capacity' who migrate to Dublin from rural areas.

Programme cover for variety show at the Theatre Royal Hippodrome, Dublin's largest theatre, on Hawkins Street.

Whatever about the shortage of housing, there is no dearth of cinemas – there are 23 in the city centre including the Phoenix, Mary Street, Bohemian, Dorset Street, Grafton, Carlton, Rotunda, Inchicore, Lyceum, Camden and La Scala, Ireland's largest with 1,900 seats. Every day there are nearly 16,000 seats available in the city's picture houses. These new temples of entertainment greatly outnumber traditional theatres, of which there are just six – the Theatre Royal is the largest with 2,011 seats and the smallest is the Abbey, the national theatre, with 562.

The most visited sites in the city are the Royal Botanic Gardens, with over 350,000 visitors a year, and the Zoological Gardens with 123,000 people.

Looking at a map of the city, one would think it was reasonably well-endowed with parks and open spaces.

A drawing by Countess Markievicz of a Dublin slum and its diseased occupants.

There are numerous squares, as well as the delightful expanse of the Phoenix Park's 1,752 acres. But three of the squares – Mountjoy, Merrion and Fitzwilliam – are closed to the public and reserved for the private use of the residents of the squares. Apart from the Phoenix Park, there are just 227 other acres of public space in Dublin. By comparison, the similarly sized city of Edinburgh has 1,836 acres.

Dublin is a city of students. Trinity College is the largest with 1,800 – 1,150 are studying arts, 530 medicine, 68 engineering, 50 law and 30 divinity. In UCD, there are 1,200 students, of whom 450 are studying arts, philosophy and Celtic studies, 425 medicine, 130 commerce, 120 science, 78 engineering and 40 law. The next largest is the Royal College of Surgeons which has 470 medical students.

Given the nearly 1,500 medical students in the city, one would think that Dublin must be one of the healthiest in Europe. But due to continued poverty and chronic overcrowding, disease, particularly tuberculosis, is rampant. A startling statistic is that one quarter of all deaths each year in Dublin are of children who have not yet reached their fifth birthday.

Dublin is decades behind others in terms of modern planning. But the survey's authors are not without optimism. 'Dublin,' they state, 'is a city redolent of charm: a city of castle, sea and distant hills; a city full-charged with the glory and pathos of the past. Let her citizens resolve that Dublin shall have a great future.' With the survey now complete, a 'Final Town Plan' to guide the growth of Dublin until the end of the twentieth century can be formulated.

Thursday, 11 February 1926

Tonight is the third performance of Sean O'Casey's *The Plough and the Stars* at the Abbey Theatre. The play's opening night was the high-water mark of public interest in the work of the national theatre. Located in the heart of the city, until recently the Abbey was almost exclusively the preserve of plays depicting rural Ireland, 'real' Ireland. This image of 'Irish Ireland' is not one that generally features Dublin. However, O'Casey's works are different.

O'Casey grew up in the East Wall and his plays see the world through the eyes of the city's poor. Instead of characters with 'peasant quality', there are people from the Dublin tenements who have so far gained little from the new Ireland. His characters are not heroes and heroines of legend but those who survive in the city slums. *The Plough and the Stars* features bricklayer Jack Clitheroe and his wife Nora, Peter Flynn, labourer, Fluther Good, carpenter and Mrs Gogan, a charwoman.

Bookings for his play, about how the working classes of the city went about their business while history was being made during Easter week 1916, have broken all box office records.

The opening night was a great success but there were signs of trouble on the second night as a handful of people voiced their objections to members of the Irish Volunteers bringing an Irish flag into a public house.

Tonight there are disturbances from the start. There is stamping of feet, hissing and shouting. During the second act it gets worse.

During Act III, which starts off with Mrs Clitheroe's description of what she saw during the fighting, there is bedlam. Twenty women rush from the pit to the stall, with two managing to reach the stage. When these two women are thrown back into the orchestra, a young man attempts to perform a similar feat, but is cut off by the lowering curtain. However, the man grabs the curtain and begins swinging out of it, trying to pull it down. Some women rush to help him in his endeavours but then the man is sent into the stalls by a punch from one of the actors.

Panic breaks out among the audience, many of whom run to the exits.

Shortly afterwards, the curtain is raised again but as soon as it is up a young man rushes onto the stage and grapples with two actresses. Immediately, two actors rush from the wings and send the intruder off the stage. Meanwhile another man gets onto the stage and is attacked by a number of actors. He is not so quickly dispelled and it is only after several blows and a particularly strong punch from actor Barry Fitzgerald that he tumbles into the stalls.

Altercations are not only taking place on the stage, as in various parts of the theatre people from either side are confronting each other.

The scene is only calmed when a group of detectives and uniformed police arrive and place themselves around the theatre.

At this point, Senator W.B. Yeats, Director of the Abbey, comes forward to a barrage of boos and hisses. He addresses the crowd, recalling the controversy surrounding John Millington Synge's *Playboy of the Western World*, but his words are only audible to those at the front and even for those it is difficult.

> I thought you had got tired of this. It commenced 15 years ago. You have disgraced yourselves again. Is this to be an ever-recurring celebration of the arrival of Irish genius? Once more you have rocked the cradle of genius. The news of this will go from country to country. You have once more rocked the cradle of a reputation. The fame of O'Casey is born tonight.

When Yeats leaves the stage, shouts of 'We want the play!' compete with 'Up the Republic!'

There is a huge cheer when the curtain is raised to continue the aborted third act. But it is soon interrupted when over a dozen women protesters who seized a number of front-row seats that were vacated by people who left the theatre begin to sing 'The Soldiers' Song'. When the police eject the women, the play finally continues to the end.

The only physical damage is the face of the man punched by Barry Fitzgerald, two broken footlight lamps, parts of the stage curtain that have been ripped, some sheets of music, and the cover of a double-bass fiddle that have been torn. However, more lasting damage has been inflicted on the reputation of the theatre-going public of the city.

❖ ❖ ❖ ❖ ❖ ❖ ❖ ❖ ❖ ❖ ❖

Sunday, 18 April 1926

Tonight, every household in the country fills out a form for the state's first census, and the first that has taken place since 1911. The information published by the Civic Survey about the physical make-up of the city is to be added to that collected on the census forms about its inhabitants. The first census offers the opportunity of planning for the future of Dublin city, a means of taking stock and assessing what has changed since the last census.

Dublin's population is now 505,000, up from 477,000 in 1911 and 405,000 in 1871. It is the only county where the numbers have increased. Dublin now has 17 per cent of the population of the Free State, having accounted for 10 per cent in 1871.

One of the main reasons for the increase is the constant influx of migrants from rural areas. Some 28 per cent of Dublin's population was born outside of the capital. Dublin is the only county in Ireland where women, who account for 54 per cent of the population, outnumber men. One of the reasons for this is that large numbers of women from rural areas go to Dublin for economic opportunities that are simply not available to them where they grew up.

The census reveals how the religious composition of the city has changed as a result of the recent political changes. The city is becoming increasingly Catholic; since 1911 the number of Protestants in the central area fell by 38 per cent and in the suburbs by 20 per cent.

But perhaps the most striking statistics show how little has changed in slum conditions five years after independence. The areas with the largest number of families of seven or more living in single rooms (with some having more than 20) are to the east of O'Connell Street, (1,799 families), to the north of O'Connell Street (1,561 families), and in the Merchant's Quay area (1,278 families). But this situation is not only to be found in the traditionally poor areas, because behind some of the most elegant streetscapes, there is poverty and overcrowding. In the area that includes St Stephen's Green, Baggot Street, Fitzwilliam Square, Earlsfort Terrace, Adelaide Road and Harcourt Street, 488 families of seven or more people are living in one room.

George Bernard Shaw, the Dublin-born playwright, wins the Nobel Prize for literature in 1926.

The census lists a plethora of ways in which Dubliners make a living: there are 154 actors (76 male, 78 female), 364 musicians (218m, 146f), 25 racehorse trainers and jockeys (all male), 685 blacksmiths (all male), 244 brushmakers (all male), 370 solicitors (368m, 2f), 778 hairdressers (678m, 100f), 942 postmen and postal sorters (915m, 27f), 1,501 charwomen and office cleaners (38m, 1,463f), 2,039 dockers (all male), 12,876 in professional occupations (6,591m,

On Thursday, 11 November 1926, George Bernard Shaw is awarded the 1925 Nobel Prize for Literature 'for his work which is marked by both idealism and humanity, its stimulating satire often being infused with a singular poetic beauty'. Among his works is *Pygmalion*, about linguist Professor Henry Higgins' attempts to pass cockney flower girl Eliza Doolittle for a duchess, *Heartbreak House*, a complex play about Europe before the war, and in 1923 *Saint Joan*, a tragedy based on the life of Joan of Arc. Shaw is not in Dublin, the city of his birth, when the award is announced – he left Dublin in the 1870s and has lived in London since then. Unlike Yeats, Shaw refuses the prize because he believes he has already made sufficient money from his works.

6,285f), 549 publicans (485m, 64f), 436 tram and bus conductors (all male), 256 journalists and authors (219m, 37f), 2,308 teachers (776m, 1,532f), 2,304 painters and decorators (2,291m, 13 f), 990 makers of tobacco and snuff (292m, 698f), 421 sugar, sweet and jam makers (135m, 286f), 1,870 dressmakers (8m, 1,862 f), 683 clergymen and 1,451 nuns, 131 bicycle mechanics (all male), 194 photographers (104m, 90f), 235 printing machine setters and minders (202m, 33f) and 259 watch and clock repairers (256 m, 3f).

❖ ❖ ❖ ❖ ❖ ❖ ❖ ❖ ❖ ❖ ❖

Thursday, 9 December 1926

Just before 8 a.m., between 200 and 300 people gather outside the gates of Mountjoy Prison.

At 8 a.m., the prison bell tolls. Shortly afterwards, the gate opens and a warder pins a note signed by the governor announcing that Henry McCabe has been executed.

Henry McCabe, originally from Enniskerry, County Wicklow, was convicted of Dublin's largest mass murder (apart from those during the recent troubles) in a house called 'La Mancha', just outside Malahide. Four members of the McDonnell family and two of their staff had been poisoned, bludgeoned and burned. The slightly built 48-year-old McCabe was the McDonnells' gardener, and although it was not shown how he might have done it or what motive he might have had to carry out the most calculated and gruesome of killings, it was proven in court that he was the only one who could have done it. Later this morning, his body will be buried in an unmarked grave within the grounds of the prison.

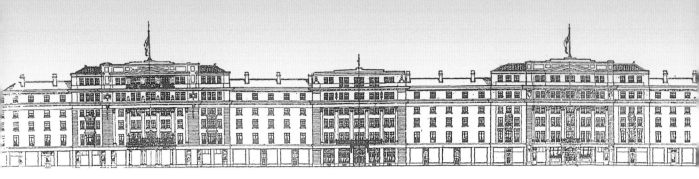

Saturday, 16 April 1927

Nearly five years after it was taken over by Republicans in 1922 and then destroyed by shelling and fire, the Gresham Hotel on O'Connell Street is reopening for guests.

The new Gresham is a combination of old and new, with a strong French accent. The eighteenth-century style façade of Portland stone is built around a modern concrete and steel structure. The entrance hall is decorated in French stucco and marble, though the floor is made of hard-wearing rubber. The 'Winter Gardens' lounge has 'blue-grey trellis decoration harmonizing with the rose and silver-coloured curtains and polished hardwood floor'. The two restaurants are 'decorated in the French style' and all of the hotel's light fittings have been imported from Paris. The 120 bedrooms, many with sitting rooms and private bathrooms, feature the latest type of pedestal wash basins (with hot and cold water), telephones and concealed central heating that can be controlled by the occupants of each individual room.

Top: Dublin Corporation architect Horace O'Rourke gives clear design styles for new buildings to be erected on O'Connell Street in the years after the Civil War fighting.

Right: The fully reconstructed Gresham Hotel reopens in 1927.

Wednesday, 25 May 1927

Work on the restoration of the GPO continues behind specially erected hoardings. While the workers are cleaning the exterior of years of soot, grime and the scorch damage caused by the flames of 1916, the large carved relief of the British Royal Coat of Arms that had once stood proud is being removed from the pediment at the top of the façade.

Seamus Murphy, Chairman of the City Commissioners, writes in the foreword to the Dublin Civic Week General Programme on Saturday, 17 September 1927 of the under-appreciated importance of Dublin to Ireland:

'The average Dublin citizen has his finger on Ireland's pulse. This is a fact as obvious as that the heart sends life-giving blood circulating through the body. Yet of this he is unaware and were one to tell him so, he would be surprised, if not amused.

Such is our appreciation of civic pride! But the average Dubliner cannot be blamed, for the importance of his city, the part it plays in the country's life, the share it has in the shaping of the nation's destiny have never been pointed out to him. He cannot know that Dublin's inner life is very real, and that daily, at his very door, mayhap, are being set in motion the forces which direct and develop that inner life.'

A street trader and shoppers on South Great George's Street in 1927.

Sunday, 25 September 1927

This year has seen the greatest sporting crowds in the history of the city.

In February, 40,000 attended the rugby international between Ireland and Scotland at Lansdowne Road – it was the occasion of the opening day of the new East Stand. The following month, 25,000 watched Drumcondra FC draw with Brideville, a club based in the Liberties, in the Football Association of Ireland Cup Final at Dalymount Park. Then, in August, a record 67,000 attended the city's most important sporting and tourist event, the RDS Horse Show – numbers were boosted by the recent introduction of a new international team jumping competition, the Nations, Cup, whose winners receive a trophy donated by the Aga Khan. Three weeks ago a crowd of 24,000, watched the Dublin hurling team win the All-Ireland again. Today 36,000 attend the All-Ireland football final in Croke Park between Kerry and Kildare.

A new Bewley's Oriental Café opens on Sunday, 27 November at 78–79 Grafton Street. It is Bewley's third establishment in the city after its George's Street and Westmoreland Street cafés.

Saturday, 30 June 1928

The city streets cannot contain the numbers this evening. People escape the crowds by perching on window ledges, bridge parapets and rooftops and cling to the inanimate figures of the city's statues while concerned mothers take refuge with their children in shops and St John Ambulance men rescue those who faint in the crush.

No one could have envisaged such a scene three months ago.

On 26 March at 4.30 p.m., three Germans arrived at Baldonnel Aerodrome, west Dublin, in the *Bremen*, a Junkers single-engine monoplane, after a nine-hour flight from Tempelhof Aerodrome, Berlin.

In the *Bremen* was the project's financier Baron von Huenefeld – a 36-year-old 'slightly built', 'highly strung' and 'sensitive' aristocrat who sports a monocle and jauntily angled yachting cap. The pilot was Captain Kohl, a short, broad-shouldered, good-natured Bavarian who had been a squadron leader during the war.

Baldonnel was not the *Bremen*'s final destination. The Germans had come to the most north-westerly capital in Europe to do what had never been done before.

They had come to Dublin to fly east to west across the Atlantic. Last year, Charles Lindbergh had flown from America to Paris but both he and his plane had to take the boat back. For transatlantic travel to become commercially viable, the return journey, the challenge of flying against the prevailing winds and weather systems, has to be made.

While the *Bremen* waited at Baldonnel for favourable weather, its mechanic returned to Germany, leaving a spare seat in the plane. This was soon filled by a Free State Air Corps' commandant named James Fitzmaurice, who would act as navigator.

The son of a Mountjoy Prison warder, Fitzmaurice was born in 1898 in a prison cottage. In 1915, he enlisted in the British Army and fought at the Somme. After being injured twice in battle during the Great War, he was transferred to the military school of aeronautics, where he excelled. In May 1919 he piloted the first night-time mail flight. After resigning from the RAF, he joined the fledgling Free State Army Corps in February 1922 and in March 1928 was the commandant at Baldonnel.

Last year Fitzmaurice had attempted his own flight to North America with a Captain Macintosh in the *Princess Xenia*. However, after five hours, they returned home due to bad weather. Since then others have tried, often with fatal consequences. The *L'Oiseau Blanc* disappeared in a North Atlantic storm in May of last year. Three months later the *St Raphael* and its three crew members were lost. Then *Old Glory* went down. Just two weeks before the *Bremen* landed in Dublin, Captain Walter Hinchliffe and Elsie McKay had been killed. Pioneering aviation may be glamorous but it is not for the faint-hearted. Kohl was phlegmatic about their task: 'Navigation,' he said, 'is a matter of simple mathematics, and the rest is a matter of nerves.'

When the weather finally cleared on 12 April the *Bremen* took off from Baldonnel and flew into the western sky accompanied by the hopes and fears of millions of people on either side of the Atlantic.

The *Bremen* is prepared for its journey across the Atlantic Ocean at Baldonnel aerodrome

Huge crowds including those on O'Connell Street turn out to see the crew of the *Bremen* who are the first to fly east to west across the Atlantic.

After 36 hours flying, dangerously low on fuel, Kohl and Fitzmaurice managed a controlled landing on a frozen lake in remote wilderness on the Quebec, Newfoundland and Labrador border. Although they had not reached New York as planned, Baron von Huenefeld, Captain Kohl and Commandant Fitzmaurice had done what had never been done before.

When the three aviators were brought to New York, they were given the traditional hero's ticker-tape parade, President Coolidge decorated them with the Distinguished Flying Cross and they were personally congratulated by Charles Lindbergh. Subsequently, they were feted in Chicago, Philadelphia, Milwaukee, Detroit, St Louis, Montreal and Boston before travelling to Germany where they were mobbed once again.

Today it is Dublin's turn to take part in the worldwide phenomenon of aviation euphoria. Today Dublin joins Berlin, Paris and New York.

In 1928 a 'Medical Inspection of Dublin Schoolchildren' is carried out. It is found that 50 per cent of children require immediate medical treatment, 80 per cent some dental treatment, 12 per cent have defective vision, 3.8 per cent suffer from skin diseases (a figure regarded as remarkably low), 1.8 per cent have heart defects, 0.8 per cent are stammerers, in poor areas 96 per cent showed evidence of verminous contamination and as high as 30 per cent of children in poor areas had *pediculosis corporis* caused by lice, while children in good areas often had no body vermin but 15 per cent were found to have had nits.

When the three aviators finally reach O'Connell Street, they mount a podium erected in front of Clerys. After the speeches, which go largely unheard amid the constant cheers of the thousands packed into the street, the group retires into Clerys for a gala dinner following which the three aviators will be made 'Freemen of the City of Dublin'.

❖ ❖ ❖ ❖ ❖ ❖ ❖ ❖ ❖ ❖ ❖

Friday, 19 October 1928

Tonight there is a new departure in the theatre world as the Dublin Gate Theatre Studio puts on its first production in the 102-seat Peacock Theatre. The Abbey is the national theatre but the Gate was founded by actors Hilton Edwards and Micheál Mac Liammóir to meet another need. Both had returned to Dublin from London where they became familiar with London's Gate which opened in 1925 for the production of 'international theatre'. Believing that Dublin, now a European capital, 'should be the point of contact between that country and other countries, the medium of international understanding' they founded the Dublin Gate to put on the best of international theatre.

The Gate's first production is *Peer Gynt* – somehow the huge cast fit onto the tiny Peacock stage. Though the performance is a success, the company will just about break even from the returns of barely 100 ticket sales. If the Gate is to survive it will surely need to find a larger home of its own.

❖ ❖ ❖ ❖ ❖ ❖ ❖ ❖ ❖ ❖ ❖

Sunday, 11 November 1928

Dublin is a city that is not at peace with its own past.

Armistice Day is a day for those in the city to remember loved ones and friends who fought and died in the Great War. But it is also a day targeted by those who oppose any connection with Britain, or even a reminder of it.

At dawn on this Armistice Day, three British memorials in the city are damaged by explosions. A bomb explodes at the George II statue in St Stephen's Green, a fountain in Pembroke Park commemorating King Edward VII's 1907 visit is

A shrine erected by Dubliners in one of the city streets during the Catholic Emancipation centenary celebrations in 1929.

A mass on Watling Street Bridge during the celebrations.

damaged, and a land mine is detonated on the plinth of the statue of William of Orange, the Protestant 'King Billy', at College Green.

Later in the morning, memorial services take place in many of the city's Protestant churches. Thousands of veterans march in formation to the day's main commemoration event in the Phoenix Park, moved from College Green.

After the ceremony, there is trouble in the city centre. At O'Connell Bridge, two small Union Jacks are snatched from people returning from the Phoenix Park by a group of young men and ripped up. These men are then attacked by a group of ex-British soldiers. Gardaí, who had been prepared for possible trouble, are quickly on the scene. They draw batons to keep the sides apart. The flag stealers then make their way to O'Connell Street where they are caught and beaten by poppy-wearing men.

At around the same time, a crowd of some 200 women and young boys carrying a large Union Jack march down D'Olier Street. Gardaí, concerned about another disturbance, manage to persuade them to disperse, but as they do so they sing defiantly 'God Save the King' and 'The Red, White and Blue'.

❖ ❖ ❖ ❖ ❖ ❖ ❖ ❖ ❖ ❖

Thursday, 11 July 1929

Eight years to the day that the Truce that ended the War of Independence came into effect and over 13 years since it was destroyed by British shells during the Easter Rising, the General Post Office finally reopens for business.

The material used in the reconstruction of the birthplace of the new Irish nation has been sourced as patriotically as possible. The GPO's walls are made of sandstone from Mountcharles, Donegal, the marble used in the public areas is from Kilkenny, Cork and Connemara, the bronze and iron metalwork has been manufactured in Dublin, the roof slates are from Killaloe, County Clare, and the large quantities of granite are from the quarries of Barnacullia and Ballyknockan in the Dublin and Wicklow mountains.

At midday President Cosgrave's car arrives. In front of an impressive military guard, he addresses the large crowd on the significant occasion:

> War has now given way to peace, construction has replaced destruction. The restoration of this building is symbolic of a new order … On the occasion of its reopening we may well recall with gratitude and with pride the sacrifices which have enabled it to be reopened for public use by the Head of the Irish Executive in the presence of members of an Irish Parliament, surrounded by representatives of the State's new institutions. We may well be encouraged by the reflection that as this building has come back to us renewed and beautiful so too is the Irish nation progressing in the path of prosperity and peace.

The GPO finally reopens in 1929.

On Tuesday, 16 July 1929, the statue of Young Irelander, William Smith O'Brien, which has stood in the middle of the road at the O'Connell Bridge corner of D'Olier Street and Westmoreland Street since 1870, is removed to be re-erected on O'Connell Street to ease the flow of traffic.

After the Irish flag is ceremoniously raised above the roof, Cosgrave enters the GPO to become the first customer since the morning of Easter Monday 1916. He purchases the first stamp. He sends the first telegram, fittingly to the International Telegraph Bureau in Berne. He also makes the first telephone call. It is to the Governor General's residence in the Phoenix Park. However, James McNeill is not there, so Cosgrave leaves a message with his son offering greetings on the occasion of the GPO's reopening.

❖ ❖ ❖ ❖ ❖ ❖ ❖ ❖ ❖ ❖ ❖

Friday, 29 November 1929

The damage done to O'Connell Street in 1922 is now almost completely repaired. Tonight, on the site of the old Granville Hotel, on the opposite side of the road from the GPO, where Cathal Brugha had made his last stand, the largest cinema in Ireland called the Savoy is opening.

There is no doubting the popularity of the picture house. Last year, two million people attended Irish cinemas and it remains by far the most popular form of entertainment in Dublin.

Built by Associated British Cinemas at a cost of £200,000, the Savoy is not just a place to show projected images, accompanied by sound or not – the Savoy will be showing both silent and the new talkies – it is a place of escape.

A journalist given a preview of the cinema describes the main auditorium: 'Scene: a canal in Venice. Time – after nightfall. Left back and right back – stately medieval houses, built in the Venetian style. Left front and right front – weather-beaten stone walls, with big iron gates giving glimpses of old-world gardens. In the centre, the world-famous Bridge of Sighs casting its shadows on the waters on the canal beneath, represented softly on the curtain, and shimmering softly in the dim light.'

A broad marble staircase speaks of 'true elegance', while a 300-seat restaurant promises the finest of fare. In the auditorium, the seats are the 'acme of comfort' and the air 'conditioned', with its impurities filtered out. The ceiling above the stalls, balcony and dress circle is painted azure blue, suggesting 'the beauties of the far Mediterranean Sea', while a novel lighting system – with hardly a lamp visible – can turn it into a star-studded night canopy.

The Venetian style interior of the new Savoy Cinema on O'Connell Street.

An essential feature of any cinema is its organ and the Savoy's is an attraction in itself. Manufactured by the famous Compton Organ Company in London, this machine has taken several weeks to install. Containing thousands of switches, it stands on an electrically operated lift that can, in a matter of seconds, raise the organ into the auditorium, or lower it as required. But even when in view, what can be seen is only a fraction of this monster, because in three rooms off-stage are the motor generator, blowing apparatus and hundreds of pipes.

This evening begins with a news bulletin which is followed by the premier screening of a specially commissioned government film called *Ireland*. The first reel features the sites of the Free State's capital including such landmarks as the Bank of Ireland, Trinity College, College Green, O'Connell Street and Leinster House as well as suburbs such as Howth, Dalkey and Dún Laoghaire. After tonight, Associated British Cinemas will show it in all their picture houses across the water which, it is hoped, will lead to many future British visitors.

Finally comes the main feature. It is Warner Brothers' *On With the Show*, which is billed as 'the first 100% Natural Colour, Talking, Singing, Dancing Picture'.

1930–1939

Housing, the Church and Traffic

Tuesday, 14 October 1930

It is the start of a new era of municipal government as the myriad of public bodies that once governed the city are amalgamated into Dublin Corporation, Dublin County Council and a new 'coastal borough' of Dún Laoghaire. These bodies are not being run directly by councillors with their own staff, as had been the case before the commissioners took over, but by a paid 'manager' with professional staff (dealing with Finance, Public Health, Streets and Waterworks) who will report to the councillors.

The review of Dublin's local government that had led to the changes had also proposed the abolition of the office of Lord Mayor as anachronistic, outdated, part of the trappings of British rule, not in keeping with a new Irish State, a waste of money. But tradition won out and the office of the Lord Mayor, dating back to 1665, is about to be filled for the first time in six years.

Alfie Byrne TD is proposed. The son of a docker and described as 'one of the greatest friends of the poor', he had been an Irish MP in the House of Commons before being elected as an independent to the Dáil in 1922. Though an independent, Byrne is aligned to the Cumann na nGaedheal party and the question of his partisanship is bitterly debated in the City Hall chamber.

After three acrimonious hours, Byrne is elected by a vote of 20 to 13 (defeating the challenge of Sean O'Kelly, deputy leader of Fianna Fáil). When the chain of office, a gift to the city from William of Orange, is put over his shoulders, a woman in the public gallery shouts 'God Save the King!' and 'Ireland for England!', perhaps in reference to the chain and its donor, or the retention of the word 'Lord', or maybe because the new Lord Mayor had once sat in the House of Commons.

Following the reorganisation of local government in the city, Alfie Byrne is elected Lord Mayor in 1930.

Thursday, 30 October 1930

The highest-ranking police officer in the country, Eoin O'Duffy, is in Government Buildings giving evidence, behind closed doors, to the Committee on the Criminal Law Amendment and Juvenile Prostitution Acts. In the chair sits barrister William Carrigan.

From his position O'Duffy has a unique view of the city and its illicit habits.

The police raid on Monto in 1925 might have closed down Dublin's brazenly open red-light district, but it did not eradicate the trade in sex. O'Duffy estimates that there are 100 prostitutes in the city who no longer work in the open, but operate in 'secret brothels'.

O'Duffy is not unsympathetic to the plight of the prostitutes. He tells Carrigan, 'There is nothing inherently bad in the majority of our young Irish girls who drift into this unfortunate class.' For him the issue of prostitution is one inextricably bound up with conditions in the city's tenements. In the slums, 'the rudimentary fundamentals of society' are undermined as 'large families sleep in one or two beds, in a common room, clothes barely sufficient to cover their nakedness, and no consideration possible as regards dressing, undressing, sleeping and complying with the demands of nature'.

In recent years, sexual assaults and rapes on children have increased. It is even worse than the statistics show, as O'Duffy estimates only 15 per cent are reported. This is due to parents' fear of stigmatising their child, the difficulty of proving a sexual assault in court, and the fact that even when someone is convicted of 'taking advantage' of children, they often get off with just a six-month sentence, sometimes only a fine.

When a rape results in a pregnancy, the final hurt is inflicted as the unmarried mother is fired from her job, cast out of her home and shunned by society. In such situations she is all too often forced into prostitution in order to survive in the city.

Commissioner O'Duffy's comments must be causing Carrigan some unease. Because last year was the centenary of Catholic Emancipation and it was recently announced that Dublin is going to host the Catholic Church's Eucharistic Congress in 1932.

❖ ❖ ❖ ❖ ❖ ❖ ❖ ❖ ❖ ❖ ❖

Monday, 17 November 1930

This morning, people in all corners of the world look to Dublin.

The city buzzes with anticipation.

Because this morning, the first Irish Hospital Sweepstakes draw is taking place in the Mansion House.

When the Sweepstakes' promoters are challenged on the ethics of their venture, they argue that they are doing nothing immoral, only selling 'anticipation' and inducing the not normally charity-minded to contribute to the running costs of Dublin's outdated, overrun and dilapidated hospitals. Jervis Street, Sir Patrick Dun's, St Ultan's, Harcourt Street Children's, the National Maternity Hospital and the Dental Hospital will divide £131,724 between them to help clear debts, get wards re-opened and buy modern equipment. How can that be immoral?

At 9 a.m., the counterfoils are brought into the Mansion House and piled onto 40-foot tables surrounded by scores of women who delve their arms into the counterfoils and mix.

Sixty Gardaí keep watch while auditors Craig Gardner are on hand to ensure that all is above board.

At 10 a.m., 20 nurses from the hospitals bring sacks full of counterfoils into the Round Room. Under the glare of floodlights that have been set up for the benefit of newsreel cameramen, they pour the tickets into an 18-foot-long drum decorated with the city's coat of arms.

A parade through the streets prior to a Sweepstakes draw.

An invited audience that includes members of the Oireachtas, the judiciary, lawyers, medical men, prominent sports men and fifty of the world's journalists take their seats.

Anticipation reaches its climax at 11 a.m. as the 'Ceremony of the Drawing' begins with a 'certifiably blind' boy from St Joseph's Asylum, Drumcondra, led to the larger drum. With the impartiality of the unseeing, he reaches in and draws out the first lucky ticket. When it is announced that it is Mordie Poirier's of Moore Street there is a cheer for what is thought to be a Dublin winner. However, cheers turn to laughter as the next line of the address is read – Mordie is not from Dublin's Moore Street, but one in Boston, USA.

The first Irish ticket drawn is from Cork and it is not until the twentieth counterfoil is taken out by one of the boys that there is a Dublin winner. It is that of Mr J.E. Ryan of 13 Croydon Gardens, Fairview, a typesetter for Independent Newspapers, who draws 'Empire Builder'.

All this takes time.

When the draw finally ends after four hours, there are 11 winners from Ireland, two from Dublin. The highest number are drawn from England, with others from Northern Ireland, Scotland, Wales, Canada, South Africa, the United States, the Philippines, Burma, Malay and Demerara (Guyana).

The lucky ones have a week to wait for the Manchester race. While everyone drawn – even those with non-runners – will get a substantial cash prize, the ticket holder whose horse wins will receive the almost unimaginable sum of £200,000 – more than all the hospitals combined.

For everyone else, well, tickets will soon be on sale for the second Sweepstakes draw. This time it will be for the Aintree Grand National in March.

Now, there is something to anticipate.

In March 1931, a song is released by Jimmy O'Dea and Harry O'Donovan called 'Biddy Mulligan the Pride of the Coombe' about a widowed street trader on Patrick Street who for 64 years has sold apples, oranges, nuts, sweet peas, bananas and sweet sugar sticks, and on Fridays, fish – her herrings are the best – and on Saturdays, second-hand clothes.

Sunday, 5 July 1931

The north side of the city is leading the way in what is being called the 'new architecture'. A house named *Wendon* on Mobhi Road in Glasnevin is one of the first to be constructed in Ireland in the style of Germany's Bauhaus School of Art and Architecture.

Built of reinforced concrete and steel, *Wendon* is the ultimate in no-nonsense straight-line, utilitarian architecture. The simplicity of the structure is supposed to appeal to today's aesthetics, but it also achieves substantial savings through the elimination of unnecessary frills, decoration and any features that are without a 'definite structural reason'.

Today at Kincora Road, Clontarf, three miles from *Wendon*, overlooking the seafront of Dollymount, the first of 42 houses built in the new style are open for viewing. According to one journalist, the general effect is of 'a house built of children's square blocks, but built by a master and artistic hand'. Brilliant white 'snocrete' finish, flat roofs and steel windows are features that Irish sensibilities will take some time getting used to.

Lord Mayor Alfie Byrne is launching the scheme. But as he does so, he clearly has something else on his mind. For, while admiring the houses and their innovations, he remarks that it would be a great service to the nation if the architects could manage to devise a new flat that could be built at a reasonable price in order to house the working classes of the city.

❖ ❖ ❖ ❖ ❖ ❖ ❖ ❖ ❖ ❖ ❖

Tuesday, 14 July 1931

A week after launching the Kincora Road houses, the Lord Mayor hosts a meeting at the Mansion House at which a 'War on the Slums' is declared. Those in attendance regard the Dublin housing situation as the greatest national problem. Because, despite the fact that since 1922, in the most stringent of times, £2.5 million has been spent on 3,686 new family working-class dwellings, the Dublin slum evil remains.

In England, overcrowding is legally defined as 'any room occupied by a man, his wife and a child over ten years of age, without proper facilities for the segregation of the sexes'. But such are the conditions endemic in Dublin, if every overcrowded building was cleared, a huge tenement problem would, in an instant, become a problem of mass homelessness.

An extract from this month's Corporation Housing Report describes just one of thousands of Dublin houses:

In the top left room lives Mrs A. with her husband, three daughters and one boy, whose ages range from 20 to 8 years. The boy is in the Free State Army. The husband is a builder's labourer, and was idle from Christmas until the 8th July 1931. The family was 17 years in occupation of the room at a rent of 3/- weekly. The top right room was occupied by Mr B a widower, with two sons, aged 21 and 16 years. They live on outdoor relief, have been 18 years in occupation of the room, the rent of which was 3/- weekly. The left drawing-room is occupied by Mr C and his wife and six children, whose ages ranged from 12 to 1 years. They live on outdoor relief. The rent is 3/9 weekly. The family had been 14 years in occupation. The right drawing-room is occupied by Mrs X, a widow, with three sons whose ages range from 23 to 17 years. One has an Army pension of 26/8 and another boy earns 11/- weekly. The rent is 3/9. The family has been 12 years in occupation. The left parlour is occupied by Mrs X, a widow, with one boy and three girls, whose ages range from 22 to 6 years. The total income is 17/2 and the rent 3/9. The family has been 25 years in occupation. The right parlour is occupied by Mrs X, her husband, and eight children, whose ages range from 14 years to 3 months. The husband is a coal-heaver, and the income of the family is about £2 a week. The rent is 3/9. The family has been in occupation for 13 years. The left kitchen, one of the underground dwellings that have been so often mentioned, is occupied my Mrs C. her husband and ten children whose ages range from 21 to 3 years. The man is a builder's labourer who, after being unemployed for a considerable time, had just been re-employed. The rent was 2/3. The family were in occupation for 16 years. The right kitchen was occupied by Mrs C., her husband and eight children whose ages range from 16 years to 6 months. The income was 18/6. The husband has a pension of £18 yearly from the Free State Army. The rent was 2/3. The family was in occupation for 18 years.

On Thursday, 1 October 1931, the Four Courts finally reopens for business, nine years after its destruction during the Civil War.

The Four Courts
from the steps of
St. Audoen's Arch.

Wednesday, 3 August 1932

Ten years after independence, a new era in public housing begins as the Housing Act comes into effect. The legislation is almost revolutionary.

Until now, the administrative process of slum clearance has been cumbersome, time-consuming and one heavily weighted in favour of those – notably the landlords – whose interests are vested in their perpetuation. It has also been expensive. Not only have tenement landlords greatly inflated their properties' values, they have also been compensated for profits earned from packing sometimes more than 20 people into single rooms. It was a system that virtually rewarded the creation of overcrowded slums.

Today's legislation removes many of the obstacles to solving the problem.

In anticipation of the Housing Act, Dublin City Manager Sherlock has already outlined a five-year plan to build 2,000 dwellings a year. To deliver the programme the corporation is creating a Housing Department, with a chief architect, Herbert Simms.

Simms was born in London in 1898 and served with the Royal Field Artillery in the Great War. After studying architecture and civic design, he moved to Dublin where, after working in a private practice for a time, he joined Dublin Corporation in 1925 as an architect. This unassuming, reticent man now has the daunting task of solving Dublin's housing problem.

For Simms, the solutions to the problem are dictated by mathematics and money.

In order to alleviate overcrowding, the majority of people in the tenements will not be able to stay in the areas where they have been living. If ten acres of slum where 3,000 people live is cleared, only 1,000 will be able to return there. Therefore the other 2,000 will have to live somewhere else. And that somewhere else is in the suburbs. That is simple mathematics.

Many people regard the construction of healthy 'cottage type' two-storey houses on the outskirts of the city as the ideal solution. These houses will all have running water, central heating, two or three bedrooms, kitchens, parlours, front and back gardens, fresh healthy air and open spaces near their houses for children to play.

But because of money they cannot be for everyone.

The suburban houses are going to be expensive to build and therefore have high rents. They will also require people to travel to their work, which means they will have to pay for bus or tram fares to the city centre.

Simms' solution is a new type of structure known as 'working-class flats' that will be built in blocks several storeys high. These will house the poorest of the poor on the sites of demolished slums. But even before they are constructed, his policy is being criticised, with some believing that these will become nothing but overcrowded 'tenement flats' and recreate an 'evil to vex future generations'. Others are concerned that by concentrating the poorest of the poor in these blocks, the city is just storing up future social problems.

❖ ❖ ❖ ❖ ❖ ❖ ❖ ❖ ❖ ❖ ❖

Sunday, 26 June 1932

This morning, someone on the Dublin Mountains looking down on the expanse of the Fifteen Acres field in the Phoenix Park would be witnessing a curious phenomenon. Because as the sun climbs over the city, the Fifteen Acres, considerably larger than its name would suggest, is gradually darkening as hundreds of thousands of people assemble for the penultimate event of the 1932 Eucharistic Congress.

It is the end of a week during which the vast majority of Dubliners have shown their loyalty to Rome – 'All the Catholic world knows it,' the papal legate, Cardinal Lorenzo Lauri, remarked, '… and admires you for it.'

Even before today's mass, the Congress has been the largest single event ever staged in Ireland.

There has been an influx of Catholics from every county in Ireland, from Britain, Canada, the United States, Uruguay, Argentina, New Zealand, Italy, Spain, Armenia, China, Poland, Austria, Belgium, the West Indies, Nicaragua, Ethiopia, the Fiji Islands and elsewhere. Numbers have far exceeded the city's official accommodation and thousands have been put up in private homes, converted national schools, libraries

Planes from the Irish Air Corps flying in cross formation above Papal Legate Cardinal Lorenzo Lauri ship as it steams into Dún Laoghaire harbour.

Left: Midnight mass at Iona Road.
Right: People crowding onto a tram to bring them to the Phoenix Park mass.

and town halls, tented villages in Artane, Cabra and Terenure and more than 50 ships used as floating hotels that are moored on the Liffey and in Dublin Bay.

The main thoroughfares of the city are decorated with 60 miles of garlands, bunting, coloured shields, papal flags, Congress flags and Irish flags. Public buildings have been illuminated at night, while searchlights have spelt out onto clouds drifting across the city *Laudamus*, *Glorificamus* and *Adoramus* (We praise, We glorify and We adore). But what has impressed visitors most are not the official decorations. It is the 'furnaces of colour' and 'fountains of light' in the slums off the main streets, erected with the meaningful sacrifice of the poor.

Since the papal legate arrived at Dún Laoghaire and was greeted by a twenty-one-gun salute, a benediction from the air by the Air Corps flying over in cross-

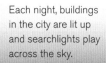

Each night, buildings in the city are lit up and searchlights play across the sky.

formation and 50,000 people crammed onto the embracing piers, Dublin has been a 'city of hymnal song; of spiritual chant; of sacred harmony'. There have been religious meetings, daily services for the various nationalities, midnight masses, garden parties at Blackrock College, a women's mass attended by 200,000, a children's one attended by 100,000.

It has not only been those attending the events who have been able to take part. In what is believed to be the most extensive public address system installed anywhere in the world, 500 loudspeakers erected throughout the city have broadcast the collective acts of worship. Dublin has been one vast temple.

This all comes to an end today.

At 1 p.m., the 'Solemn Pontifical Mass' begins in the Phoenix Park. A million people face an altar with a dome and curving colonnades reminiscent of Rome's St Peter's. The Bell of St Patrick, loaned by the National Museum, is rung, a choir 2,000 strong leads the hymns and papal count John McCormack sings an unforgettable 'Panis Angelicus'.

The final blessing on O'Connell Bridge brings the Congress to an end.

Girls attending the
Eucharistic Congress.

But the mass is not the end. There is one more event. It is the concluding blessing at O'Connell Bridge, under the statue of Daniel O'Connell, the man responsible for the emancipation of Catholics in Ireland.

In order to get the faithful from the park to the city centre safely and in reasonable time, the crowd is divided into four groups who take different routes.

The main group consists of, in a strictly pre-determined order, Christian Brothers, the No. 1 Army Band, the first portion of the choir, regular and secular clergy, the priests' choir, the canon of Dublin, then the Blessed Sacrament with the cardinal legate carried on a platform drawn by eight young priests, preceded by torch-bearers and flanked by a military guard of honour

Girls attending the
Eucharistic Congress.

and thurifers. After this come the cardinals (in order of seniority), archbishops, bishops, members of the Eucharistic Congress Committee, other prelates, ministers of state, members of the judiciary, foreign ministers, the second portion of choir, representatives of the Dáil and Senate, consuls, bearers of papal titles, members of Dublin Corporation, Dún Laoghaire Borough, the six Northern Ireland counties, various other corporations, county councils, harbour boards, vocational councils, urban district councils, boards of public assistance, the National University, and then, finally, representatives of women's groups, a special group of female singers and 'other women'.

As the hundreds of thousands walk, they join in hymns and prayers in Irish, English and Latin that are being broadcast over the loudspeakers. Eventually, they congregate in the area around O'Connell Bridge. The hymns cease. There is a sharp military command. Trumpets ring. The legate raises the monstrance high and the multitudes kneel. A great hush falls over the city.

Then the *Te Deum* and other benediction hymns are sung by the throng. At the blessing, the trumpeters sound the general salute. Then there is 'intense prayerfulness' as the city's gulls wheel and cry overhead.

Finally, the legate prays 'that the most abundant blessings descend on the clergy and people of this beautiful Isle of St Patrick, that God may preserve this Ireland now and in the future, as God in his mercy has done in the past, and keep it always and ever the Ireland of Saints'.

With that, an extraordinary week in the city comes to an end.

It is a week that has put the church firmly in the centre of Irish public life. The Eucharistic Congress has changed not only how Ireland is viewed, but also how Ireland views itself.

Thursday, 1 December 1932

In offices at Government Buildings, a delicate meeting takes place between James Geoghegan, the new Fianna Fáil Minister for Justice, and the Bishops of Limerick and Ossory and Thasos. The purpose of the meeting is to discuss the recently completed Carrigan report.

Carrigan had first presented his report to the Cosgrave government a year ago. What Carrigan had put in his report was an edited, even censored, version of what various people had told his committee. Among the evidence that was omitted was much of what Commissioner O'Duffy had presented. While the report does make reference to prostitution in the city, the association between child abuse, prostitution and the city's social conditions is nowhere to be seen.

Carrigan's main concerns are not cruel abuse that goes on behind closed doors but the visible signs of sexual activity. He is concerned about unregulated dance halls and the illicit uses to which motor cars are put on public roads – the report quotes the Fairview parish priest describing 'men in motor cars who patrol the streets, stopping here and there to invite young women to whom they are unknown to accompany them for drives'. The only reference to the issue of sexual abuse is that the children of the city are particularly vulnerable in their homes when both parents are out working.

At today's meeting, the bishops express their concern to the minister about the impression the report would create if it should be made public. Anyone reading it would have little choice but to conclude 'that the ordinary feelings of decency

The St Patrick's day military parade has become one of the most popular events in the city.

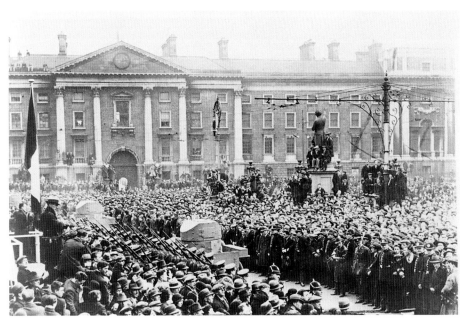

and the influence of religion have failed in this country'. That is not an impression they want the world to have. In their opinion, 'it is clearly undesirable that such a view of conditions in the Saorstát should be given wide circulation'. The report, they recommend, should remain confidential. And Minister Geoghegan puts up no argument; there are some things that the public do not need to know.

❖ ❖ ❖ ❖ ❖ ❖ ❖ ❖ ❖ ❖ ❖

Wednesday, 29 March 1933

Dublin may not be a hotbed of communism such as Berlin or Paris but the very existence of a few has drawn the ire of the city's religious figures. Emboldened by the Eucharistic Congress, the city's Catholic leaders decide that they are not going to tolerate a 'red menace' in Dublin.

Tonight a crowd of men and women march on a small two-storey red-brick terraced house on Great Strand Street. Called 'Connolly House', it is the headquarters of the recently founded Irish Revolutionary Workers' Group, Ireland's communist party.

In the last few weeks the city's Catholic clergy have enthusiastically taken up Pope Pius XI's encyclical *Caritate Christi* that labelled communism 'the greatest evil of our time'. Weekly anti-communist sermons have been delivered in various parish churches. Last month, the well-known priest and novelist Rev. Owen Dudley spoke to a large audience in the Theatre Royal on the 'menace of communism'. During it he warned of the threat posed by even a small cadre of communists in a city with such wretched poverty – it is no coincidence that the communist building is located in the middle of an area with some of the worst slums. What precisely sparked off direct action is not known, but last week, a communist meeting held at the corner of Capel Street and Lower Abbey Street was broken up by a large crowd who, after singing 'Faith of Our Fathers', stormed the platform, the speakers having to be bundled onto passing trams by Gardaí.

On Monday, following a vehemently anti-communist sermon in the Pro-Cathedral, Connolly House became a centre of Catholic anger.

It was the same last night.

Tonight the crowd is numbered in the thousands. Maybe it is because of the stubborn defiance that has been shown during the week by the dozen or so communists. Or perhaps the news in today's papers of the burning of the Reichstag in Berlin by, allegedly, a lone Dutch communist, shows what even one communist is capable of doing. Or maybe it is just that numbers are swelled with those who had been watching the largest fire seen in the city since the Civil War that is raging in a furniture warehouse nearby on Bachelors Walk.

But whatever the cause, 60 gardaí are struggling to contain the crowd who are far from content to sing 'God Bless Our Pope' and 'Hail Glorious St Patrick'. They charge the police, while those inside Connolly House rain missiles down on their attackers. Sixteen people are arrested and 33 are brought to Jervis Street Hospital to receive treatment.

Eventually, after 11 p.m., when a neighbouring building is set alight, the occupiers of Connolly House flee for their lives over rooftops. Then the protesters ransack the communist headquarters and litter Great Strand Street with various leaflets, including some advocating 'The Irish Case for Communism' and others explaining the views of 'Marx, Engels, Lenin on the Irish Revolution'.

❖ ❖ ❖ ❖ ❖ ❖ ❖ ❖ ❖ ❖ ❖

Monday, 19 June 1933

The new 'Dublin Municipal Gallery of Modern Art' opens in Charlemont House, Parnell Square. Added to the opening of the new Gate Theatre in 1928, around the corner at the Rotunda Hall, the area is fast becoming a key cultural part of the city. A curious aspect of the gallery's opening is an empty room. Not many galleries open with an empty room on public display – curators tend to abhor blank walls. But that is precisely what happens at this gallery, as one room has the solitary bust of Sir Hugh Lane, a man who died nearly 20 years ago.

It has been left vacant for 39 paintings that form what has become known as the Hugh Lane Bequest Pictures. During the last three decades, nothing has been more controversial in Irish art than the saga of these paintings.

The story started in 1908 when Dublin Corporation opened a Gallery of Modern Art at 17 Harcourt Street. Widely regarded as the first gallery of modern art in the world, it mainly housed paintings that had been loaned by one of Europe's foremost collectors of impressionist paintings, Sir Hugh Lane. Among these were 39 'Continental Paintings' that included such works as Édouard Manet's *La Musique aux Tuileries*, Edgar Degas' *Sur la Plage*, Claude Monet's *Waterloo Bridge* and Pierre Auguste Renoir's *Les Parapluies*.

The terraced house, with its limited space and poor lighting, was only ever intended as a temporary home, until such time as the corporation could establish a proper gallery.

Among the various sites for the new gallery were Lord Edward Street, Merrion Square, the Old Turkish Baths on Lincoln Place, a site beside the Mansion House and a disused skating rink at Earlsfort Terrace. But each was discounted, mainly because the cost of purchasing them was too high.

Then Lane proposed a 'gallery bridge' to replace the Metal Bridge and asked English architect Edwin Lutyens to design a new pedestrian bridge with an open-air art gallery. Lane promised significant financial support to the corporation – the most it would have to outlay was £22,000. However, it rejected Lane's proposal for a number of reasons. One remained the cost – £22,000 was still a considerable sum. Another was that, while the corporation did not oppose the demolition of the Metal Bridge, it wanted any new bridge to carry vehicular traffic in order to relieve traffic congestion at College Green. It also wanted the bridge designed in such a way so as not to block views along the river, which was already a problem with the Loop Line Bridge.

In the end, that little footbridge remained in place and a miffed Lane transferred his paintings from Dublin to London's National Gallery. It was this failure of the Dublin authorities to secure the Lane paintings that had provoked William Butler Yeats to write 'September 1913', his castigating criticism of the city – 'adding the half pence to the pence' – being both a comment about the city authority's parsimoniousness and an obvious reference to the Metal Bridge's toll.

But that was not the end of the story.

In May 1915, Lane, along with nearly 1,200 others, perished when the *Lusitania* was sunk off the Cork coast by a German U-boat. When his desk was being cleared a codicil to his will was discovered. This codicil stated that the 39 pictures then in London, 'I now bequest to the City of Dublin providing that a suitable building is provided for them within five years of my death'.

Unfortunately, the codicil was not witnessed and therefore had no legal standing. Since then, despite numerous official requests for the return of the paintings and the 'moral right' that Dublin asserted over them, the British National Gallery has consistently refused to hand them over.

And that is the reason that today, at the grand opening of the Municipal Gallery of Modern Art, there was that empty room, reserved in the hope that one day its walls would be adorned with 39 impressionist paintings that had once belonged to Sir Hugh Lane.

Tension is high in the city on Sunday, 13 August. For days, people have been waiting to see if the National Guard, also known as the 'Blueshirts', under former Garda Commissioner Eoin O'Duffy, will proceed with a banned march to a cenotaph in memory of Michael Collins and Kevin O'Higgins on the lawn of Leinster House. Strongly influenced by European fascists, its members take part in parades and route marches in distinctive blue shirts with shoulder straps and black berets.

Amid fears of a Mussolini-style march on Rome, 300 police, some armed, are on duty at Government Buildings. An armoured car prowls up and down outside, while lorries with armed police patrol the city and suburbs. But the day passes peacefully, with just two unidentified women arriving to the lawns of Leinster House to pay their respects.

The Corporation's Playground Committee opens its first playground on Tuesday, 1 August 1933. It is in the tenements in Foley Street. Although the new playground will accommodate 500 children, another 10,000 children will have to continue dodging the traffic as they use the streets as playgrounds.

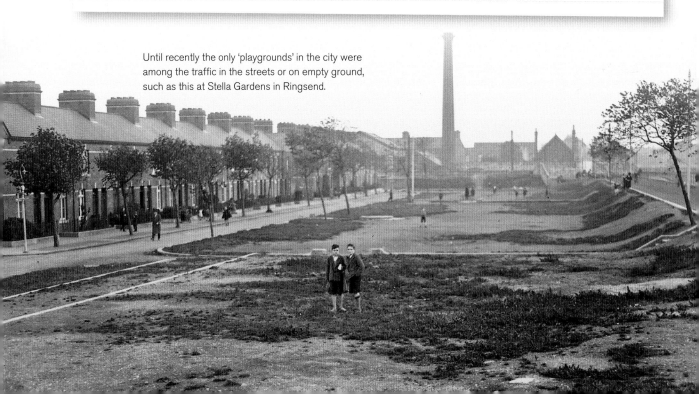

Until recently the only 'playgrounds' in the city were among the traffic in the streets or on empty ground, such as this at Stella Gardens in Ringsend.

Amid fears of a march on Dail Eireann by members of the Blueshirts, an armoured car patrols the road in front of Leinster Lawn.

Sunday, 26 November 1933

In a New York courtroom the final judgement in a case known as 'United States v. One Book Called *Ulysses*' is delivered. Random House, the publisher with the American rights, had started the proceedings to resolve the central question as to whether or not the book set in Dublin on 16 June 1904 is 'obscene'.

Judge John M. Woolsey's verdict is considered, erudite and significant. He rules that *Ulysses* is neither obscene nor pornographic. In his opinion, Joyce was sincere and honest in his attempt to show how the minds of his characters worked. According to Woolsey, if he had failed to portray their thoughts fully – however lewd they might be – it would have been 'artistically inexcusable'.

Within minutes of Woolsey's verdict being delivered, Random House typesetters are fast at work printing *Ulysses* for the lucrative American market.

When Joyce hears the news in Paris, he comments that 'one half of the English-speaking world surrenders; the other half will follow'. Except, he knows, Ireland. Because not one Dublin bookshop or any of its riverside bookstalls has a copy of *Ulysses*. This is not because the book is banned in the country of his birth. It is because no one has dared attempt to import or print it, knowing that such an exercise would be both expensive in terms of legal fees and entirely futile.

'At O'Connell Bridge I stopped a taxi and got out. I walked up the quays past the Custom House. There were several trading steamers lying in the river. The evening sky was blue and cloudless and there was a breeze with a feint salt-sea smell blowing up the river. More than the scent of any flower, that scent to me is full of romance. I think of the world saturated by it like a woman in the dark with a strange subtle perfume, and if one knew nothing else of her one would fall in love with her because of that alone.'

Francis Stuart, *Things to Live For: Notes for an Autobiography*, 1934

Tuesday, 11 December 1934

While the issue of housing the poor has been occupying much attention, the construction of private houses, aided by the same low-interest loans being provided to local authorities, is booming.

Some of the largest and most fashionable homes are on the Merrion Park Estate in south Dublin. Built on land once owned by the Fitzwilliam family, these are not homes for former slum dwellers.

At Merrion Park, there are just six houses to the acre. There are more than 50 different house designs with prices ranging from £650 to £1,600.

Though the estate has the characteristics of a rural idyll with many ancient trees retained – some in the middle of roads – Merrion Park houses are far from rustic. They all have the modern amenities that will give '100% comfort to the housewife'.

Crowds queue to get into number 22, the 'Electricity Demonstration House', that is open for viewing. Developed with the assistance of the Electricity Supply Board, the house showcases the role that electricity can play in domestic life.

Although the kitchen is dedicated to the housewife's twin tenets of minimising labour and maximising service, there are men on hand to explain how the novel appliances work. Of particular interest is the new way of washing and drying clothes: put the clothes in the electric clothes-washing machine, then through the electric mangle, place them in the electric drier, shut the door, turn on the current, and take them out clean and bone-dry an hour and a quarter later!

It seems as if the developers of the Merrion Estate believe that relationships in a modern home will be different because the traditional kitchen table has lost its central place in the kitchen and is now consigned to running the length of the wall under a window. At the other side of the room stands a 'frigidaire', nests of little drawers, a meat safe and cupboards with lights that come on when the doors are opened.

The dining room is the only room that has a traditional open fireplace.

But even here, modernity intrudes with 'electric fire panels' to either side that can produce heat at a moment's notice.

In the master bedroom, there is a reading light in the headboard, while a button at the bedside turns on an electric fire 'to get the room properly warmed up before you adventure your toes from beneath the blankets on a cold winter morning'.

❖ ❖ ❖ ❖ ❖ ❖ ❖ ❖ ❖ ❖ ❖

Saturday, 7 April 1934

There may be a boom in private housing but two years after the 'war on slums' was declared by the Lord Mayor and legislation passed to solve the problem there has been little progress. In fact, the Corporation's Housing Department has spent most of the time preparing the ground for the housing programme, rather than building.

The targets set in the five-year plan in 1932 are now but a memory. In the last 18 months, there have been just 650 families moved from slums into new corporation dwellings. Among these are the first flat-dwellers at Mercier Street and Mary's Lane.

The Mary's Lane flats, whose first residents moved in in April 1933, are the first in a new style of tenement flat complex that will be repeated at various sites around the city including Bridgefoot Street, Cook Street, James's Street and Hanover Street. Their 'expressionist' design, intended to give a sense of identity and pride to its inhabitants, is inspired by Dutch housing schemes visited in 1925 by members of Dublin Corporation and features balconies and walkways overlooking central courtyards.

Meanwhile, the largest of all the corporation's housing projects is being built at Crumlin.

Crumlin is quite different from the flats. It is a garden suburb on Dublin's outskirts and is being built on a vast scale. There will be 2,915 houses in an area ten times the size of St Stephen's Green. Fifteen thousand people will live there, more than the population of the town of Drogheda.

That Crumlin is intended to be a world away from the tenements is emphasised not only by open spaces, gardens, wide streets and views of the Dublin Mountains, but also by the fact that former slum dwellers will live on roads named after places that are distant from Dublin, as though they will be able to pretend they are living far away at Ardagh, Armagh, Bangor, Benbulbin, Blarney, Brandon, Carrow, Cashel, Clonard, Clonmacnoise, Clonfert, Comeragh, Derry, Downpatrick, Durrow, Galtymore, Kildare, Kells, Kilfenora, Knocknarea, Monasterboice, Lismore, Mourne, Slievemore or Sperrin.

Two of a series
of colorised
photographs
taken by American
Branson DeCou in
the early 1930s –
Top: A farmer leads
his cattle down the
North Circular Road
to the cattle market
at Prussia Street.
Bottom: Fruit and
veg sellers.

Sunday, 26 April 1936

Tonight Dubliners fill out the forms for the country's second census.

One of the most striking facts is that in the decade since the last census, while every county outside of the capital has experienced population decline, Dublin's has increased by 16 per cent. There are now 587,145 people living in the capital, compared with 505,484 in 1926. Dublin now accounts for 20 per cent of the Free State's population – up from 17 per cent a decade ago.

In the last ten years, about 16,000 people have moved to the city from other parts of the country. The counties with the largest populations in Dublin are Wicklow with 11,934 followed by Cork, Kildare, Meath and Tipperary.

Not surprisingly, the capital is also Ireland's most cosmopolitan place with 4 per cent of its people coming from abroad. The main foreign-born are the just over 20,000 from England, Scotland and Wales while there are 1,300 people from the Unites States of America, 900 from India, 400 from what was Russia (now the Soviet Union), 300 from Germany, 170 from France and 2,500 from various other countries.

With the increasing population, the advent of the omnibus and the prevalence of the automobile, the city is expanding. The construction of individual houses, large housing estates and roads is making it increasingly difficult to know where the city ends and the countryside begins.

Much attention is given to the corporation's houses and flats, but a remarkable number of private developments are also being constructed. These private houses are generally larger than those being built for the working classes and instead of being terraced they are detached or semi-detached. However, another thing that differentiates them is a feature that is now regarded as an essential component of middle-class life: the bay window.

Corporation workmen shovel snow into the River Liffey in 1936.

On Wednesday, 27 May 1936, a six-seater De Havilland 84 Dragon biplane crosses the Irish Sea on its way to Baldonnel Aerodrome. It is the first daily service between Dublin and Bristol being operated by a new Irish airline company called Aer Lingus with the Blackpool and West Coast Air Services – they are operating the service under the joint name of Irish Sea Airways.

H.V. Morton, one of the airline's first passengers, later writes of this entirely new way of arriving in Dublin: 'A rim of land grew clearer and slowly the Wicklow Hills shouldered their way out of the sea. My first impression of them was that they were foreign hills. They were not like any hills in England or Scotland, and it was difficult to say why. The light was, perhaps, different over them; even the clouds seemed to be Irish clouds … First one mountain and then another comes into view until the gorgeous panorama embraced by the mountains of Dublin and Wicklow forms a living map on the earth below, with the City of Dublin stretched for miles between the sea and hills. Nelson's Pillar is plainly visible in the centre of the main street, while such buildings as the Custom House and Four Courts on the banks of the river lend grace and magnificence to the scene.'

While middle-class houses are being built on the north side at Castle Park, Rosemount Estate on Calderwood Road, Glandore Road, off Griffith Avenue, Glenbeigh Road in Cabra, Hampstead Hill Estate in Glasnevin, Strand Road at Sutton Cross and Whitehall Road, Drumcondra, it is on the south side where most private developments are being constructed.

Apart from the Merrion Estate, new middle- and upper-class developments are also under construction at Trimlestown, the Clonkeen Estate in Foxrock, Highfield

A painting by Harry Kernoff. An Irish painter of English–Russian extraction, he has drawn numerous scenes around the city. Here is the entrance to St Stephen's Green at the top of Grafton Street.

Park, Annaville and Braemor Park in Dundrum, Richmond in Monkstown, Mounttown Road in Dún Laoghaire, Stradbrook Road and Maretimo Gardens in Blackrock, the Nutley Estate in Donnybrook, on Rathfarnham Road and the nearby Castle Park Estate, Merton Park in Ranelagh, Adelaide Road in Glenageary, Fortfield and Hazelbrook in Kimmage, Gilford Road and Wilfield Road in Sandymount, Cowper Road in Ranelagh and Westfield Estate in Harold's Cross.

Indicative of the distinction that is developing between the north side and south side is an advertisement by Kelly's, the builders of the Merrion Estate, which proudly announces that they *only* build on Dublin's south side.

❖ ❖ ❖ ❖ ❖ ❖ ❖ ❖ ❖ ❖ ❖

Wednesday, 21 October 1936

A series of articles on Dublin's housing crisis that has been running in the *Irish Press* since 1 October is coming to an end. The articles were prompted by the census findings which showed that the rate of Dublin's population growth has been underestimated and the slum situation will remain unless something drastic is done.

In the last ten years, the populations in some of the most overcrowded city wards – Inns Quay, Arran Quay, North City, Fitzwilliam, Merchant's Quay and South Dock – have barely changed. The most shocking of all the findings is that of the more than 33,000 families who live in the slums, in excess of 27,000 live in single rooms, an increase of 2,000 families since the last census.

According to the *Irish Press*, the first step to solving the terrible problem is for people to realise that one exists. It is a curious premise, given that the slums have been around for decades and are hardly hidden from view. It is now estimated that 20,000 new working-class houses and flats are needed. It is an immense task considering that fewer than 4,000 dwellings have been built since 1932.

There is no shortage of reasons for the slow progress. Assembling of sites for clearance in the city has not been as quick as hoped. Until 1934, the Housing Department was scattered around the city in various offices. In 1935, there were virtually no houses built as the corporation found it impossible to borrow money on the open market due to the poor international financial situation. The increased demand for labour caused by the housing programme, private developments and the start of the Sweepstakes hospital works (the first hospital in Dublin to benefit from the Sweeps is the National Maternity Hospital, which has been entirely rebuilt

IN A DUBLIN TENEMENT:—This Dublin family, eight including father, has to live in this typically over-crowded one-room tenement in the City's slums.

Two newspaper cuttings from a 1936 *Irish Press* series of articles on the slum conditions in the city. The woman to the left is Winifred O'Rourke. Five of her children have died, another is in hospital with lung trouble, while she is also seriously ill.

at Holles Street) increased the cost of labour, thereby reducing the amount of units that could be built. Another difficulty is that the whole financial basis of flat construction has been turned on its head. Instead of being cheaper, the flats are turning out to be much more expensive than suburban houses. The average cost of building a house is about £500 while each flat costs around £750 – about the same as one of the smaller houses in the Merrion Estate.

As a result, 14 years after independence, Dublin is still in danger of being taken over by overcrowded, vermin-ridden, disease-sodden, death-trap slums.

The *Irish Press* articles feature human stories from the tenements.

William Behan of 5 Upper Rutland Street, who has four young children, tells the newspaper, 'I am living in a back parlour in this house condemned by the corporation five years ago. The ceiling is held up by six planks – one across the ceiling, on the floor and four more uprights … The rain comes down from the top room to the next one, and through my ceiling, which is water sodden and one day must fall in on us.'

Dr Collis of the National Children's Hospital states that 'Dubliners are wont to describe their city affectionately as 'an old lady'. When visitors admire her outer garments – the broad streets, the old eighteenth-century houses, Fitzwilliam Square and St Stephen's Green – they smile complacently and feel proud. Lift the hem of her outer silken garment, however, and you will find suppurating ulcers covered by stinking rags, for Dublin has the foulest slums of any town in Europe. Into these 'quaint old eighteenth-century houses', the people are herded and live in conditions of horror.'

He writes of a mother's reply when told that her daughter, who had been suffering from 'rheumatic heart disease', was being sent home for 'rest'. 'But how can she get rest in bed?' the mother asked. 'The bed is crawling with bugs which eat her alive. Seven others sleep in the same attic room on the sixth floor. The roof is leaking. The only water supply is in the yard. The only lavatory is down six flights … And you say she is to *rest* there in bed!' Collis tells of how TB wiped out one family in nine months. 'In a room 14 feet by 11 feet a father lay … dying of consumption. In the bed also slept his wife and new-born baby, while the remaining three children lay on the floor, which they showed crawling with bugs and brown beetles. Some months later, the baby was brought to the hospital screaming. She had tuberculous meningitis. Six months went by, two more of her children were affected. Then at last the father ceased coughing and the Corporation buried him.'

In a mice- and rat-infested house in Marrowbone Lane 'there was a child stricken by a curious malady resembling meningitis. The case has proved of great fascination in London and America because the little girl had caught a very rare and interesting disease of mice.'

At the front line are the 1,600 'basement dwellers' who live in horrendous conditions in the low-lying area around the Four Courts. At high tide, the soil here is turned into a morass by the backed-up flow of the Liffey and its tributaries. Subterranean putrid air seeps into the basements, sewage wells up in drains, cockroaches skitter and children grow up in terror of 'roof rats'.

One of the basement dwellers pleads simply, 'Take us out of this terrible place.'

Perhaps the *Irish Press* articles will galvanise popular opinion and the city's leaders – in light of the articles, City Manager Sherlock has already set a new housing target of 3,000 units per year. But even after the three weeks of articles, there must be doubt. Because although they have been given one- or two-page spreads in the centre of the paper, the housing crisis has never featured on the front pages. Instead, the front-page news has been General Franco's triumphal march on Madrid, clashes between fascists and communists in London and Paris, President de Valera's call for the revival of the Irish language, the publication of Ernie O'Malley's *On Another Man's Wound* and the consecration of the Most Reverend Dr Thomas Keogh as Bishop of Kildare and Leighlin.

Which leads one to wonder, if the harrowing stories are not important enough for the front page, just how interested are people in solving the problem of the slums?

❖ ❖ ❖ ❖ ❖ ❖ ❖ ❖ ❖ ❖ ❖

Monday, 8 March 1937

Patrick Abercrombie, now Professor of Town Planning at the University of London, and Sydney Kelly, architect, are returning to Dublin, not to finish the work they started in their 1922 plan, but to make a new one.

Without great enthusiasm the corporation adopted the provisions of the 1934 Town Planning Act last January. Some members of the city authorities still remain lukewarm on the whole concept of 'town planning', regarding it as a 'questionable

A scene from the Zoological Gardens.

innovation' and a 'fanciful experiment' promoted by 'faddists'. As a result, the City Manager only recommended the adoption of the Act on the condition that the plan would be an outline one 'on broad lines, to be dealt with gradually'. He wants no unrealisable grandiose schemes, no Parisian-style innovations, nothing like the 1922 plan. No, he wants a 'sketch' plan.

A libel case against Oliver St John Gogarty and the publishers of his memoir *As I Was Walking Down Sackville Street* is settled on Wednesday, 12 May 1937.

In one of the uncontentious passages, Gogarty writes about the natural amenities that Dublin enjoys. No doubt the sentence 'Dublin has one advantage: it is easy to get out of it' will be quoted for years to come by the city's detractors. But instead of being a criticism, it is a compliment. Because, as Gogarty continues: '... Dublin has the country and the streamy hills very near, and nearer still the sea ... You can get a horse for an hour's canter on Merrion Strand at Serpentine Avenue ... The morning sky is a sight worth more than a morning's sleep. Before the reek ascends from the old houses in which now nearly every room holds a fire – so different from the days when one family held a whole house – there is always a glint of sunlight to be found at the edge of the distant tide. The little waves that cannot rise to any height on the level sands may be the better part of a mile away, and you can canter for five minutes before you meet them and watch them bearing rainbows and spreading on the tawny sands their exquisite treasures brought, as it were, overseas from the inexhaustible and sunny east ... On the right is the smooth outline of the Dublin Mountains, rising like cones and rippling into nipples like the Paps of Jura, where Wicklow shows Bray Head.

We inhale the Atlantic vapours and they turn us into mystics, poets, politicians, and unemployables with school-girl complexions; thus these vapours have lost their enervating and transforming powers before they reach England. And yet her only thanks is to send us for April her eastern winds, whose influence is influenza.'

Friday, 27 August 1937

At the junction of Clare Street and Merrion Square, a large crowd gathers to watch the latest innovation in traffic management being tested. It is Ireland's first set of 'traffic lights'.

To assist the public, leaflets have been distributed and notices published in the press giving basic instructions: 'GREEN means YOU MAY GO (with due care and

The Christmas pantomime remains a firm Dublin favourite.

Gaiety Theatre

Telegrams: " Gaiety, Dublin."   Telephone 21404

Proprietors ....THE GAIETY THEATRE, DUBLIN. Ltd
Resident Manager.............................R. F. McCARTAN
Musical Director.......................ERNEST BROADHURST

WEEK COMMENCING MON., 27th DEC.
6.45—TWICE NIGHTLY—9.0
MATINEES EACH WED. AND SAT. AT 2.30

O'D PRODUCTIONS LTD.
PRESENT

THEIR ANNUAL CHRISTMAS PANTOMIME

"MotherGoose"

Written by HARRY O'DONOVAN
(Based on the HICKORY WOOD Version)
Lyrics by HARRY O'DONOVAN
Additional Music by JOE CAREY

Ballet and Incidentals by
CONNIE AND MICHAEL RYAN

BEAUTIFUL SCENES

MAGNIFICENT   ORIGINAL
COSTUMES   EFFECTS

NOVEL SPECIALITIES

Produced by JIMMY O'DEA

for the safety of others), AMBER (alone) means stop before entering the intersection unless you are so close to the intersection when AMBER first appears that you cannot stop with safety, in which case you may go on and get clear of the intersection. RED means STOP (do not pass stop line), RED and AMBER mean PREPARE TO START. You must not start before GREEN shows.'

Like all busy junctions in the city, this usually has a garda attired in white gloves and armbands on point duty, but today four are needed to manage the confusion caused by drivers stopping their vehicles as soon as they see the lights turn red, rather than continuing up to the junction, horse-drawn carts that are too slow to get across the intersection before the lights change again, and the fact that pedestrians are simply ignoring the very existence of the new lights.

At the end of the day, despite the difficulties, the traffic light experiment is deemed a resounding success. In no time people, in Dublin can look forward to traffic lights regulating and easing the flow of traffic at junctions throughout the city.

❖ ❖ ❖ ❖ ❖ ❖ ❖ ❖ ❖ ❖ ❖

Monday, 20 December 1937

While there are many in Crumlin who are delighted to have got out of the tenements, who take walks in the country fields and who grow vegetables in their new gardens, not all is well in the garden suburb.

Instead of being close to work, the residents of Crumlin have to travel. Instead of scores of shops close at hand there are just a few, whose prices are high. Instead of a strong community spirit imposed by living in close proximity, some find it soulless and isolating. The houses may be their own, but they lack the beautiful fanlights (albeit with broken glass), the elegant staircases and other traits of a grandiose past. There are wide streets but no street lighting, and while it was intended that they would benefit from the fresh air and the proximity to the mountains, one resident likens the area to the Russian Steppes.

Crumlin is also still short on amenities. Almost the only civic building that was in place when residents first arrived was the centrally located 900-seat Catholic church. Two years after the first tenement dweller moved in, the children of the area still have to travel back to their old schools in town because the new ones are not finished – not surprisingly, truancy is rampant.

Another problem has been the difficulty of simply getting into town as the bus service cannot run frequently enough to take the numbers. There has been talk of bringing the army in to help, but the issue should improve today with the introduction on the Crumlin route of Ireland's first double-decker buses built at the United Tramways Company's Inchicore works.

❖ ❖ ❖ ❖ ❖ ❖ ❖ ❖ ❖ ❖ ❖

Monday, 3 January 1938

The latest attempt to ease the city's traffic congestion is coming into effect. A forest of blue-and-white traffic signs have been erected around the city centre, and 70 gardaí are on duty to enforce the new regulations.

It is no longer permissible to park anywhere one wants, for as long as one wants. In the area between Parnell Street, South King Street, Kildare Street, Pearse Street, Butt Bridge and Lower Gardiner Street, there are now 900 specially designated 'parking spaces', with parking restricted elsewhere to 20 minutes.

❖ ❖ ❖ ❖ ❖ ❖ ❖ ❖ ❖ ❖ ❖

Monday, 11 April 1938

As the city is being changed due to new housing, the influx of people from the countryside, and the obliteration of historic sites and familiar vistas, there is a growing interest in its history.

At the forefront is the Old Dublin Society, founded in 1934.

Each week, the society's lecture attracts up to 250 people. According to Annie Smithson, novelist and secretary of the Irish Nurses' Association, when members are at the lectures they forget about the Dublin of the twentieth century: 'We are back with the Danes, watching while they beach their boats at the top of Pearse Street; we watch while St Patrick's and Christchurch cathedrals slowly lift their spires to heaven; we go with Henry Grattan to the old Parliament House; we buy an orange from Peg Woffington at Crowe Street Theatre; we see Robert Emmet in Trinity; we stand by while the body of Wolfe Tone is being "waked"; we see O'Connell at his studies in the long night hours and we are present at the foundation of our hospitals.'

Today, the society publishes its first journal, the *Dublin Historic Record*. Based on talks that have been given to the society, it features articles on 'Dublin Castle', 'Beginnings of Municipal Government in Dublin', 'Vagabonds and Sturdy Beggars', 'Poverty, Pigs and Pestilence in Mediæval Dublin', 'Dublin's First Railway', 'Mulhuddart Queries', 'Place-names in and Around Dublin', 'Dublin Slang Songs' and 'Hidden and Vanishing Dublin (Part I)'.

❖ ❖ ❖ ❖ ❖ ❖ ❖ ❖ ❖ ❖ ❖

Saturday, 16 April 1938

In the expanding city, former slum-dwellers who had been deprived for years of the benefits of running water are plunging into baths and flushing toilets with such enthusiasm that the city is running out of water. Conservation measures including shutting off supply to the city's fountains and reducing water pressure at night – much to the chagrin of restaurants and the fire brigade – are not enough. To address the problem, work has started in the Dublin–Wicklow Mountains on a five-storey-high dam.

Due to be completed in 1940, the dam will hold back the flow of the River Liffey to create a 5,000-acre lake capable of supplying Dublin with 20 million gallons of water a day. That is far in excess of what it currently needs and, it is believed, more than sufficient to ensure that never again will the city experience water shortages.

The dam is not only being built with the intention of supplying water. Poulaphouca is a joint project between the corporation and the Electricity Supply Board and will create Ireland's second hydro electric power plant (after Ardnacrusha on the Shannon). Because as much as Dublin needs water, it also needs power.

Driven by the 'liberal provision of wall sockets' in new houses and the ever-increasing sales at the ESB showrooms of such modern conveniences as irons, vacuum cleaners, kettles, toasters, coffee percolators, milk warmers, cookers, washing machines, refrigerators and immersion heaters, the demand for domestic electricity in the city centre doubled between 1934 and 1937 and nearly trebled in suburban areas. Dublin's electricity consumption is now nearly twice that of the rest of the country combined.

❖ ❖ ❖ ❖ ❖ ❖ ❖ ❖ ❖ ❖ ❖

Thursday, 7 July 1938

Dublin, like all historic cities, is a palimpsest, with historic layers creating the patina of the experience of being in the city.

The earliest known map of Dublin is John Speed's from 1610.

Speed's map depicts a Dublin that had changed little in the three centuries before it was drawn. But the city was on the cusp of its first great period of expansion. Just over three centuries after it was drawn, it is interesting to see what still exists from Speed's time and what has changed.

Though the houses shown on Speed's map are almost all gone and the city walls largely demolished, the street pattern of the medieval city still exists, as do many of the street names – Winetavern Street, Fishamble Street, Thomas Street, High Street and Wood Quay.

In Speed's map, there is Trinity College, simply called 'The College', founded just two decades before the map was produced. There is only one bridge over the Liffey, called 'The Bridge' at the site of Baile Átha Cliath's 'Ford of the hurdles', now occupied by the recently renamed Father Matthew Bridge, after the nineteenth-century temperance campaigner. There are some of today's churches including St Michan's, St Werburgh's and St Andrew's. There is St Patrick's Cathedral, there is Christchurch.

One of the most noticeable aspects of his map is just how far west the city of Dublin once was. Dublin was founded not on the bay, but on the River Poddle and then expanded to higher ground to the west, where Christchurch Cathedral stands. Until the seventeenth century, there had been virtually no development east of Dublin Castle. But since Speed's time, Dublin has edged ever closer to the bay through the construction of the quays, bridges over the river, the railway skirting the southern shore of the bay and the development of coastal suburbs.

The bowl of water held between the sentinels of the Baily Lighthouse on Howth

Dún Laoghaire baths, one of the most popular seaside destinations in Dublin.

Head and the obelisk on Killiney Hill has gradually come within the city's ambit. But although one of its great amenities, on most days one would not know it from the numbers that use it.

On those precious few hot summer days, the bay's beaches – if not the water – are packed with day-trippers, crowds frequent Dún Laoghaire's baths and the nearby piers, others stroll the recently completed two-mile promenade at Clontarf. But generally, on days when the weather is more typical of the city the bay is the preserve of the few.

Among them are the sailors from the Royal St George, National and Royal Irish yacht clubs whose sails billow in summer breezes. There are those who walk the expanse of strand at Dollymount or Sandymount and others who, regardless of weather or time of year, frequent the bay's various coves and little harbours, some walking from their houses in their dressing gowns, to take morning dips, and who try to convince others that the water is lovely and warm, despite the disturbing blue tinge to their skin.

In the last ten years, there have been a number of proposals to change this situation, to make the bay, its shallow waters and expanse of mud flats more 'useful', to more people.

In 1929, a 'Dollymount–Sutton Marine Lake' or 'Blue Lagoon scheme' was proposed for the area behind the Bull Island. As part of this scheme, a dam would trap water at high tide to create a natural sea lake which could then be used for aquatic sports. However, this proposal has become embroiled in arguments over cost, sea levels and engineers' reports.

In 1930, the 'Coastal Development Movement' organised a day of events at Dollymount. Over 100,000 people attended displays of aeronautics and fireworks, which showed what could be done if the 300 acres of marshland and mudflats 'lying completely useless' could be put to productive use.

A National Sports Stadium has been proposed for Bull Island. However, cost and local opposition – according to one objector 'the establishment of a pleasure centre of this sort will seriously affect the amenities of the district, and lower the value of property' – ended the dream of its promoters.

A novel proposal for the south side of the bay was made in 1935 by Desmond McAteer in *Studies: An Irish Quarterly Review*. He suggested reclaiming the mudflats at Sandymount Strand by constructing a three-mile sea wall built between Sandymount and the South Wall, at the mouth of the River Liffey, and building an airport on the infill.

Now, tonight, it seems as though another proposal for the bay is going to go by the wayside.

A meeting is being held in response to Dún Laoghaire Borough's plans for a new coastal amenity at Sandycove which would turn this already popular area into 'a great national seaside resort', Ireland's equivalent to Bournemouth or Torquay.

However, the local rate-payers at this evening's meeting are far from happy.

Their main criticism is that the amenity would be built in Sandycove and not Dún Laoghaire, where most of them are located. The businesses in the town believe they will gain little from the development while having to foot the £100,000 bill. Given the tone of tonight's speeches, there is no doubt that they are going to vote against it.

❖ ❖ ❖ ❖ ❖ ❖ ❖ ❖ ❖ ❖ ❖

Saturday, 13 May 1939

There is no shortage of places to buy books in the city. There are the second-hand bookstalls along the Liffey, and there are ten main bookshops: Brown and Nolan, Hodges Figgis and Fred Hanna on Nassau Street, Combridge's on Grafton Street, James Duffy's on Westmoreland Street, the Grafton Bookshop on Harry Street, Greene's on Clare Street, Humphries on Trinity Street, the Three Candles on Fleet Street and, the only one on the north side, Eason and Son on O'Connell Street.

Unsurprisingly, the most popular recent titles include Adolf Hitler's *Mein Kampf* and Benito Mussolini's *My Autobiography*, but outselling everything is Margaret Mitchell's international bestseller *Gone With the Wind*, being bought by those who have just watched the movie.

A number of Irish books have also been doing well, including Edward McLysaght's *Irish Life in the Seventeenth Century* and Pat 'the Cope' Gallagher's *My Story*.

Recently some of the most unusual novels ever published have been written by Dublin authors. Each of these seem to care little for the traditional novel form.

Last year *Murphy*, written by Samuel Beckett from Foxrock, who now lives in Paris, was published in England. It is based mainly in London, but also features

Dublin. In one of the more memorable passages, a character leans against the railings of Nelson's Pillar and curses 'first the day in which he was born, then – in a bold flash-back – the night in which he was conceived'. *Murphy* is an absurdist work that was hardly intended to compete with the likes of Mussolini or Mitchell. It had a print run of just 1,500 and has not done well. Last year, it sold just over 500 copies, mainly outside Ireland. This year virtually nothing. The future of Beckett's writing career must be in doubt.

Flann O'Brien, the pseudonym of civil servant Brian O'Nolan, has written *At Swim-Two-Birds*. It has sold better in Dublin than *Murphy* and this week even featured on some of the bookshops' bestseller lists.

O'Brien was born in Strabane, County Tyrone. He came to Dublin with his family at a young age. After going to Blackrock College, he studied at University College Dublin. *At Swim-Two-Birds* is unmistakably set in Dublin – there is St Stephen's Green, Grogan's pub, Parnell Street, Croppies' Acre, Fosters Avenue, University College Dublin and Dundrum. However, like *Murphy*, *At Swim-Two-Birds* is far from straightforward. It is a novel with competing plots and with characters who rebel against the author. According to one reviewer, 'This is an odd, astonishing, and – in places at any rate – a vastly entertaining book. What its title means I don't know, what it is all about I have been unable to discover, and how to describe it I am at a loss. Yet it has moved me to mirth more often than any volume that I have read for a long time.'

If *Murphy* is obscure and *At Swim-Two-Birds* not to everyone's taste, *Finnegans Wake* by James Joyce is another thing altogether.

Finnegans Wake is Joyce's first novel since *Ulysses*. Its opening sentence is intelligible enough, if one has some knowledge of the geography of Dublin Bay: 'Riverrun, past Eve and Adam's, from swerve of short to bend of bay, brings us by a commodious vicus of recirculation back to Howth Castle and Environs.' But after that *Finnegans Wake* is impenetrable to almost everyone.

❖ ❖ ❖ ❖ ❖ ❖ ❖ ❖ ❖ ❖ ❖

Sunday, 18 June 1939

On hearing the roar of dive-bombing aeroplanes, hundreds of people enjoying the peace of the Iveagh Gardens at Earlsfort Terrace look up, somewhat alarmed, to the sky.

Then a siren blares. There is a loud explosion. A cloud of yellow smoke billows from behind shrubbery. Two further blasts are followed by what sounds like machine-gun fire. People stagger through the smoke and fall to the ground. St John Ambulance men with gas masks and protective clothing run with stretchers to assist the 'casualties'.

But not to worry. This is just an elaborate drill, a 'public air raid precaution demonstration', to bring something of the horror that may come to the citizens of Ireland's capital as Europe lurches ever closer to war.

❖ ❖ ❖ ❖ ❖ ❖ ❖ ❖ ❖ ❖ ❖

Sunday, 3 September 1939

Members of Dáil Éireann leave Leinster House at 5 a.m. with weighty matters on their mind. Without waiting for Britain's ultimatum to Germany regarding the suspension of aggression against Poland to expire, they have just passed the Emergency Powers Act that officially declares Ireland's neutrality. Also leaving are members of the diplomatic corps in the public gallery who took a keen interest in the proceedings, including Mr Cudahy, the American Minister, Dr Hempel, German Minister, Mr Goor, the Belgian Minister, Marquis Malsaspina, Secretary of the Italian Delegation and Mr Dobryzynski, Polish Minister.

War comes as no surprise, and preparations have started. Air raid trench shelters with six-inch-thick concrete walls and over four-inch reinforced concrete roof slabs capable of holding 2,000 people are currently being dug in Mountjoy Square, St

As war breaks out, Dublin is one of the safest capitals in Europe.

Patrick's Cathedral, Spitalfields and Brabazon Square. The complex in Mountjoy Square is the most extensive, with twelve 68-foot-long trenches.

On Friday, after Germany's attack on Poland, people tuned in to the BBC radio broadcasts and crowded around anyone with the latest newspaper. Dubliners contacted relatives in Britain appealing for them to return home. The Holyhead–Dún Laoghaire mailboat has been busier than usual with emigrants returning to the safety of neutral Ireland, Germans trying to make their way back to their homeland and British Army reservists who have been called up for active service.

Despite neutrality, some people in the city fear that Dublin will become immediately involved in the war. There has been some panic buying of food and the city's coal merchants have been besieged.

Dubliners were requested to take blackout precautions and so on Saturday night, windows around the city were covered in dark material or painted black, cinema and shop signs were turned off, buses and cars ran without headlights and only one out of every five streetlights was working. In fact, one of the few buildings in the city that was fully illuminated was Dáil Éireann as the TDs went through the provisions of the Emergency legislation.

Shortly after members of the Dáil leave Leinster House, a thunderstorm, perhaps an ominous portent of things to come, sweeps over the city, flooding roads and houses.

Later, as Slovakia declares war on Poland and Britain and France declare war on Germany, the main interest in Dublin is the All-Ireland hurling final between Kilkenny and Cork. Ten minutes into the second half, there is another thunderstorm. Lightning flashes, thunder cracks and the stadium is lashed with sheets of rain. Despite the conditions, it is instantly regarded as a classic, with Kilkenny scraping to a one-point victory.

Maybe the normality of staging the hurling final breaks the tension in the city. Because in the evening when an *Irish Times* journalist goes out and about to gauge the mood, he does not find fear.

People are going about their lives 'as if all was still well with the world'. People coming out of cinemas talk about the pictures. There is no mention of war. There are longer than normal queues at bus stops but conversation is confined almost entirely to complaints about how few buses there are. It is only when he gets on a tram that he hears two soldiers discussing the speed of the British bombers and how long one of them would take to fly from London to Berlin. But when they are joined by another person, their conversation turns to the weather. They agreed that it had been 'shockin'. They had never seen anything like the rain.

And so as parts of the continent take their first steps into a violent abyss, the people of Dublin settle down for the night in what is one of the safest capitals in all of Europe.

1940–1949

From War to Republic

Friday, 19 January 1940

It is 6 a.m. and 'Packie' Bourke is the first to arrive at Dublin's new airport at Collinstown, eight miles north of the city centre. It is bitterly cold. The city is in the grip of the longest cold snap anyone can remember – there is a water shortage as cisterns are emptied nightly to stop pipes from bursting, the building trade has been closed down for two weeks and people have been skating on the Zoo's frozen pond.

Last night the mercury in the airport thermometer plummeted to minus 21 degrees Fahrenheit, so this morning Packie's most important job is to put heaters on two Aer Lingus Lockheed 14s. Because at 9 a.m. they will take off for Liverpool as the airport's inaugural flights.

The need for a civilian airport has been obvious since the national airline, Aer Lingus, was established in 1936. Until today it has been sharing Baldonnel with the Irish Air Corps. Mixing civil and military aircraft was far from idea!, but more importantly, a new airport was required to cater for the rapidly increasing numbers of air travellers. In the last two and half months of 1938 just over 3,000 civilians had used Baldonnel. For the same period last year it was 1,300.

Although there was no argument about the need for a civilian airport, there was much discussion about where it would be. Sandymount Strand,

Dublin airport terminal building under construction.

Fairview, Finglas and the Phoenix Park were all mooted, but the site of the former British military base in Collinstown was chosen for a number of reasons. There are clear flight paths over open countryside, it is located away from turbulent sea and mountain air, the site is not susceptible to mist and fog and 268 of the 700 acres required were already in state hands. Construction began in April 1937 and since then, up to 1,000 men have been working at Collinstown.

Today heralds the start of the era of international commercial air transport in Dublin, but one would not know it from the handful of officials present to watch the first flights. The reason is that the immediate future of civilian air transport is bleak. It had been hoped that when the airport opened there would be daily flights connecting Dublin with the delights of London, Paris and Amsterdam. But due to the war, the only flights will be to and from Liverpool, and the future of even those are in doubt.

It is a pity that the airport's terminal building is not yet finished. Masked by lattices of scaffolding, it is already being regarded by architects as one of Ireland's most significant buildings. Larger than London's Gatwick, more elegant than both Berlin's Tempelhof and Paris's Le Bourget, if it were not for the war and the fact that Dublin is on the edge of Europe the terminal would surely be heralded as a ground-breaking building in the 'International Style'. The sleek horizontal lines and shining glass have been designed by the young architect Desmond Fitzgerald and a team that includes Dermot O'Toole, Daithí Hanley, Charles Aliaga Kelly, Kevin Barry and Harry Robson. While from the air, people will see that it is shaped like an aeroplane's wing span, from the ground, it will resemble the sleek form of an ocean liner, with the bridge represented by the air traffic control room and the decks by the viewing platforms from where people will watch planes take off and land.

The new Dublin airport from the air.

Monday, 3 June 1940

Since December, New Zealand caricaturist Alan Reeve – who arrived in neutral Dublin last October from his travels in Europe – has had a weekly caricature feature in *The Irish Times* called 'Drawing the Crowd'.

Among the people Reeve has drawn are John Larchet, Professor of Music at UCD, Kerry author Maurice Walsh who now lives in Dublin, James Brontë Gatenby, Professor of Zoology at TCD, Frederick Summerfield, the Irish agent for Chrysler cars, recently nine-time Lord Mayor of Dublin Alfie Byrne TD, landscape artist Paul Henry, the elderly Sir John Lavery, Alan Kidd, Honorary Secretary of the Golfing Union of Ireland, poet, playwright and novelist Austin Clarke, Hilton Edwards of the Gate, Lord Longford, theatrical socialite Joseph Holloway and many more.

Before Reeve leaves for America, he is holding an exhibition of his works at Brown Thomas on Grafton Street.

The largest image on display attracts the most attention. Called *Dublin Culture*, it depicts a group of 40 of the city's literary and artistic set in their regular habitat, the back room of the Palace Bar on Fleet Street.

At the centre of *Dublin Culture* is the generously proportioned Bertie Smyllie, editor of *The Irish Times* and one of the most influential figures in Dublin's literary circle. There is Flann O'Brien, to whom Smyllie has recently given a weekly column which he writes under the nom-de-plume 'Myles na gCopaleen', and Monaghan poet and novelist Patrick Kavanagh, recently arrived from London. Among the others are Brinsley McNamara, best known for his first book *The Valley of the Squinting Windows*, about the claustrophobic and spiteful life in a fictitious village

New Zealand cartoonist Alan Reeve depicts Dublin's wartime (male) literary, artistic and theatrical set in *Dublin Culture*. The artist is in the bottom left corner.

in Westmeath, poet and manager of the Abbey Theatre F.R. Higgins, from Foxford, County Mayo, Belfast sculptor William Conor, novelist Francis MacManus from Kilkenny, and artist Harry Kernoff, a painter among whose works are *A Bird Never Flew on One Wing* which features two Dublin pub 'characters', pints of stout in hand, standing in front of a wall daubed with the names of what must be every pub in Dublin.

There is poet Donogh MacDonagh, son of executed 1916 leader Thomas MacDonagh, another poet Ewart Milne, who recently took part in the Spanish Civil War on the Republican side, Seamus O'Sullivan, editor of *The Dublin Magazine*, and the Jew A.J. Levanthol, who succeeded Samuel Beckett as French lecturer in Trinity.

Though the New Zealander came to Dublin without having any connection with the city, in *Dublin Culture* Reeve has captured the city's cultural milieu at a moment when most of the rest of Europe is in the throes of mass destruction.

The 1940 Armistice Day commemorations have moved from the Phoenix Park to a specially laid out War Memorial Gardens in Islandbridge, overlooking the River Liffey. Built by former British and Irish National Army soldiers, it has been funded by the British Legion and Irish government. The eight-hectare gardens, designed by Sir Edward Lutyens, feature a 'War Stone', a great granite cross with truncated arms, and four 'Bookrooms' that will hold Books of Remembrance listing the names of every Irish soldier killed in the war.

Tuesday, 10 December 1940

In City Hall Dublin Corporation's General Purposes Committee adopts the 62-page *Sketch Town Planning Scheme for the City of Dublin*, prepared by Patrick Abercrombie, Arthur Kelly and Dublin-based Scottish town planner Manning Robertson.

Reading the sketch plan, it is striking how little has changed in the city since 1922. The shortage of housing for the poor is still the city's main problem. To meet these needs the planners have identified over 1,000 acres of land for mass working-class housing estates. The plan further exacerbates the social division of the city between the two sides of the River Liffey. Apart from Ballyfermot, in the west of the city, all of the sites are on the north side – at Larkhill (off the Swords Road), Cabra, between the Finglas and Ballymun roads and between the Swords and Coolock roads.

Addressing the continuing shortage of public parks, they recommend the conversion of St Anne's Estate, Raheny, recently purchased by the corporation from Bishop Plunkett, into a public park, reclaiming 780 acres of mud flats at Merrion Strand, creating a 50-acre park at Bushy Park, another at Monkstown and 'parkways' along the Dodder and Tolka rivers.

To deal with the ever-increasing traffic problem, they recommend two new bridges. One downriver of Butt Bridge, connecting Cardiff Lane on the south side with Guild Street on the north, would bring traffic travelling between the south-east and north-east of the city away from the central area. The other bridge would finally replace the Metal Bridge that has stubbornly stayed in place.

The planners state that they have given the Metal Bridge's removal the most 'prolonged and careful attention' but have concluded, again, that it will have to go to ease congestion at College Green and O'Connell Bridge.

In a city where so many people are originally from elsewhere in the country, a provincial bus depot is badly needed. At the moment those who refer to themselves as 'exiles' in the capital and go home for weekends and holidays have to

Dublin street character Johnny Forty Coats with an unknown child.

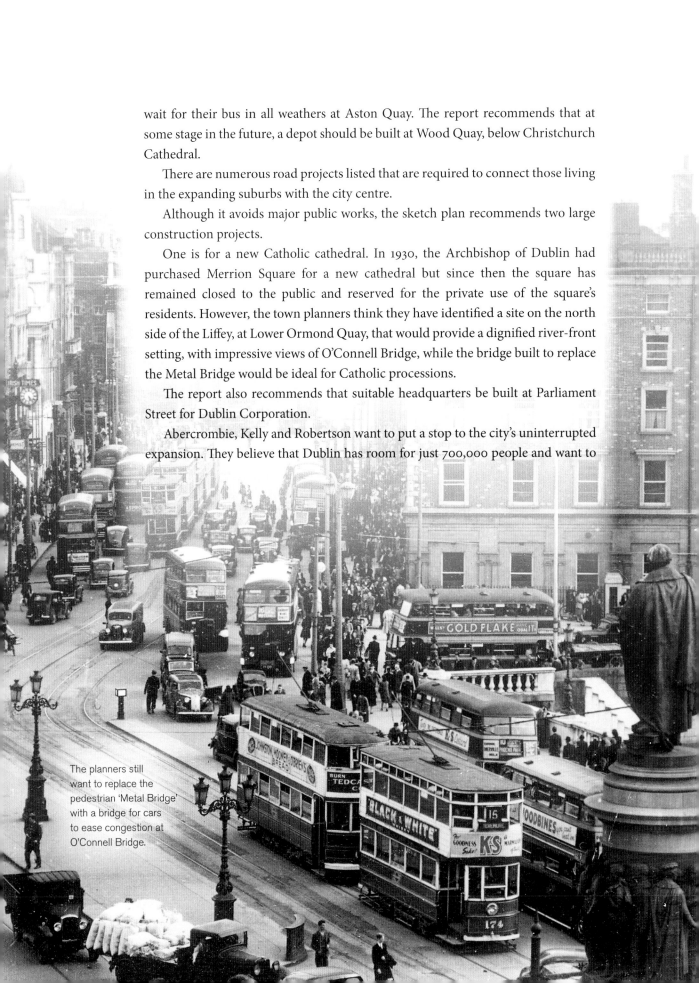

wait for their bus in all weathers at Aston Quay. The report recommends that at some stage in the future, a depot should be built at Wood Quay, below Christchurch Cathedral.

There are numerous road projects listed that are required to connect those living in the expanding suburbs with the city centre.

Although it avoids major public works, the sketch plan recommends two large construction projects.

One is for a new Catholic cathedral. In 1930, the Archbishop of Dublin had purchased Merrion Square for a new cathedral but since then the square has remained closed to the public and reserved for the private use of the square's residents. However, the town planners think they have identified a site on the north side of the Liffey, at Lower Ormond Quay, that would provide a dignified river-front setting, with impressive views of O'Connell Bridge, while the bridge built to replace the Metal Bridge would be ideal for Catholic processions.

The report also recommends that suitable headquarters be built at Parliament Street for Dublin Corporation.

Abercrombie, Kelly and Robertson want to put a stop to the city's uninterrupted expansion. They believe that Dublin has room for just 700,000 people and want to

The planners still want to replace the pedestrian 'Metal Bridge' with a bridge for cars to ease congestion at O'Connell Bridge.

designate a 'green belt' around the city where only limited development would be permitted at Malahide, Portmarnock, Swords, Blanchardstown, Castleknock and Tallaght. Beyond this, people would live in 'satellite towns' to the west and north.

The satellite town policy is argued on traditional planning grounds. A reasonably sized city with a ring of satellites is 'infinitely better and healthier' than 'the sprawling and overgrown town'. But war makes it even more sensible as satellite towns are less vulnerable to aerial attacks than large cities.

The sketch plan's many recommendations could reshape Dublin in the second half of the twentieth century. But the report also argues that change should not compromise the 'most characteristic streets in the city' at its Georgian centre.

So finally Dublin has a plan. However, with the war continuing, nothing is going to change quickly. It will be some time before Dubliners know exactly how this 62-page report will alter their city.

❖ ❖ ❖ ❖ ❖ ❖ ❖ ❖ ❖ ❖ ❖

Wednesday, 15 January 1941

Over 750 miles away from Dublin on a hill in a Zurich suburb, James Joyce is being laid to rest in the Fluntern cemetery.

Last month, Joyce had moved from Paris to neutral Switzerland to escape the war. Shortly afterwards he suffered a perforated ulcer. He passed away two days ago, just three weeks short of his fifty-ninth birthday.

His wife Nora, son Giorgio and 50 of Zurich's literary community stand around his grave to pay their respects.

Although Joyce is regarded by many as one of the world's greatest writers, the Irish legate in Berne has refused to attend today's funeral – Joyce remains unpopular in official Irish circles. So the honour of speaking on behalf of the international community falls to Britain's Swiss representative, Lord Derwent.

Though Derwent is a published poet and knew Joyce from his Paris days, he obviously finds this current task rather awkward. It is impossible to ignore the obvious, so he makes a passing reference to the snub from Joyce's homeland by remarking, somewhat disingenuously, that he is not aware of how Joyce is thought of in the country of his birth. However, Derwent emphasises how important Ireland was to the writer – Joyce 'had no creative thought in his mind that was not intimately connected with the Ireland of his birth'. But given Ireland's official absence, Derwent goes on to claim Joyce, and his characters, for the wider European literary community and expresses his honour at 'bidding farewell as an Englishman to this noble wielder of our language'.

❖ ❖ ❖ ❖ ❖ ❖ ❖ ❖ ❖ ❖ ❖

Monday, 10 February 1941

Teachers and civil servants are on duty at 70 city schools to register people who want to be evacuated from Dublin in case of an attack.

This is the culmination of over two years' work. As long ago as December 1938, the Department of Defence, already anticipating a European war and Ireland's possible unwilling involvement, began to consider what should be done in the case of a serious aerial attack on Dublin. The matter took on a degree of urgency when Germany began large-scale bombardments of British cities last September. When German planes dropped bombs on Terenure and the South Circular Road last month it showed how accessible Dublin is to modern, long-range bombers.

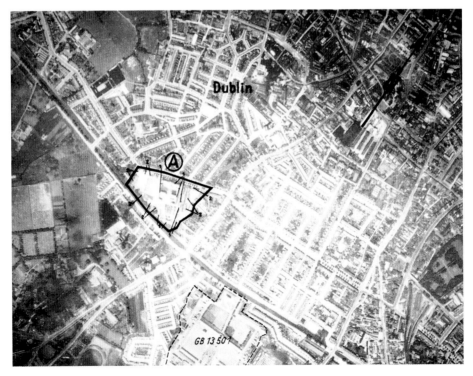

One of the Luftwaffe's aerial photographs of Dublin highlighting strategic targets. In this one Griffith barracks on the South Circular Road is marked 'A'.

In the event of an evacuation only those described as 'non-essential' will be permitted to leave the city. This includes children under six years of age, who may be accompanied by their mother or another female adult, children aged between six and 14 who will have to go unaccompanied, expectant mothers, the aged, the infirm and inmates of institutions if 'desirable and feasible'. It is estimated that there are 160,000 such people in the city.

If the evacuation order is given, the city will be surrounded by the army and Local Defence Force members to stop people fleeing into the countryside.

Inside the cordon, the city will be divided by security forces into three zones. The only movement allowed between them will be for people who find themselves in a different zone from where they are supposed to depart.

The West zone contains the entire area lying west of Drumcondra Road, Dorset Street, Clanbrassil Street, Harold's Cross Road and Rathfarnham Road. Extending from the Phoenix Park to Crumlin, it will have 68,000 potential evacuees destined for midland and western counties. Some 54,000 will leave on trains departing every 20 to 30 minutes from the Liffey Junction station in Cabra, with the other 14,000 taking buses from Ashtown and Blanchardstown. All going well, the non-essential population of the West can be evacuated in 18–24 hours.

The North-East zone, north of the Liffey and east of Dorset Street and Drumcondra Road, contains 36,000 people who will be evacuated on buses leaving from Griffith Avenue for midland counties. The full evacuation of this area can be completed in 18 hours.

In the South-East, south of the Liffey and east of Rathfarnham Road, Harold's Cross Road and Clanbrassil Street, there will be an estimated 41,000 people. They will all leave on Great Southern Railways trains from the various stations to counties in the south-east. They could all be removed from the city in 18–24 hours.

While registration is taking place, preparations are being made in Roscommon, Monaghan, Cavan, Longford, Wicklow, Leitrim, Meath, Westmeath, Wexford and Laois for the billeting of the 160,000 Dubliners. Surveys are being carried out of large country houses, and thousands of households are being sought to take in evacuees.

So, as registration begins, that is the plan. However, the Department of Defence is aware that it is not without its difficulties.

In the Western zone, there is potential for considerable confusion and distress because people from the southern part of this section, including thousands in the new suburb of Crumlin, may have to walk up to five miles to reach their departure point. For many, this may well be difficult enough, but if the four bridges they can use to cross the Liffey are destroyed, they might not be able to leave the city at all.

The plan for the North-East also has its problems as the buses will have to travel on secondary roads with overhanging trees, making it unsuitable for double-deckers. The roads are also too narrow on long stretches to allow two buses heading in opposite directions to pass each other.

For those in the South-East sector, there is no plan B if the railway tracks are destroyed.

Added to this are some fundamental issues not being publicly discussed by the government. In what precise circumstances will an evacuation take place? How severe might such an attack be? What will the condition of the city be after an aerial bombardment? What degree of panic will there be – will people be paralysed by fear, will there be uncontrolled panic? How will the members of the gardaí and defence forces keep control? What, in short, will happen if the 'fog of war' envelops Dublin?

❖ ❖ ❖ ❖ ❖ ❖ ❖ ❖ ❖ ❖

Monday, 24 March 1941

While much of the rest of Europe is enduring privations and rationing, the situation in Ireland is much less severe, as can be seen from the goods on offer by these Moore Street traders.

Tonight, well-known paediatrician Dr Robert Collis is in the Gaiety Theatre for another run of his play *Marrowbone Lane*. It is the story of a girl from Mayo, played by Shelah Richards, who marries a Dublin builder's labourer and comes to the city dazzled by his stories of life in the capital. But having won her, he brings her to his cockroach-infested tenement. She struggles to exist in the slums and when she is finally offered one of the city's new flats it is on the day that her child dies.

Collis addresses the audience before tonight's performance. He criticises the fact that despite the country governing itself for two decades, little has been done to improve the health of the poor. While conditions were bad before the war, they are now chronic. He estimates that there are 40,000 people with just 6d for food and heat. Then he tells a story: 'Only a matter of weeks ago another young mother carried her sick baby from hospital door to hospital door. At the fourth hospital she was told there was no bed that night. She took the baby home. At 2 a.m. she tried a fifth hospital. When the nurses there unwrapped the bundle she was carrying, they found the baby was dead.'

Tenement life remains largely unchanged since independence and, with the war bringing an end to the housing programme, there is no end in sight.

❖ ❖ ❖ ❖ ❖ ❖ ❖ ❖ ❖ ❖ ❖

Saturday, 31 May 1941

Dubliners have become used to unidentified planes flying over the city and are familiar with the firing of the army's anti-aircraft batteries at Conquer Hill Road in Clontarf, Collinstown, Dalkey, Trimlestown, Baldonnel Aerodrome, Ballyfermot,

Ringsend Park, the Hibernian School in the Phoenix Park, a field by Dún Laoghaire Golf Club, Sundrive Road in Kimmage, the Fifteen Acres in the Phoenix Park, St Vincent's Home on the Navan Road and the fields by Grace Park Terrace in Drumcondra.

But tonight it is different.

Shortly after midnight, between 20 and 40 planes fly over the city. By their distinctive engine drone people know they are Luftwaffe.

Almost from the start people notice something unusual. Instead of being bunched in a tight formation, on their way somewhere else – Belfast, Liverpool, Manchester – they are loose, circling the city. The searchlights on Killiney Hill, Howth Head and Ballyfermot dance across the night sky.

Warning shots fire from the gun batteries at 00.18. But the planes do not leave. At 00.35, the anti-aircraft batteries around the city open up the most intense firing yet seen in Dublin. Although all of this is unusual, the air raid wardens do not sound the alarm. In fact, people come out of their homes to watch the show.

After a brief lull, the anti-aircraft fire resumes, with increased intensity.

Sometime after 1.30 a.m., an aircraft flies out towards the airport. When it is fired upon, it turns back towards the city and begins flying in an unusual manner, banking, diving, circling at low altitude over the rooftops. It is as though the pilot is seeking something. Or trying to figure out where he is.

Why the pilot finally decides to drop his payload is not clear. But just after 2 a.m. there is a whining, whistling sound, followed by a huge explosion on the North Circular Road. Then other bombs explode, not far away, at Summerhill Parade,

Some of the devastation at North Strand Road.

at North Strand Road and near the Dog Pond in the Phoenix Park. Two more are dropped on Summer Street and Fairview but they fail to detonate.

The North Circular Road bomb destroys a shop and a house. At Summerhill Parade, a house is destroyed. The one that explodes in the Phoenix Park does the least amount of damage, breaking windows in the residences of the president and the American ambassador and alarming animals in the Zoo – a startled elephant falls over. But at North Strand Road, there is carnage.

Ten houses are destroyed between the Five Lamps and Newcomen Bridge. Others have their roofs blown off, windows shattered, doors blown in.

Under the glow of flames flaring from a burst gas main, emergency workers and volunteers in human chains remove rubble to reach the trapped. Rescuers call with megaphones into the debris for survivors. Children scream for mothers, mothers for their children.

People buried in the debris suffer burns, asphyxia and crush injuries. Among the dead and dying are carpenter Patrick Murray, Josephine Fagan, her father Thomas Carroll, two-year-old Patrick McKeogh, seven members of the Brown family – Mary (75), Harry (37), her son, his wife Mary (33) and four of their children, Maureen (7), Nan (5), Edward (3½) and Angela (2) – and Patrick McLoughlin and his two-year-old child – they had been at Summerhill when the bomb fell there and had come to what he thought was safety at North Strand.

❖ ❖ ❖ ❖ ❖ ❖ ❖ ❖ ❖ ❖ ❖

Sunday, 1 June 1941

While workers are still clearing rubble at North Strand, where the death count has risen to 30, a building collapses on the other side of the city. A tenement at Bride Street falls, floor upon floor, not because it has been bombed but because of neglect, cynicism, greed, apathy.

The only warning for the occupants at Bride Street was the sight of the walls coming apart around them, ceilings buckling. Some managed to get out just in time, but others are not so lucky. In the pile of bricks, joists, masonry, roof slates, tables, chairs, bedsteads and life's trinkets, are the remains of 72-year-old Samuel O'Brien, who had been in the top storey, Bridget Lynskey, aged 35, and her four-month-old baby. Bridget had only just received the key to her new Crumlin home. She was due to move tomorrow.

While German forces are closing in on Leningrad, British and Soviet troops invading Iran to save the oilfields from German capture and Japanese troops consolidating their hold on Indochina, in Dublin, journalist and author, Denis Ireland attends a play in the Gate Theatre on Tuesday, 26 August where he makes the following observations:

'In spite of flying bombs over London and war clouds over Europe, conversation sparkles, rumours seethe like a bath of acid. There are mountainy young women from remote Georgian country houses, looking as if they had been dragged through a hedge backwards, earls, mountebanks, playboys, dramatists who once had a play on for a week at the Abbey, hungry looking authors, even respectable bookmakers and publicans. It is Bloomsbury translated so far west that no one would bat an eyelid if some of the authors, or the sprigs of nobility gone native in corduroy trousers, were suddenly to produce six-shooters and start 'shooting up' the chandeliers.

The authors, bookmakers, publicans and mountainy young women with wild hair surge noisily into the auditorium and arrange themselves for conversational mayhem in the stalls. The play is *The Importance of Being Earnest*... and it had better be good.'

'The shops are full of good things to eat, the streets full of people who cannot afford to buy them. Light and heat are desperately short, for there is very little coal, and turf is scarce through lack of transport. The coal ration is three-eighths of a tonne every two months ... Doctors and government inspectors have less petrol than the average English motorist, the great country houses have the bath night once a week, bread is rationed, tea and coffee very scarce, trains run slowly on inferior fuel, the Archbishop of Dublin has inaugurated free soup kitchens ...'
Cyril Connolly *Horizon Magazine*, January 1942

Friday, 15 May 1942

Recently crime has become a big topic.

Going through the Dublin courts at the moment are nine young men on charges of riotous assembly and attempted murder. Their cases relate to events that occurred at a junior cup final soccer match between Stephen's Celtic and Mountainview in Tolka Park in March. With 30 minutes remaining in the match, members of the Stafford Street Gang, from the north side of the city, went to the ground, some arriving by boat, others scaling a wall, to attack members of the Coombe's Ash Street Gang. For 20 minutes, a battle was fought between the gangs, who used flagpoles, knives, iron bars, wooden batons, even bayonets, as weapons.

'A Bird Never Flew on One Wing' by Harry Kernoff shows two men drinking stout in front of a wall covered with the names of well-known Dublin public houses.

While the 'Battle of Tolka', as it is being called, is the most violent incident in the city for some time, the weekly fare in the Dublin District Court is not the stuff of dime store novels. It usually consists of minor work-related thefts, indecent exposures, shoplifting, refusal to pay taxi fares, drunkenness, driving motor cars at speed. As wartime restrictions bite deeper, the crime rate has been increasing. And one crime is affecting thousands of people.

In 1938 1,160 bicycles were stolen in Dublin. This year the number is going to be treble that. There is no doubt that some of the thieves, or those in receipt of stolen bicycles, are themselves the unfortunate victims of the same crime – having had their bicycle stolen, they take another to get home, or buy a stolen bicycle on the black market to replace their own.

Shortages of materials and petrol rationing have made the bicycle an increasingly valuable item. More than 50 are being stolen each week and much garda time and resources are being spent investigating the thefts. Supervised cycle parks are being established, while gardaí are put on special duty outside churches during mass – a particularly popular time for thieves. Perhaps most significantly, the judges in the city courts are starting to get tough.

This week George Dudley, a 17-year-old newsboy from Corporation Buildings, John Nash, also from Corporation Buildings and Joseph McDermott from Corporation Place are each given several months' imprisonment for stealing bicycles. Patrick Quinn of Corporation Buildings is given nine months' hard labour and Thomas Whelan from Killester, 'a first-class mechanic', is convicted of dismantling and reassembling bicycles, and given three years' penal servitude. It is hoped that such sentences will bring an end to this plague.

An attendant keeps watch on bicycles parked on O'Connell Street.

Tuesday, 15 September 1942

With every extension of the theatre of war being preceded by aerial bombardments, the number of public air raid shelters has been increasing in Dublin. Now in the event of an attack, 50,000 people will be able to find shelter, if not complete safety.

Apart from private shelters provided by employers and at newly constructed flats such as Sister Mary Aikenhead House on Thomas Street, a variety of public shelters have been provided throughout the city.

More trench shelters have been dug at Fitzwilliam Square, Merrion Square, Fairbrothers' Fields, Ormond Square and Custom House Square.

Professor Erwin Shroedinger on the left, President Hyde in chair with Taoiseach Eamon de Valera on the right.

132

The basements of large buildings such as the King's Inns, the Law Library, Independent House on Abbey Street, the Russell Hotel, the Stephen's Green Club and the College of Surgeons have been converted into underground shelters for up to 20,000 people.

But of increasing importance for the protection of the population are 650 overground shelters. Capable of holding 50 people, these large huts have 15-inch-thick concrete walls and roofs of concrete reinforced with steel bars. They have been erected almost everywhere – along the quays, on bridges, in the middle of roads. Though they have been built to withstand the effects of German – or British – bombs, they have been no match for a much more local threat – Dublin's vandals.

As a result of this vandalism, new shelters will have doors and old ones are being fitted with them. These will remain locked until an air raid warden comes with a key, which hopefully will be in time to save people from an attack.

❖ ❖ ❖ ❖ ❖ ❖ ❖ ❖ ❖ ❖ ❖

Friday, 26 February 1943

Academics, students, religious figures and leading politicians file out of the lecture theatre on the top floor of the Physics building in Trinity College at the end of the last of three lectures on what is possibly the biggest of all subjects: 'What is Life?' But the content of the talks has been of things that are so small they cannot be seen except without the aid of high-powered microscopes. Some only exist in theory.

The lectures have been delivered by Professor Erwin Shroedinger, an Austrian intellectual refugee from the war. He is the one of the leading figures in mathematical physics.

In 1927, he put forward a new theory of wave mechanics. In 1933, he was awarded the Nobel Prize 'for the discovery of new productive forms of atomic theory' and since 1935 his theoretical experiment known as 'Shroedinger's Cat' has attracted much attention. With the rise of Nazism, Shroedinger became an itinerant academic and ended up in Dublin at the invitation of Taoiseach de Valera to join the staff of the School of Theoretical Physics at the newly established Dublin Institute for Advanced Studies.

Since moving to Dublin, Shroedinger has lived with his wife at Kincora Road in Clontarf – though rumours of affairs with Dublin women abound. He is now a familiar figure cycling in his waterproof cycling suit and beret along the seafront to his Merrion Square office. He has settled in very well and almost feels at home:

Less than a month after Shroedinger's last lecture, Taoiseach Éamon de Valera delivers a St Patrick's Day speech on national radio that harks back to an Ireland that is far from quantum mechanics. In it, the Taoiseach outlines his vision for an ideal Ireland. In it Dublin does not feature. The city has no place in his image of an 'Irish Ireland':

'The ideal Ireland that we would have, the Ireland that we dreamed of, would be the home of a people who valued material wealth only as a basis for right living, of a people who, satisfied with frugal comfort, devoted their leisure to the things of the spirit – a land whose countryside would be bright with cosy homesteads, whose fields and villages would be joyous with the sounds of industry, with the romping of sturdy children, the contest of athletic youths and the laughter of happy maidens, whose firesides would be forums for the wisdom of serene old age. The home, in short, of a people living the life that God desires that men should live.'

'... the mentality of the people, their attitude towards life, it is like that of our own people in the Alps'.

In his Trinity lectures, Shroedinger has addressed the stuff of 'life' not from the traditional biological point of view but from that of physics. He is particularly concerned with why living things defy the Second Law of Thermodynamics which states that all order in the universe eventually breaks down. But life goes on, from generation to generation.

In the lectures, Shroedinger has not answered his own question. But he has argued that this information must be hidden, somewhere within a molecule. There has to be a 'hereditary molecule' containing some sort of 'code script', or biological information book, which determines the pattern of an individual's future development.

When that molecule is found, scientists can then set about breaking the code of life. Perhaps someone at the lectures, or who reads them when they are eventually published, will be inspired to further the inquiry through the science of physics. Perhaps they will be the one who will discover the answer to the question 'What is life?'

❖ ❖ ❖ ❖ ❖ ❖ ❖ ❖ ❖ ❖ ❖

Thursday, 9 September 1943

Today the 'Irish Exhibition of Living Art' at the Gallery of the National College of Art at Kildare Street opens. The exhibition features not just the 'traditionalists' whose work is displayed annually at the Royal Hibernian Academy which puts a premium on 'the accurate rendering of the human form' and what is called 'correct drawing'. There are also 'moderns' whose work is not appreciated at the Academy.

Organised by people who had either studied in Paris or been influenced by artists based there, the exhibition is immediately recognised as one that will change the future of Irish art. Among the artists are Jack B. Yeats, Sean Keating, Louis le Brocquy and Jerome O'Connor, but what is also most notable is the high percentage of brilliant work by Irish women artists. Among these are Mainie Jellett, Mary Swanzy, Beatrice Glenavy and May Guinness.

Louis Le Brocquy, artist and founding member of the Irish Exhibition of Living Art, and Elizabeth Curren, secretary of the exhibition, standing in front of Le Brocquy's painting 'Spanish Shawl' at the IELA in 1943.

❖ ❖ ❖ ❖ ❖ ❖ ❖ ❖ ❖ ❖ ❖

Tuesday, 25 January 1944

Daily city life is not something that is often recorded. Thousands of episodes, events and happenings take place every day which go unnoticed, leaving no trace, but make up the essence of city life. But for the last 16 months, a twice-weekly column called 'City Commentary' in the *Irish Press* has tried to do that. It is written by Monaghan poet Patrick Kavanagh under the pseudonym 'Piers Plowman'.

Though Kavanagh's writings are generally rooted in rural Irish life (his most notable work to date is his 1942 poem *The Great Hunger*), 'City Commentary' is 'a

Children playing on Dominick Street.

countryman's impression of city life for the benefit of my friends in the country. I
want to reveal in a simple way the usual – and unusual …'

'City Commentary' has featured bedsit dwellers, artists, writers, newspaper boys
(those with a good patch such as a window ledge on the GPO can make over £3
per week, 'But the others! Misery and hardship'), the 'Battle of Trinity' during the
annual rag week, city fashion shows, a junior cross-country run in the Phoenix Park,
a visit to the Central Catholic Library, boys sitting on a Ringsend quay wall fishing
at midnight, Christmas Eve ('the evening of evenings'), the Stock Exchange, a self-
service laundry attached to the Tara Street corporation baths (boiling water supplied
at three half pence an hour, bring your own soap), the 'receptacle for misfares' at bus
stops (Kavanagh admits to having never contributed to this honest man's conscience
box), the working patterns of Dublin's window cleaners, the National Library
(whose earlier closing time of 9 p.m. has hit students hard), pigs being driven down
Abbey Street, the best way to negotiate the city's busy footpaths if in a hurry (do not
walk with the traffic but against it, with a determined look that will part the crowd
'like the Red Sea before the Israelites'), the starlings that assemble on the trees of
O'Connell Street, the film censor's studio, the fair day of the Association of Juvenile
Catholics, a meeting of the Magicians of Ireland, the retirement of George Crawford,

'a tall, military looking man', from the Trinity College Library after 40 years' service showing visitors the Book of Kells, 'Guard 236' who has been 17 years on traffic point duty at the Henry Street side of Nelson's Pillar, sculptor Seamus Murphy, the rugby cup final at Lansdowne Road, the shortage of potatoes, the paucity of good actresses, the overheard conversations ('No, it was John that made me promise'), O'Connell Bridge the day before an All-Ireland (people up from the country asking gardaí for directions to 'the Museum, then Woolworths and finally the whereabouts of the best dance hall'), Dublin's poverty ('One of the things that most surprises a man fresh from the country in Dublin is the terrible poverty that exists. Nothing like it is known in a country place …').

The column is not high literary fare but sometimes the poet captures aspects of city life that can define it at least as well as the town planners do with their surveys and maps. In one column he wrote:

> On Saturday night I wandered about the streets seeking adventure. Nothing that is called news was happening, but adventure, yes. Here on these streets were crowds of individuals passing by, each man and woman with a story whose plot is woven in the Eternal Web. Lounging against the houses on both sides of Westmoreland Street were men like rows of statues; had they no place to go? What was their secret? As I came over O'Connell Street a breeze like a draught in the haggard

A barge on the River Liffey.

caught my cheek. The pavement artist had gone home and his chalk pictures of Mr de Valera, Mr Jim Larkin, film stars, etc. were fading. But another artist was re-marking their outlines and later on I saw this lad waiting beside his cap, against which was the legend: 'All my own work and I got no training'.

In another he describes walking in St Stephen's Green:

Facing the duck-pond as we go in the direction of the memorial gate at the Grafton Street end I observed the rows of people sitting on the free seats in the shadows. One man with a grey face and a ragged expression on his clothes was reading a very old torn newspaper. A little girl wheeling a small boy in a broken pram. A toddler trying to reach out for a gull near the edge of the pond. These names may not make news in the modern superficial sense, but they do make life. It is in their unwritten stories we find the history of the human race.

❖ ❖ ❖ ❖ ❖ ❖ ❖ ❖ ❖ ❖ ❖

Sunday, 24 September 1944

The Football Association of Ireland Cup Final is Dublin's most popular domestic sporting event. Since 1922, there have been just three finals that have not featured a team from Dublin. Shamrock Rovers, founded in Ringsend but now based in Milltown, has 11 cup final appearances, St James's Gate, founded as part of the Guinness Brewery's sport and social club, has four, Shelbourne four, Brideville from the Liberties two, Bohemians, founded in a Phoenix Park Gate Lodge in 1890 and now based at Dalymount Park, three, Drumcondra FC, based in Tolka Park, two, and Dolphin, from Dolphin's Barn, two. In the 22 years since independence, only five teams from outside the capital have won the cup.

The most popular sporting events for Dubliners are rugby and soccer internationals. Both are suspended due to the war but they usually pack Lansdowne Road and Dalymount Park with up to 40,000 spectators.

But in terms of scale, the GAA's All-Irelands are in a different league altogether. The All-Ireland football final is the city's largest sporting event. After that comes the hurling final. Both usually attract a crowd of between 45,000 and 55,000 to Croke Park.

Although Dublin might be the venue for its finals, the city has not fully embraced gaelic games. In fact, in the last ten years, the finals that Dublin contested have been the most poorly attended. This year's hurling final, played two weeks ago between Dublin and Cork, drew a crowd of just 27,000 (Cork won).

Despite petrol rationing, which made travel from the competing counties difficult, today's clash between Kerry and Roscommon has broken all previous attendance records for an Irish sporting event.

The thousands of people from Kerry and Roscommon who live and work in the city have rarely felt more at home, as last night the city was taken over by supporters from the west and south. With every hotel, guesthouse and bed and breakfast booked out, many walked out to the suburbs to knock on strangers' doors to ask for a bed, couch or floor for the night. The unsuccessful slept in doorways, parks and train stations.

An hour before today's match started, Croke Park was packed. The official attendance was given as 79,245 but the actual figure is certainly higher – the time-honoured tradition of lifting children over turnstiles was well observed, while others broke through gates.

Even with 10,000 more people crammed into the stadium than ever before, thousands of others had to be locked out.

After the match, the city is taken over once again by the supporters from both counties. For those who want to know the result of the match all they have to do is walk across O'Connell Bridge where the Roscommon supporters are dancing jigs in the middle of the traffic.

❖ ❖ ❖ ❖ ❖ ❖ ❖ ❖ ❖ ❖ ❖

Monday, 28 May 1945

There is good and bad news about the city's health.

According to a survey of cases at Cook Street Hospital, diphtheria is on the decline. Largely as a result of an immunisation programme introduced during the planned evacuation of the city, the number of cases in the hospital has fallen from 70 in 1934 to just 24 last year. Among other improvements has been a decline in scarlet fever cases, from 478 in 1934 to just 104 last year, and just one death from measles, which had killed nine in the hospital in 1934.

However, there are new diseases at Cook Street. Among these are whooping cough, which led to just one death in 1937 but last year accounted for 34, and polio, of which there were never more than three cases in any year in the 1930s but over 30 last year.

Another Dublin hospital has seen a rise in instances of a different type of illness. Dr Steevens', the city's main venereal disease hospital, reports a sharp increase in sexually transmitted diseases during the war. From a low point after independence of 600 cases in 1938, in 1942–43 it treated over 1,300 despite increased emigration and more men in the army, where they receive treatment. The rise was caused by promiscuity, the lack of prophylactic contraception and the fact that people receive no information about the disease.

However, the biggest killer in Dublin remains – and this will be the case for the foreseeable future – tuberculous meningitis. There are an estimated 5,000 cases of TB in the city, meaning that one in every 100 Dubliners is infected with the disease. More people between the ages of 15 and 35 die from TB than every other illness put together.

To celebrate its tenth anniversary, the Mount Street Club, founded to help the city's unemployed, publishes *What To Do: A Survey of the Unemployment Problem* in April 1945. In it a chapter written by Patricia Hutchins outlines the idle, wasted life of one of the ranks of Dublin's unemployed:

'He shuffled one foot sideways against the wall of the bank, marked in brown patches, shoulder high, by the men who spent most of their lives there, and lit the butt of a cigarette. Frayed trouser-ends, pockets shaped to hands constantly in them, scrap of cloth at the neck, with a cap once checked black-and-white, now with a leather-like band of grease to the peak, Michael O'Toole was an unnoticeable part of a Dublin street, as inevitable as the old people who sorted the battered dustbins and buckets on the steps of the houses opposite. Torn lace curtains across the windows competed with broken panes mended with pieces of board, to give a patchwork, shanty effect, though they were solid shale-coloured houses; what remained of shattered door-lights were as incongruous as an 18th century embroidered fan might have been in the hands of one of the women talking there ...

'It had been wet in the city earlier that morning but now the sun slanted across the road, making the contrast of light and shade deeper. Michael could feel the moisture of the pavement through the soles of his shoes, the slim, dandyish type used for dancing. He shifted again, for the unemployed have a formula for standing; as boy, youth, man, each seems to develop this ability to watch others hurry about their business, meet, talk, pass on; feeding on the apparent monotony, to find in it the drama of repetition, of changing pattern.'

Today at the Mansion House, the Irish Red Cross Society is holding a 'Tuberculosis Exhibition' to raise awareness of the causes of the disease. The overriding message to everyone, but particularly parents and their children, is that TB is not handed down from generation to generation, it is one that is passed from person to person.

The exhibition features films such as *Defeat Tuberculosis* and *Goodbye Mr Germ*. There is a 'Choric Dance Fantasy' about 'the Great Destroyer', with 'the Harbinger of Disease' being fought by Hope, Rest, Air, Sunlight and Health. There is also a lantern slide drama *Crime Comes to Lungtown* featuring the 'bacillus gangsters', 'Tony Tuberculosis', 'Scarface Sputum' and 'Commissioner Corpuscle'.

A warning of the dangers of Tuberculosis, still Dublin's greatest killer.

❖ ❖ ❖ ❖ ❖ ❖ ❖ ❖ ❖ ❖ ❖

Monday, 7 May 1945

At 2 p.m., BBC radio announces the end of the war. After 2,094 days and tens of millions of dead, Germany has surrendered. There is peace in Europe.

On hearing the news, the mainly Protestant students of Trinity College celebrate by hanging Union Jacks at the corners of the building overlooking College Green.

Fearing a disturbance, gardaí enter the college to have the flags removed. However, a short time later, another 100 students make their way to the rooftop to sing the British and French national anthems, 'Rule, Britannia!' and 'It's a Long Way to Tipperary'.

Outside, a crowd on College Green grows in size, their numbers swelled by UCD students from Earlsfort Terrace.

The students on the rooftop hoist four flags on the flagpole. At the top is the Union Jack, then the red flag of the Soviet Union, the French tricolour and, at the bottom, a somewhat grubby Irish flag. The crowd below are angered at the lowly positioning of the Irish flag. While the Trinity students sing 'God Save the King', a Union Jack is burned by the UCD students below. Young men in the crowd rush the college gates, thought they do not manage to break through.

Then the Trinity students hoist a solitary Stars and Stripes before setting fire to the Irish flag and throwing it from the roof.

Before things get completely out of control, a squad of detectives arrive and enter the college. The flags are taken down, the students leave the roof and peace is once again restored to College Green.

The Military Exhibition and Tattoo at the RDS, the most popular event in the city for years, comes to an end on Saturday, 8 September 1945. Organised to raise money for the Army Benevolent Fund, it has run every day for two weeks. Some 219,000 people have been to the exhibition where they have looked at, sat in and handled armoured cars, Hurricane bombers, tanks, heavy artillery, mine detectors, anti-aircraft guns and every other piece of modern military equipment. Another 200,000 have watched the Tattoo in the showjumping enclosure with massed pipe and drum bands, motorcycle trick riders, a re-creation of the 1646 Battle of Benburb – one of the few battles in history that was won by the Irish – and a parade of Irish soldiers including the Fianna, the Red Branch Knights, the men of 1798, of 1916, the War of Independence and the modern-day army. But absent from the parade is any sign of the hundreds of thousands who fought, and the tens of thousands who died, in the First World War.

> *Another Fine Display*
> THE
> **MILITARY TATTOO**
> AND EXHIBITION
> at the R.D.S. Showgrounds,
> **Ballsbridge, Dublin**
> AUGUST 27th ——— SEPTEMBER 8th
> (in aid of the Army Benevolent Fund)
> Independent Newspapers, Ltd.
> 24

Thursday, 17 April 1947

The general contents of Dublin guide books have changed little since the 1920s. Almost invariably, they direct visitors to the familiar sites of the city, to the General Post Office, the Bank of Ireland at College Green, Trinity College, the Mansion House, the National University at Earlsfort Terrace, St Stephens' Green, Dublin Castle, Christchurch and St Patrick's cathedrals, the Custom House, the Guinness

Poet Patrick Kavanagh has lived in Dublin for over five years. On Thursday, 3 October 1946 the *Irish Press* publishes a poem of his called 'Dark-Haired Miriam Ran Away'. Few people know it but the poem is about Kavanagh's love not for 'a dark-haired Miriam', but stunning-looking medical student Hilda Moriarty, from Kerry, who lives in Ballsbridge, near Raglan Road. When Hilda teased him about only ever writing about turnips, cabbages and potatoes he penned this poem:

On Raglan Road on an autumn day I met her first and knew
That her dark hair would weave a snare that I might one day rue;
I saw the danger, yet I walked upon the enchanted way,
And I said, let grief be a fallen leaf at the dawning of the day.

On Grafton Street in November we tripped lightly along the ledge
Of the deep ravine where can be seen the worth of passion's pledge:
The Queen of Hearts still making tarts and I not making hay –
Oh I loved too much and by such and such is happiness thrown away.

I gave her gifts of the mind, I gave her the secret sign that's known
To the artists who have known the true gods of sound and stone,
And word and tint ... I did not stint, for I gave her poems to say
With her own name there and her own dark hair like clouds over fields of May.

On a quiet street where old ghosts meet I see her walking now
Away from me so hurriedly my reason must allow
That I had wooed not as I should a creature made of clay –
When the angel woos the clay he'll lose his wings at the dawn of day.

Brewery and the National Library, National Museum and National Gallery. However, a new book, *In Dublin's Fair City*, written under the pen name G. Ivan Morris, purports to be an insider's guide to Dublin for visitors from Britain 'drawn by the aroma of the juicy unrationed steaks of the Dublin hotels and restaurants; the cream, eggs and other delicacies, which abound on every hand ...'

Morris describes various parts of the city including Moore Street's 'symphonic smell'; there are the clientele of second-hand bookstalls along the Liffey quays: 'Old men with long white hair, young fellows with longing looks, prosperous businessmen and even children, stand along the stalls examining the books and magazines which

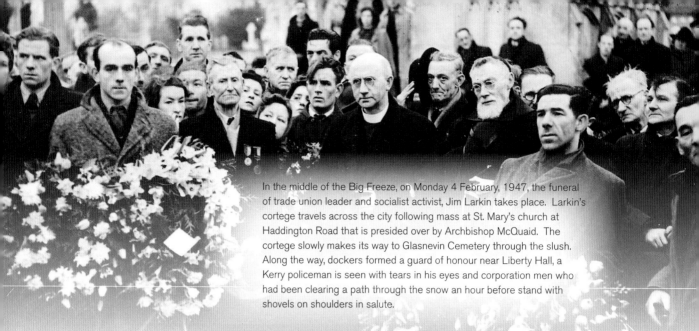

In the middle of the Big Freeze, on Monday 4 February, 1947, the funeral of trade union leader and socialist activist, Jim Larkin takes place. Larkin's cortege travels across the city following mass at St. Mary's church at Haddington Road that is presided over by Archbishop McQuaid. The cortege slowly makes its way to Glasnevin Cemetery through the slush. Along the way, dockers formed a guard of honour near Liberty Hall, a Kerry policeman is seen with tears in his eyes and corporation men who had been clearing a path through the snow an hour before stand with shovels on shoulders in salute.

even through the scarcity of the war years abounded.' Saturday evening crowds on Camden Street that surge 'up and down the old thoroughfare in thousands' looking at the low-priced shops and the wares of street traders, while on Grafton Street, 'intermingled with the [fashionable] human clothes dummies are the arty young men in corduroy pants, carelessly-worn neckties, and out of shape sports jackets, and, of course – in every second instance – the inevitable facial embellishment in the form of a beard or a moustache'. There are the city's cyclists who 'are a sight to behold, especially during lunch hour and between five and six o'clock in the evening, when they appear in their thousands amidst the traffic of O'Connell Street'.

Among Morris's less flattering passages in the book is one describing the general appearance of the average Dubliner:

> Although they have a natural freshness that is delightful, it is doubtful if the Dublin women are quite as attractive as those of London or other large cities. They are certainly not as smartly dressed and turned out, and seem to lack the ability to get the best out of themselves and their clothes … The men of Dublin deserve a sharp rebuke in the matter of clothes. It is not too much to say that utter carelessness is the outstanding feature of men's wear. A test made in O'Connell Street, at mid-day, over a hundred-yard stretch revealed the astonishing fact that less than one man in a hundred had his trousers properly pressed. Most of them were baggy-kneed, and obviously had not creased their pants for a considerable period … Everyone says that the women walk very badly. Few of them seem to know how to carry themselves … Indeed, were it not for the charms which Nature has given them, including the soft brogue and the witty sally, the women of the Irish cities would be very far down the scale of feminine attractiveness.

DUBLIN SINCE 1922

Monday, 7 April 1947

Today the sun shines and the air is warm. Windows throughout the city are thrown open, painful joints are loosened, clothes are aired, the fear of death recedes and people greet one another as if for the first time, as though this day was never going to arrive. As though it would forever be winter.

The city was in the grip of arctic weather between 22 January and 7 March. During that time, the temperature never climbed above five degrees Celsius.

The first snow fell on 24 January; heavier snow came two days later. For children the 'gift from the gods' made for snowballing and sledding, but it challenged bus drivers' skills of avoiding catastrophic skids, cyclists' ability to navigate ice and snow and cattle drivers' patience with cattle slipping while being driven along the streets of the north side to market.

Heavy snowfalls on 21 February produced the busiest time for hospitals for many years with dozens injured – mainly dislocated shoulders and fractured ribs. After hopes were raised that the weather would break even heavier snow fell on 24 February.

Such was the constant state of winter that there were just 16 hours of sunshine in Dublin in the entire month of February.

One of the worst problems has been the lack of fuel. To preserve their own supplies, Britain stopped all fuel exports on 6 February. To conserve fuel, the city's tram services were cut by 25 per cent, mainline passenger rail services were reduced and then eventually stopped altogether, Radio Éireann shortened its broadcasting hours so people could turn off their radios, and all external electric signs in the city were banned. Gas rationing saw the reappearance of the dreaded 'glimmerman'. Carrying nothing more sinister than a pen, notebook, torch and authorisation from the gas company, he walked the streets looking for houses burning gas that remained in the pipes, when the supply was turned off. Hundreds of offenders had their gas supplies completely cut off.

The fuel shortage was not just an inconvenience.

During the height of the fuel crisis one *Irish Press* journalist joined the women of poor families who queued at the Bridgefoot Street fuel depot:

> The women talk about nothing else. The search for fuel has eaten so deeply into their time and energies that there is no room for any other feeling, any other topic of conversation … Those that have gas are the envied ones. Kettle after kettle is boiled and rushed to neighbours' rooms … They have relatives safe and warm in hospital, thank God;

they have babies stored away at home in rags and wrappings; they have children at school; they have sick husbands roaring and bawling out of the bed for this and that; they have infirm neighbours who have to be tended with gentle hands and not forgotten in the fuel fight.

In addition to deaths from influenza, the cold has been a silent killer. Although there are no figures published, everyone knows that hundreds of people have fallen victim to 'the White Death' having been frozen to death in houses and tenements with fireless grates.

March started with a brief thaw but even this brought its own tragedy as three boys drowned when the ice in a Kimmage quarry cracked open underneath them.

But the respite was brief as it snowed on the ninth and then again on the twelfth. Those who hoped that the weather would turn with the national holiday were disappointed when a snow blizzard on the sixteenth was followed by torrential rain. St Patrick's Day was less colourful than for many years with shamrock scarce and many events and sporting fixtures cancelled.

March turns out to be the wettest since 1924.

Finally today, Easter Monday, it is bright, and if it is too windy to be warm, it is not too cool. There is also news that the fuel shortage is ending, with 2,000 tonnes of coal due to arrive in the city tomorrow and 7,500 more tonnes being loaded in Baltimore, USA. The crisis is over. Today is the first day of spring.

On the coast of north County Dublin a new concept in Irish holidays opens at Red Island, Skerries in March 1948. According to the newspaper advertisements, 'Young people, Red Island is your holiday dream come true!' And they may well be right.

Red Island features the largest ballroom in the country, a roller-skating rink, hotel-like accommodation (as opposed to Butlin's-type chalets), the delights of Skerries Beach and plenty of organised activities including talent competitions, quizzes, sing-songs, table tennis, dancing and cinema shows.

The camp will no doubt be popular with British tourists who are now coming in record numbers. But Red Island's major selling point is that it caters exclusively for single people. The message is quite clear: there will be plenty of opportunities for everyone to 'mix with boys and girls your own age'. Red Island will be the 'Rendezvous of Young Ireland'.

And with all of this being made available for an all-in price of five pounds fifteen shillings per week, it is sure to be popular.

Thursday, 22 July 1948

People are gathering in the grounds of Leinster House, outside the National Library, National Museum and on Kildare Street because the statue of Queen Victoria is finally being removed. For 40 years, she has brooded from her 15-foot-tall pedestal, 26 of those looking down on Oireachtas members going about the daily business of running an independent Ireland. But her inanimate reign is about to end.

The three-tonne bronze statue has been the largest in the city. In preparation for today, three figures at the base that had portrayed 'Hibernia at War', 'Hibernia at Peace' and 'Fame' as well as an inscription which read 'Victoria, Queen of the United Kingdom of Great Britain and Ireland, Empress of India, erected by her Irish subjects', have already been removed.

Having survived in an independent Ireland for so long, what is bringing her down today? Is it national sentiment? The wish to erase the past? The obvious irony of a statue of a queen of England lording it over the Irish parliament? No, apparently it is because the members of Dáil Éireann need more car parking.

At 3.20 p.m., a crane shifts her off her perch with a sideways jerk. 'We are not amused,' someone in the crowd quips. In a few minutes, to cheers from the onlookers, she is freed from her support. Floating in the air, she surveys her dominion for the last time. Then she is loaded onto the back of a lorry and, in a distinctly undignified supine position, is driven out of the gates of Leinster House.

With Queen Victoria now dethroned, the only statues in Dublin remaining of Ireland's former rulers are Admiral Nelson on his O'Connell Street Pillar, Prince Albert behind the National Museum and Lord Gough on his horse in the Phoenix Park. But the statues must know that their days are numbered. Because it is becoming evident that for a statue to survive in this city, it needs to have been on the winning side.

❖ ❖ ❖ ❖ ❖ ❖ ❖ ❖ ❖ ❖ ❖

Friday, 1 October 1948

Two days ago Herbert Simms, Dublin Corporation's housing architect since 1932, was found badly injured on the railway tracks at Dún Laoghaire. He had been struck by an early-morning passenger train. He was rushed to hospital but died of his injuries later that day. This morning he is being buried in Deansgrange Cemetery.

New working-class houses in Drimnagh, part of the legacy of Herbert Simms.

Simms had died by suicide. Before going to Dún Laoghaire to take his own life he had left a note for his wife in which he wrote that he feared overwork was driving him insane.

Though he clearly despaired, Simms leaves behind a significant legacy of 17,000 new working-class houses in the city. According to one obituary, 'It is not given to many of us to achieve so much in the space of a short lifetime for the benefit of so many.'

On Easter Monday, 18 April 1949, nearly 33 years after the Easter Rising, the Irish Republic comes into being. Around the city, the national flag and papal flag fly from various buildings. Bonfires have been lit in rural areas and on the hills overlooking the city. Messages of goodwill have been received from the Pope, King George and President Truman. All evening, people have been arriving at O'Connell Bridge where a gun battery has been set up by the army and searchlight batteries focus their beams directly overhead.

Buses festooned with streamers in the national colours have brought nationalists from Northern Ireland. Cars decorated in green, white and orange have come into the city from outer districts all evening while thousands packed buses. At 11.30 p.m., the crowd between the Metal Bridge and Butt Bridge is so large that they burst through the police cordon and swarm across the bridge. Rooftops are lined with people.

At one minute past midnight there is a fanfare of trumpets and a roll of drums. A 21-gun salute – delayed by some minutes as part of the crowd pushes its way too close to the guns – is fired downriver from O'Connell Bridge, the flames from the muzzles scorching the bridge's balustrade. After a reveille, the ceremony ends with the singing of the national anthem, cheering, and ships moored at the North Wall sounding their horns.

Sunday, 10 July 1949

It is the end of an era as tonight the last trams run in the city centre. The tram's demise in Dublin was first decided upon in 1938, but the war gave it a stay of execution. Tomorrow, what was once one of the most extensive city tram networks in the world will cease operations.

Tonight the Dún Laoghaire and Dalkey routes will be the last to run. Tomorrow the city will be completely given over to the bus. Officially the buses are being hailed as an improvement because, although they are noisier and belch fumes, there will be more of them and they will shorten journeys. But the trams will be missed by Dubliners.

Thousands have come to O'Connell Street to watch the last trams follow the rails for the last time. Radio Éireann's plans to record the departures for posterity and the intention of the Irish Transport and General Workers' Union band to lead the tram out of town have had to be abandoned as the last two are swarmed upon by hundreds of people.

Stuck on one of them is journalist and playwright Denis Johnston who had taken the tram into town when he found himself unable to get off. He becomes an unintentional witness to the occasion.

The scenes on O'Connell Bridge the night that Ireland is finally declared a Republic.

The journey out is 'a fantastic ride'. All the way out the 'crazy poltergeists' are taking the tram to bits. First the lights, then the curtains and the fittings are wrenched off, and next the Fare Sheets, Byelaws and Board of Trade Regulations disappear. At Haddington Road, the very seat underneath Johnston is removed. From there to Ballsbridge he stands up with nothing to hold on to, because nothing is left. All the while, ghostly figures wave and call from the pavement, and at Ballsbridge, where he gets out, a bonfire is blazing in the middle of the road.

Like a spectre, the darkened, half-wrecked tram crosses the Dodder Bridge and clanks its way out past the RDS Showgrounds. From the blackened interior comes 'the howling of many banshees'.

More than two hours after departing, what remains of the tram finally reaches the Blackrock depot. Another crowd is on hand but gardaí are there to help CIÉ staff to get the tram in to safety. When they do manage to pull the huge depot doors closed, they bring the era of the Dublin tram to an end with a rendition of 'Auld Lang Syne'.

1950–1963

A Conservative City with
a Rebellious Streak

Friday, 17 March 1950

Two Aer Lingus Dakotas take off from Dublin Airport, not on one of the airline's scheduled flights to Paris, Amsterdam, Birmingham, Glasgow, the Isle of Man, London, Manchester or Shannon, but to fly low over the city. Below, thousands of people line a route between O'Connell Street and St Stephen's Green to watch the procession of vehicles and bands that make up the new St Patrick's Day Parade.

Until this year, the national holiday has been marked by military parades. In the early years there was the new army, horse-drawn 18-pound cannons and Crossley armoured cars, but the weaponry became more and more sophisticated with Bren and Thompson machine-gun-toting soldiers, caterpillar-tracked armoured weapons carriers, anti-tank guns, anti-aircraft guns, Swedish armoured cars and howitzers trundling past the reviewing stand at College Green.

Today's parade is completely different. It has been organised by the Industrial Development Association, founded last year to promote both home-grown and foreign businesses in Ireland. Their first project is the new St Patrick's Day Parade.

At the head of the parade is the Irish Transport and General Workers' Union band, followed by members of the Dublin Council of Irish Unions who carry placards carrying the message: 'If it's Irish, it's best'. Then, for the next hour, a moving shop window features the best of Irish industry.

Among the companies taking part are Aer Lingus (in addition to the two Dakotas flying overhead, they have a busload of uniformed air hostesses in the procession), chocolate company Fry-Cadbury which has a lorry displaying a huge Dairy Milk bar with two glasses of milk being poured magically into the wrapper, and Fleming's Fireclays with six lorries loaded with varieties of drainpipes. Monument Creameries

In difficult economic times, the traditional St. Patrick's Day military parade is replaced with an 'industrial parade' to promote employment.

has a replica cottage, Bord na Móna a 15-foot figure of a turf worker, the ESB has wires, cables, electricity poles and a huge 58-volt transformer, CIÉ has a motor coach, a cattle truck and a furniture removal van and Muintir na Mara has a group of fishermen around a boat.

When it is over, the crowds leave for home, the Zoo or the Botanic Gardens, or else attend one of the city's holiday sporting events – at Croke Park there are the GAA's Railway Cup finals, at Lansdowne Road the opening match of rugby's Leinster Senior Cup, at Dalymount Park a League of Ireland selection is playing a team from the Northern Irish League and at Baldoyle, the races are on. Whoever fancies buying a drink is going to have to go to the Irish Kennel Show at the RDS in Ballsbridge because since 1927 it is the only place someone who is not resident in a hotel can buy a drink on the national day.

❖ ❖ ❖ ❖ ❖ ❖ ❖ ❖ ❖ ❖ ❖

Wednesday, 18 July 1951

Shortly after midnight, flames are seen licking the windows of a rear room of the Abbey Theatre. The blaze soon spreads and in two hours, the roof of Ireland's National Theatre since 1904, collapses. While staff and actors manage to save portraits of Yeats,

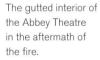

The gutted interior of the Abbey Theatre in the aftermath of the fire.

'The effects of urbanisation on the family in Ireland ... are extensive and swift. Despite certain radical continuities between the farm family and the family in Dublin, by the time the children of the immigrants from rural areas have reached full adulthood and founded their families, the total round of change has reached the point where the distinctive pattern of the family life of the countryman is no more. The countryman has been transformed literally into a citizen.'

Alexander J. Humphreys, *New Dubliners: Urbanization and the Irish Family*, 1966 (based on fieldwork carried out in 1949–51)

Lady Gregory, Lennox Robinson and others who have contributed to the history of the theatre, along with the building 50, years of history, memories, props, sets, costumes and scripts are destroyed.

Even as firemen fight the fire, decisions are already being taken. One is that the next performance of *The Plough and the Stars* must go ahead in the Peacock Theatre. People are already busy trying to find sets and costumes because, in the true tradition of theatre, the show must go on.

The other is that the Abbey must be rebuilt, but in a modern form. There had previously been plans to build a new theatre, but these had been shelved. Tonight, though, it seems that the theatre has made the final decision.

❖ ❖ ❖ ❖ ❖ ❖ ❖ ❖ ❖ ❖ ❖

Tuesday, 18 December 1951

In a year that saw the destruction of the Abbey Theatre, one of the longest-running plays in the history of the city, seen by over 100,000 people, comes to an end tonight at the Gate. Produced by Hilton Edwards and Micheál Mac Liammóir, *Tolka Row* has been the hit of the year. It is a story of modern working-class Dublin. A follow-up to her play *Liffey Lane*, which was set in the slums, writer Maura Laverty has shown herself to be what many describe as the only voice of Dublin since O'Casey. *Tolka Row* has run for ten weeks and is only being put off the stage to make way for the traditional Christmas productions.

Dubliners cannot get enough of seeing themselves portrayed on the stage. And *Tolka Row* is a story that many of them can identify with. It centres on Dan Dempsey who, in the autumn of his life, sells his cottage in the country to live in Dublin with one of his married daughters. He is at sea in the city among the new housing estates on the outskirts, bewildered by the lives the people lead, lives that are so different from the one he has been used to.

Tonight's performance is particularly special, not just because it is the last but because in the audience is the great American actor and director Orson Welles. In a way Welles has come back to the start of his career because the director and star of *Citizen Kane* began his acting career in the Gate in 1931 when on a visit to Dublin. As a 16-year-old, he made his debut in *Jew Suss* and altogether appeared in five plays at the Gate.

Before the performance of *Tolka Row*, 30 members of what is described as the 'Catholic Cinema and Theatre Patrons Association' protest outside the theatre against the American and what they regard as his communist beliefs. Inspired by the activities of Senator Joseph McCarthy in America, they carry placards reading 'Welles' actual home is Moscow: Stay out of Ireland' and 'Not Wanted Orson Welles; Stalin's Star'. Before Welles arrives, they are moved away from the theatre's front entrance by the guards.

Following the performance, a crowd in the region of a thousand gathers outside the theatre. But now they are mainly supporters of Welles and they push aside the protesters. However, in the meantime, Welles has made his way out of the theatre by another exit.

❖ ❖ ❖ ❖ ❖ ❖ ❖ ❖ ❖ ❖

Saturday, 4 April 1953

Tomorrow sees the start of An Tóstal, a national festival inspired by the recent Festival of Britain, to instil the thought that 'every exile would regard it as a matter of obligation to return to the Motherland at least once in a lifetime'. This 'national reunion' is being celebrated throughout Ireland, but most events are taking place in Dublin. The city's hotels are full with many Irish-Americans, and excitement is building before tomorrow's big parade in Dublin.

When the pubs close at 10 p.m.,word gets around that the hoarding surrounding the 'Bowl of Light' sculpture that is being specially erected for An Tóstal on the island in the middle of O'Connell Bridge is going to be removed, and thousands head for the bridge – Dublin is not blessed with an abundance of night-time entertainments.

The Pageant of St. Patrick at Croke Park opens the 1955 Tóstal festival.

By midnight, the crowd has become so large that traffic on the bridge is blocked. With no sign of the hoarding being removed, good humour gives way to impatience. Young men catcall and shout insults at the 50 gardaí on duty. The gardaí in turn are becoming impatient at the hold-up to traffic. When they try and clear the bridge, sections of the crowd are uncooperative. Gardaí draw batons to force them back, but as soon as a path is cleared, the crowd surges back.

While this is going on, some men tear down part of the hoarding to reveal a disappointing copper bowl from which emerges coloured plastic flames.

Then the crowd becomes even more unruly. A gang of youths rip up flowers from the base of the O'Connell monument and throws them at the gardaí and cars. More youths, pursued by gardaí, make their way up O'Connell Street, smashing shop windows.

The Dublin Unemployed Association is concerned about the fact that there are thousands of people out of work in the city. They hold public meetings at the unemployment exchanges on Werburgh Street, Gardiner Street and Abbey Street, in the working-class suburbs of Cabra, Crumlin and Dolphin's Barn and at various places in the city centre including Foster Place and outside Dáil Éireann where they chant 'We want work' and hold banners claiming '55,000 Houses Wanted, 22,000 Builders Idle' and '90,000 Idle Today, You Tomorrow'.

Monday, 19 October 1953

Today a building opens immediately behind the Custom House that is unlike anything else in Ireland. Although the Custom House is widely regarded as one of the city's three most important buildings, the design of the new structure makes no reference to Gandon's masterpiece. In fact, it does not tip its architectural hat to anything in the city. The reason is that the architects have taken their cue from buildings in Paris.

One is the Pavillon Suisse at the Cité Universitaire, south of Montparnasse, that was completed in 1932 to accommodate Swiss students. The Pavillon Suisse is a large glass box sitting on short concrete stilts called *pilotis*, which take the entire weight of the building while also allowing people to walk 'under' it. The other, less than two miles away and close to a railway cutting running to Gare d'Austerlitz, is the Salvation Army's Cité de Refuge. The Cité de Refuge is a similar slab of a building, with sheer glass walls.

Each was designed by the Swiss-born naturalised French citizen Charles-Édouard Jeanneret-Gris, otherwise known as 'Le Corbusier'.

Le Corbusier is the world's most influential thinker about cities and their development. Describing a house as 'a machine for living in' and cities as 'man's grip on nature', his buildings are based on mass production techniques. Inspired by Greek and Roman architecture, he wants to purge the modern city of chaos, which he regards as anything that is not steel, plate glass and concrete.

158

Le Corbusier's Paris buildings have influenced a group of UCD architecture students including Patrick Scott, Wilfrid Cantwell and Barry Quinlan.

In 1946, after qualifying, these students went to work for architect Michael Scott. At the time, Scott had been commissioned by the new bus company Córas Iompair Éireann to build a 'long-distance' bus station in Dublin.

Nearly a quarter of Dublin's population is from other parts of Ireland. A familiar ordeal for people who go back 'home' on weekends or holidays has been the uncomfortable Friday evening wait amid chaotic queues at Aston Quay, where the only facilities are a waiting room the size of a small shop and one toilet. There has been a chronic need for a provincial bus depot.

The 1941 sketch plan had selected Wood Quay as the site for the station but instead it has been built at Store Street which is nearer to the centre of the city, the port, main roads out of the city and Kingsbridge railway station.

Originally, the station was to have been a modest, two-storey circular structure. But when CIÉ decided to centralise its city offices at Store Street, the building was increased in size from two to four storeys. However, the company's financial difficulties led them to sell the site to the government, while retaining the right to rent the bus depot. When the government used the opportunity to build a ministerial department the size was increased again, this time to eight storeys. However, due to objections that it would dwarf the Custom House, as well as the fact that it was too tall for the city's fire ladders to reach the upper floors, two storeys were taken off the top and a three-storey block was added at 90 degrees at one end.

Busáras – a new kind of bus station.

A pantomime audience at the Father Matthew Temperance Hall on Church Street.

The new building is unlike anything most people have ever seen. With 380 windows, it is described as a 'honeycomb on stilts'. It has been visited by many foreign architects and is already being regarded as a 'masterpiece of contemporary architecture'. At a cost of £1 million, it is the most expensive and largest building in the city. In fact, it is one of the largest office buildings constructed anywhere in Europe since the end of the Second World War.

Six months ago, civil servants moved into open-plan offices that were fitted out at a cost of nearly £90,000. They sit at work stations ten feet apart. There are acoustic ceiling tiles, linoleum floors, fluorescent lights and air conditioning.

Following a campaign by the Irish-language movement, this most international of buildings is called Áras Mhic Dhiarmada, after one of the leaders of the 1916 Rising, with the bus station part being called Busáras. Although the majority of the building is given over to offices, it is as a bus station that most people will use it.

And this is not just any bus station. Passengers enter under a 50-foot bronze canopy with 125 recessed lights, then pass through an electrically heated porch and into a huge two-storey concourse capable of holding 5,000 people.

From a control tower, the station master uses a tannoy to inform passengers and guide the buses from the likes of Boyle and Ballyshannon, Cahir and Kiltimagh, Mullingar and Mountmellick through the spaces under each block created by Le Corbusier's *pilotis*.

For those who have time to kill before their bus arrives, there is a theatre in the basement where they can watch the latest newsreels, cartoons and short features. There are also four shops, a restaurant, a bar, cloakroom, baggage and freight room, a rest room with a trained nurse on duty, telephone kiosks and toilets, with special urinals, and concealed flushing pipes.

There are some who regard the new structure as symbolic of Ireland's progress as a nation. But it is a building wrapped in an irony. Because, although the glass and steel may tell people that Dublin is the capital of a modern and prosperous country, Áras Mhic Dhiarmada houses the Department of Social Welfare where the claims of the tens of thousands of the city's unemployed are processed.

❖ ❖ ❖ ❖ ❖ ❖ ❖ ❖ ❖ ❖

Wednesday, 16 June 1954

Today is the fiftieth anniversary of the day on which the novel *Ulysses* is set. Some are calling it 'Bloomsday', after Leopold Bloom, the book's main character.

Thirty-two years after it was published, *Ulysses* is still not for sale in Dublin's bookshops – although copies are sometimes offered for sale in newspaper small ads (with exorbitant prices and a PO box number) – but there has been a growing interest in the book in the city in which it is set.

Recent summers have seen the arrival of 'handsome, long-legged American girls with their easy enthusiasm, the young men from Amherst or Harvard with the questions and note-books, the professors from unfamiliar universities, all peering down a 50-year vista towards a bright June day'. But it is not just visitors who are interested. The attitudes of Irish people towards a book that most of them have not read seem to be changing.

Patricia Hutchins' 1950 book *James Joyce's Dublin* describes the sites featured by the writer. Davy Byrne's public house on Duke Street proudly advertises its association with *Ulysses* – Bloom stops in Davy Byrne's for a sandwich and a glass of burgundy. But never has there been as much interest as today. A Prescott's Cleaners' newspaper advertisement highlights the fact that the firm cleaned Molly Bloom's Paisley shawl in *Ulysses* – to mark the day they publish a portrait of Joyce specially commissioned from artist Sean O'Sullivan. Tonight, Radio Éireann is broadcasting a 15-minute programme entitled, somewhat surreptitiously, 'The Bloom of the Day'. However, there is a much more extensive offering on BBC radio with 255 minutes dedicated to 'Music in *Ulysses*', the themes of *Ulysses*, as well as readings.

Recognising the potential significance of today's anniversary, *The Irish Times* editorial asks if this June 16th might be a turning point in the city's attitude towards the book and its author. It asks if on the one-hundredth anniversary of Bloomsday, in 2004, Leopold Bloom will have been forgotten about or will he 'stand in stone effigy as high as Nelson stands today'?

Today's only 'event' begins in a Sandycove home built in the international style by its architect owner Michael Scott. Known as *Geragh*, it is as modernist in architectural terms as *Ulysses* is in literature.

There is a small crowd to start the day under the parapet of the Martello tower where at the beginning of *Ulysses*, 'Stately, plump Buck Mulligan, came from the stairhead, bearing a bowl of lather on which a mirror and a razor lay crossed.' Among them are poet Patrick Kavanagh, John Ryan, owner of the Bailey pub and editor of the literary magazine *Envoy*, writer Flann O'Brien and Anthony Cronin, editor of *The Bell* magazine. They have been joined by Tom Joyce. Being James Joyce's cousin, he provides a direct link to the late writer, though Tom has never met his cousin nor read *Ulysses*.

After talking and drinking in Joyce's honour, the group sets off in two brougham cabs to continue their Bloomsday. If they were going to follow the book's chapters, they would go south to Summerfield House in Dalkey where the character Stephen Dedalus, and Joyce in real life, had taught. Instead they go north, along Dún Laoghaire's seafront.

Approaching Monkstown, they debate whether or not Goggin's public house features. It does not. But they decide to go in anyway.

The Bloomsday party stop briefly at Sandymount Strand. From left to right are John Ryan, Anthony Cronin, Flann O'Brien, Patrick Kavanagh and Tom Joyce.

By the time they leave Goggin's, Flann O'Brien is already worse for wear and needs help just to get back into the cab.

They continue along the coast to Sandymount, where one of the scenes that led to the banning of the novel takes place – at Sandymount strand, Bloom sits on a rock and 'pleasures himself' while watching a young woman lift her skirt. But with the tide in, they are content with relieving their bladders against a wall before continuing.

At Ringsend, approaching Smith's pub, they argue whether it features in *Ulysses*. It does not. But, agreeing that they should not be too literal in their interpretation of Joyce's work, they go in for more drink.

After Smith's, they get back into their cabs and decide, unsurprisingly, that instead of going to 7 Eccles Street, where Bloom lived, they would go to Davy Byrne's public house. And that becomes the last stop on this strangest of literary pilgrimages.

❖ ❖ ❖ ❖ ❖ ❖ ❖ ❖ ❖ ❖ ❖

Wednesday, 11 August 1954

Led by the Archbishop of Dublin, John Charles McQuaid, the first 47 of 1,000 Dublin diocesan members on their way to Lourdes, France, board two Aer Lingus planes at Dublin Airport. They are on a pilgrimage to honour the year that the Pope has dedicated to the worship of Mary Immaculate. While this group flies out,

St Michan's House on Greek Street was one of the first block of flats to be built in the city in the 1930s. Initial optimism that such developments would solve the social problems of the city has given way to a much starker reality.

the main body of pilgrims are leaving Dún Laoghaire by boat. Before sailing, well-wishers join them in singing 'Faith of Our Fathers'.

Few countries have so enthusiastically embraced the Marian year as Ireland. Processions have taken place throughout the city. The largest was in May when 25,000 set off from the Pro-Cathedral behind a life-size statue of the Virgin Mary, complete with a halo of light, that was carried on a flower-decked float pulled by 40 children.

Meanwhile around the city, shrines are being erected to the Virgin Mary in Cabra, Monkstown, Harold's Cross, Lucan, Stillorgan, Artane and elsewhere which will act as permanent reminders of the people's devotion to Mary in Dublin in 1954.

❖ ❖ ❖ ❖ ❖ ❖ ❖ ❖ ❖ ❖

Friday, 28 October 1955

The Pike Theatre on Herbert Lane seats 55 people. Its stage measures just 12 feet by 12 feet. In spite of its size, the Pike has been making a big impact on the city's theatrical scene since it was opened two years ago by husband and wife Alan Simpson and Carolyn Swift. The couple's aim has been to put on plays that would otherwise not be seen in the city and to 'stir up the theatrical lethargy of post-War Ireland'.

One of the theatre's most popular productions was a play first sent to them by Dubliner Brendan Behan under the title *The Twisting of Another Rope*, which the Abbey Theatre had, unsurprisingly, refused. According to Simpson, the script was 'a rather unprepossessing document, typed with several different typewriters of various degrees of mechanical disintegration on paper of varying shapes and sizes and dubious origins'. But he was impressed with the writing and the story.

Worshipping at St Colmcille's Well, Ballycullen, Rathfarnham during Marian year.

Behan had grown up in Russell Street, near Mountjoy Square, but his family moved to a new house in Crumlin in 1937. He joined the IRA and during the Second World War was imprisoned in Mountjoy. During this time, an execution took place. Behan saw the dramatic possibilities and subsequently wrote a play. Following a suggestion from Simpson, Behan changed the title to *The Quare Fellow* – the name given to a condemned person in Mountjoy Prison. In *The Quare Fellow*, which takes place in the days before the execution, the main character is never seen, but he is a constant presence.

Despite the peculiar difficulty they had of keeping the notorious drinker Behan 'in a delicately balanced state of intoxication: not so dry as to wander off for a drink, no so "ossified" that he wouldn't stand up', the opening night was a great success.

Tonight is the opening night of *Waiting for Godot* written by another Dubliner, Samuel Beckett, who still lives in Paris.

Since it was first staged in Paris two years ago, it has been the most talked about play in Europe, and tonight in the Pike it is being given its Irish premiere. It is another play in which the main character does not appear, but it presents different challenges to *The Quare Fellow*. And to every other play for that matter.

During the play, one of the patrons becomes so fed up that when he leaves mid-performance he comments loudly, 'Bollox!'

At the end as people leave the Pike, all they know for certain is that in *Waiting for Godot* there were two tramps called Vladimir and Estragon (also known as Gogo and Didi), a curious man called Pozzo, his slave, Lucky and a young boy. Who or what this Godot was, and why Gogo and Didi were waiting for him, nobody knows.

The city's Roman Catholic church under Archbishop McQuaid, has a strong hold over the city. But it is not in full control. In October 1955 a soccer match is arranged between Ireland and the national team from communist Yugoslavia. Archbishop McQuaid calls on the city's Catholics to boycott the match. Although the crowd is a little smaller than usual over 20,000 watch Ireland lose 4-1.

❖ ❖ ❖ ❖ ❖ ❖ ❖ ❖ ❖ ❖

Friday, 25 November 1955

One does not need to wait to consult next year's census figures to find out the parts of the city where thousands who have been rehoused from tenements, or who have arrived from other parts of Ireland, now live. Because Dublin's growth can be followed through the expansion of what have become the three essential components of suburban living.

The first is the bus. Since taking over from the trams, CIÉ's bus routes have rapidly expanded and now cover over 160 miles of mainly suburban streets.

Among the bus routes introduced in the last ten years are many that connect the new suburbs with the city centre. There are the numbers 34 and 35 to Finglas, the 36 to Ballymun, the 37 to Skreen Road, the 41a to Santry, the 41b to Swords, the 74b to Whitechurch, the 55 and 56 to Walkinstown, the 79 to Ballyfermot and the 81 to Bangor Road.

The busiest routes in the timetable are those that bring people from the suburbs to their jobs, shops and entertainments in the city centre. Among the most frequent services, leaving every four to eight minutes on weekdays, are the number 3 that runs between town and Whitehall, the 8 between town and Dalkey, the 11 that crosses the city from Ballymun to Clonskeagh, the 12 between Cabra and Palmerstown, the 15 between town and Terenure, the 16 between Whitehall and Terenure, the 22 between Drimnagh and Cabra West, the 30 between town and Dollymount and the 54 between Killester and Kimmage.

The city is expanding. As the slums continue to be cleared and people migrate to Dublin from other parts of Ireland, new suburbs are being constructed. This aerial view shows hundreds of new houses at Donnycarney.

The second defining suburban feature is that of the Catholic churches. With the assistance of the local authorities, these churches have been located in the heart of the new communities.

Since 1933, 17 suburban churches have been either constructed or extended in the suburbs. They are Christ the King, Cabra, 1933, St Michael's, Inchicore, 1933, Our Lady of Perpetual Succour, Foxrock, 1934, St Agnes's, Crumlin, 1935, Our Lady of the Rosary, Harold's Cross, 1935, St Patrick's, Skerries, 1939, Corpus Christi, Drumcondra, 1941, Our Lady of Good Counsel, Drimnagh, 1943, Church of the Holy Child, Whitehall, 1944, St Philomena's, Palmerstown, 1948, Our Lady of Consolation, Marino, 1948, St Brigid's, Killester, 1952, Our Lady Help of Christians, Navan Road, 1953, Chapel of the Most Precious Blood, Cabra, 1953, Our Lady Queen of Peace, Merrion Road, 1953, Our Lady of Victories, Sallynoggin, 1955, and the most recent to receive the solemn blessing of Archbishop McQuaid, St Canice's in Finglas.

The final feature of Dublin's suburban life is the neighbourhood cinema. Since 1929, there have been 28 picture houses constructed in the suburbs. Thirteen of these have opened in the last decade, each with a capacity of at least 750 people, with some having more than twice that. There is the Adelphi in Dún Laoghaire, the Apollo in Walkinstown, the Grand in Cabra, the Kenilworth in Harold's Cross, the Grand in Whitehall, the Ormonde in Stillorgan, the Star in Crumlin, the Odeon in Dundrum, the State in Phibsborough, the Stella in Mount Merrion, the Landscape in Churchtown and the Gala in Ballyfermot.

Tonight, the largest, the Casino in Finglas, is being opened by the local parish priest. Despite the fact that his church has just been extended to seat 1,500 to cope with Finglas's growing population, it still falls short of the 1,910 seats that are available in the temple of entertainment that is the Casino.

In 1955, a book set in Dublin is published by New Yorker J.P. Donleavy. Donleavy came to Dublin funded under a GI programme and studied in Trinity College, and while here, he became a member of the city's literary circle which included Behan, Kavanagh and Flann O'Brien. After being rejected by 35 publishers, his novel, called *The Gingerman*, is published. Given that the main character is the drinking and fornicating Englishman Sebastian Dangerfield who lives in Dublin with his wife and daughter, *The Gingerman* is certain to be banned in Ireland.

Dressed in white drill coats, navy caps and white tops, on Tuesday, 2 October 1956 the country's first 20 school traffic wardens take up their duties outside schools throughout the city.

Wednesday, 31 October 1956

On the morning of 18 April at around 5.40 a.m., the lifeless body of 33-year-old Helen O'Reilly from Kilkenny was found lying on the footpath outside 16 Hume Street, near St Stephen's Green. At first, there was no reason to believe that the woman's death was suspicious. After all, Dublin is one of Europe's safest capital cities.

In the last six years, there have been just four violent deaths recorded in the city. In January 1953, the bodies of 34-year-old Deborah Aherne and her nine-year-old and four-year-old daughters were found in their house at Oaklands Drive, Rathgar. The mother had killed both her children before taking her own life – it was learned that she had been in 'a fit of emotional strain' following the death of her husband. Later that year, 24-year-old Mary Nolan from Crumlin was murdered in Beresford Lane, off Gardiner Street. She had been strangled by a seaman who had been on a ship unloading in the docks that night. Then, earlier this year, 16-year-old Matthew Paschal O'Hara killed his 26-year-old brother Peter in Ballybough.

When the autopsy was carried out on Helen O'Reilly's body, it was discovered that she had died of an embolism, caused by a botched abortion. A murder enquiry was started and suspicion immediately fell on Mary 'Mamie' Cadden who lived at 17 Hume Street.

Cadden was born in New York of Irish parents and was brought to Ireland at a young age. In 1922, she began working in a nursing home in Portland Row, on Dublin's north side. In 1929, after training as a midwife, she opened her own nursing home in Ranelagh. Business was so good that she soon moved to larger premises

In the 1950s, the health of the city improves significantly with tuberculosis sanitoria built, new hospitals including Cherry Orchard and St. Lukes constructed and the provision of improved health care for mothers and their babies.

on the Rathmines Road. Running a nursing home brought Cadden into contact not only with women who were having children, but also with others who were pregnant and did not want to have a child.

At a time when there was no legal adoption, and contraceptives had been banned since 1935, Cadden's business became very lucrative. With her distinctive blonde hair and even more distinctive red MG convertible, she became one of the best-known women in the city.

In 1939, she was found guilty of abandoning a child and sentenced to a year's hard labour and struck off as a midwife and had to sell her nursing home. After her release, she re-established herself in new premises on Pembroke Street.

In wartime Dublin, there was a crackdown on the city's abortionists. Between 1942 and 1946, there were 25 prosecutions relating to abortions. Among those convicted were William Henry Coleman of 25 Merrion Square, conveniently beside the National Children's Hospital at Holles Street, and Mary Maloney and Christopher Williams in Rathmines. In 1945, Cadden was sentenced to five years' penal servitude for attempting to procure a miscarriage. She was released in 1950 and, undeterred by her imprisonment, re-established her business at 17 Hume Street.

Though she was then 60 years of age, physically broken by imprisonment, with poor eyesight, and living in a ramshackle single room, eight feet by ten feet on Hume Street that was watched by gardaí, Cadden continued to defy the city's authorities and religious leaders.

One of her clients was Helen O'Reilly. During her procedure, Cadden's poor eyesight and unsteady hand led to an air embolism. In a desperate attempt to avoid the blame, Cadden dragged the body out into the street.

At the end of her trial for murder, she was found guilty and sentenced to death. However, today the cabinet has decided that she will not die in Mountjoy's hanghouse, but instead will spend the rest of her life in prison. With her demise, any woman that wants to have an abortion will have to travel to England.

❖ ❖ ❖ ❖ ❖ ❖ ❖ ❖ ❖ ❖

Wednesday, 9 January 1957

Everything in the city is somehow connected. When CIÉ chose Store Street to build Busáras, it left Wood Quay without an immediate purpose. That did not last long.

Wood Quay has been chosen for the site of Dublin Corporation's long-awaited

Civic Offices. But the location of the Civic Offices is proving controversial.

On 25 July, architects Jones and Kelly, who have also designed Cork's City Hall, presented plans of the new offices to the corporation. Facing the river at Wood Quay was a large, open forecourt at the front of a main building six-storeys high flanked by two four-storey buildings. They looked as though they had come straight from some American city.

The corporation approved the plans in July and instructed the city manager to get on with the job of building them.

But it has not been that simple.

The Royal Institute of the Architects of Ireland objected to the Civic Offices because there had not been a competition for the role of architect and the buildings were not in harmony with either the Four Courts on the opposite side of the river or Christchurch Cathedral immediately behind the site.

Objections were also made by the Dean of Christchurch, though his acquiescence was gained when the height of the main building was reduced by one storey.

The UCD Architectural Society has called it an 'early 20th century factory building'. Dublin Corporation's main architect took the unusual step of stating publicly that he did not agree with the Wood Quay site. Some called for the project to be killed 'for good and all'.

Today the corporation announces that the Civic Offices project is not to be proceeded with after all. According to the corporation, this is not because of the criticism of the buildings' design, or the location, but because they cannot afford to build it.

There is relief among the opponents of the Civic Offices. For the time being, Wood Quay will stay as it is. But, as many of them know, this may be no more than a reprieve. Just because a project is put aside does not mean that, should circumstances change, it will not one day be revived.

According to the Sketch Development Plan, Wood Quay was supposed to have been the site of the new bus station. Now that Busáras has been built, the site below Christchurch Cathedral is looked at for a long-awaited headquarters for Dublin Corporation, but the plan is shelved.

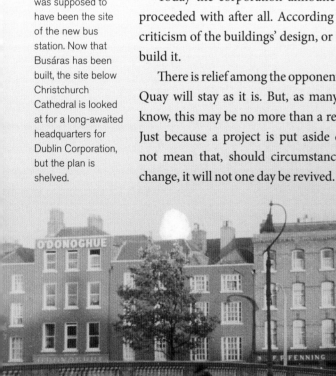

Thursday, 23 May 1957

Nine days ago, Dublin's first Theatre Festival opened as part of this year's Tóstal. Since then, there has been drama, opera, ballet and folk performances at the Theatre Royal, the Pike, the Olympia, the Gaiety, the Gate, the National Stadium, Philips Concert Hall and the Pocket Theatre – unfortunately, after six years, there is still no progress on building a new Abbey Theatre. Among the main attractions have

Brendan Behan shares a joke in a Dublin pub.

Scenes during the
police raid on the
Pike Theatre the
night Alan Simpson
is arrested.

been the 140-member Royal Ballet, starring Dame Margot Fonteyn and Michael Somes, the London Philharmonic Orchestra with violin soloist Yehudi Menuhin, a production of O'Casey's *Juno and the Paycock*, a fiftieth-anniversary performance of Synge's *Playboy of the Western World*, Denis Johnston's *The Old Lady Says No*, Oscar Wilde's *The Importance of Being Earnest* with Margaret Rutherford fresh from the film version and the operas *Aida* and *The Barber of Seville*.

The festival has been a great success but last night, controversy struck at the Pike.

The Rose Tattoo had opened the festival to rave reviews – it is the first European production in English of Tennessee Williams' play – but last night gardaí arrived before the performance and told Alan Simpson that 'objectionable passages' in the play must be omitted from the performance. The play went ahead as scripted, including a scene where an envelope was produced seemingly instead of a condom, and earlier today, Simpson was arrested for having 'produced for gain an indecent and profane performance'.

❖ ❖ ❖ ❖ ❖ ❖ ❖ ❖ ❖ ❖ ❖

Sunday, 26 January 1958

The Irish Georgian Society is founded at a tea party at Leixlip Castle by Desmond Guinness and 100 guests, to fight for the preservation of Georgian architectural heritage, particularly that in Dublin.

The catalyst for today came when two buildings were demolished in Dublin last July.

Numbers 2 and 3 Kildare Place were behind the National Museum, yards from Dáil Éireann. In July, the Office of Public Works began demolishing them because they said that it would cost £40,000 to conserve them. And that was too expensive.

But the people at Leixlip know that it is not only a question of money. There are also many people in the city who hate buildings like the ones at Kildare Place which they see as legacies of a colonial Protestant elite. When Desmond Guinness saw the work commence, he felt he had to do something.

Perhaps today at Leixlip, a start has been made. But one must doubt if large numbers of Dubliners will be joining them. Because the group is hardly representative of the city with their committee being made up of Desmond Guinness and his wife, the daughter of the Count of Württemberg, Lord Talbot de Malahide, Sir Alfred Beit, Lady Dunsany, Sir George Mahon and Desmond FitzGerald, the Knight of Glin.

When two Georgian buildings are demolished by the Office of Public Works at Kildare Place, Desmond Guinness sets out to try and save the city's architectural heritage by founding the Irish Georgian Society.

In the early hours of Tuesday, 26 August 1958, one of the last British statues in Dublin, of Archibald William, Earl of Eglinton and Winton, twice Lord Lieutenant of Ireland in the nineteenth century, is blown from its pedestal near the Dawson Street entrance of St Stephen's Green by 30 pounds of gelignite. Windows are blown in around the green and the explosion is heard far out into the countryside. It is the latest in a spate of attacks on British statues. Last year, the equestrian statue of Lord Gough, erected in 1880 and cast from cannon used by his troops in the wars against the Sikhs in the Punjab, was blown up in the Phoenix Park. Last month, also in the Phoenix Park, the statue of Lord Carlisle, former Chief Secretary and Lord Lieutenant, was also blown up in the middle of the night.

Ireland's first suburban traffic lights come into operation on Monday, 22 September 1958 at the junctions of the Blackrock Road and Booterstown Avenue and Mount Merrion Avenue.

On 1 May 1958, the inaugural transatlantic flight arrives at Dublin airport from New York.

Monday, 29 September 1958

Yesterday Dublin won its first All-Ireland football final since 1942. Despite the recent lack of success, there has been a huge upsurge in support for the Dublin Gaelic football team.

From being one of the most poorly supported counties, Dublin is now one of the best. When they lost to Kerry in the final three years ago, there was a record crowd of 87,000 at Croke Park. Yesterday that figure would have been even higher but for the fact that a new stand is under construction.

One reason for the change is that now almost the entire team comes from the city. Many grew up in the new suburbs on the north side, with the heart of the team coming from the St Vincent's club.

This morning the victorious Dublin team brought the cup to St Joseph's in Fairview where, remarkably, ten of the team had gone to school. This evening after parading through Dublin's streets on the backs of two lorries to the accompaniment of rattles, cheers and blowing car horns, the Dublin team arrive at St Vincent's, where bonfires are burning and thousands have been waiting.

At 4.25 p.m. on Wednesday, 31 December 1958, the last train to serve Ranelagh, Milltown, Dundrum, Stillorgan, Foxrock, Carrickmines, Shankill and Woodbrook stations gets ready to pull out of Harcourt Street. Some 500 people are on board for the final service to Bray. After 101 years of operation, the closure of the Harcourt Street line is the latest move by CIÉ to reduce losses. Because in the era of the motor car, fewer and fewer people take the train. Driver Ned Wheeler from Bray, who has worked on the line for 34 years, tells a reporter, 'It was a most friendly train to work; I knew most of the passengers and the stations they usually got off.'

The last ever train departs from Harcourt Street station.

People take a rest on
Dún Laoghaire's East Pier

Sunday, 14 June 1959

It is the hottest day of the year. The temperature is in the 20s and above the city is an almost impossibly blue sky. Because Dubliners know that this may not last, in their thousands they head to the beaches at Dollymount, Sutton, Sandymount and Killiney and the seaside towns of Dún Laoghaire, Howth and Bray.

Gardaí report that the roads to the city's coastal areas are busier than they have ever been. The buses are packed. The trains are full.

At the beaches people sit, lie, eat and drink. Apart from children, hardly any venture into the chilly waters for a swim. Some are even more cautious. Having driven their cars as close as they can to the water, they turn on the car radio and remain in the car, some even keeping their windows closed.

But not everyone has gone to the sea. At Croke Park, over 100,000 people are celebrating the diamond jubilee of the Total Pioneer Abstinence Association which was founded in Dublin.

People have come from every county in Ireland, from the United States (Boston, Brooklyn, the Bronx, Cleveland and Chicago), Britain (Leamington Spa, Coventry, Leicester, Birmingham, Manchester, Airdrie), Australia, Belgium, Canada and New Zealand. For the assembled, the pioneer badge is a symbol of self-denial, of reparation for the sins of intemperance and of prayers for the conversion of excessive drinkers. At the end of the celebration, the Blessed Sacrament, the emblem of the association, is carried in procession to the altar, emblazoned with the words 'For

Thy greater glory and consolation, O Sacred Heart of Jesus, for Thy sake to give good example'. In the brilliant sunshine, tens of thousands kneel and make a public act of thanksgiving.

Meanwhile, as evening comes, the beaches slowly empty. People leave behind tons of papers, bottles, cartons and the ubiquitous orange peel.

There will be plenty of uncomfortable sleeps tonight as people administer various ointments to soothe their sunburnt limbs. And others will wake up tomorrow suffering the effects of having had too much to drink on this fine day while more, enthused by their day at Croke Park, will pray for them.

❖ ❖ ❖ ❖ ❖ ❖ ❖ ❖ ❖ ❖ ❖

Wednesday 2 December, 1959

There is a crime wave in Dublin. Some think that it all started with the arrival of rock 'n' roll.

1956 saw the first recorded increase in crime since the end of the Second World War. In the same year rock 'n' roll arrived in Dublin.

On 15 June 1956, the Carlton Cinema screened the European premiere of the first rock 'n' roll musical, *Rock Around the Clock*, starring Bill Haley and the Comets which featured the title song as well as 'The Great Pretender', 'See You Later, Alligator' and 'Only You'. For three weeks, every screening at the Carlton was packed with 'mobs of rhythmically inclined young people'. After the Carlton run, *Rock Around the Clock*

A map at Dublin Castle marks the location of every crime in the city with a flag.

played in 33 cinemas in Dublin and around the country, breaking all-time attendance records in 27 of them. Nothing like it had been seen before.

At first, there had been no indication that the film would lead to crime. The Dublin showings may have been boisterous, but they were peaceful. However, as the movie's Dublin run continued, reports of riots at screenings in Oslo, Swansea, Duisburg and London had their effect in Dublin.

176

In September, there was some trouble at a showing in Crumlin. In November, the film's final showing at Mary Street Cinema was abandoned when young people ripped up seat covers and broke chairs. When gardaí cleared the cinema, 500 young people hung around outside singing, shouting and throwing stones. They only dispersed when police drew batons.

Three months later when Bill Haley and his Comets came to Dublin to play four concerts in the Theatre Royal, there were the most remarkable displays of audience participation ever seen in the city. After the final show, youths gathered on Hawkins Street and Poolbeg Street and threw bottles and stones at gardaí.

So the question has been, did the rebellious lyrics, 'freedom of movement, erratic rhythms and unexpected changes' of rock 'n roll unleash the crime wave?

There is no doubt that the city's Teddy boys, in their easily identifiable Edwardian-style clothes of single-breasted suits, long lapels, double vents, 'drainpipe' trousers, crepe shoes and hair combed in the Tony Curtis style, have been committing crime.

There have been street fights between Teddy boy gangs, most of whom have been banned from the dancehalls because of trouble. They have been involved in robberies, assaults on bus conductors, stabbings, New Year's Eve damage to property around Christchurch Cathedral, intimidation of people on the streets (a particular problem in Ringsend) and a notorious 'make-believe' bullfighting episode in a Moore Street butcher's yard in which two Teddy boys stabbed four cows so badly, they had to be slaughtered.

It is clear that, since 1956, there are more crimes being committed in Dublin. In 1957, there were 7,120 crimes reported in the city. A year later, that had risen to 8,750 – in the rest of the country there were just 5,662. In the last four years, 79 per cent of the increase in crime in the country has taken place in Dublin and its crime rate is at least three times that of the cities of Cork, Limerick and Galway.

Reinforcing the belief that rock 'n roll is to blame for crime in the city is the fact that crime is increasingly associated with young people. The phenomenon of 'juvenile delinquency' has become a significant problem.

In 1957 2,356 children aged between 8 and 18 appeared before the courts on indictable offences. Last year, the Children's Court dealt with 10,505 charges, 3,367 summonses, 1,678 school attendance summonses and 691 applications to commit children to industrial schools.

In 1957, Dublin gardaí produced a report on the causes of juvenile delinquency and tonight the *Evening Herald* distributes a free pamphlet of articles it has published on the subject.

According to those who have studied the situation, the causes of juvenile crime go far beyond Teddy boys and their music.

The main issues are family structures and home life. Problems in this area include the slum conditions, overcrowding in the city flats, lack of parental control, the link between large families and youth crime (37 per cent of juvenile delinquents (JDs) are from families with nine or more children), the result of thousands of broken homes in Dublin, the migration of fathers to England, the increasing number of working mothers and, generally, what are described as 'bad parents'.

Wider societal issues are also blamed. Among these are the weakening effects of the welfare state on parental responsibility, lenient sentences for offenders, the fact that almost none of the JDs practise religion, that there are 7,000 14–19-year-olds in the city who do not attend school or have a job, psychological disorders, poverty, 'mental sub-normality', failure to make constructive use of leisure time, lust for adventure, 'natural inclination', the fast pace and feverish atmosphere of a large city, the stress caused by high-pressure advertising for goods that are unattainable by most of the young, the distorted view of violence created when they are told to admire killing for patriotic ends and the almost complete lack of distraction for children in a city that has just two open-air swimming pools, ten playgrounds and a handful of sports pitches.

Then there is the particular influence of cinema. And it is not just *Rock Around the Clock* or films such as *The Wild One* or *Rebel Without a Cause* that are of concern. Rebelliousness in the youth is being created by desiring objects that are vicariously possessed in the dark confines of cinemas. After a movie is over, frustration leads them to steal cars or break into shops and steal cigarettes, drink, clothes or money.

After reading the articles and reports, there seems to be no end to the reasons why there is so much crime in the city. Some might continue to insist on blaming rock 'n roll for the problem but it is unlikely to decline if a new type of music comes along.

In December 1959, some of Ireland's first bean gardaí take up their posts at College Street Garda Station.

Dressed in navy skirts, tunics and laced shoes, the country's first 12 female gardaí take up their posts at College Street Garda Station on Monday, 7 December 1959. They have been trained by a woman officer from Liverpool and if anyone doubts their capabilities it should be noted that one of them attained the highest mark for any recruit, male or female, since 1952. Two of the bean gardaí are from Dublin, with the others from Donegal, Roscommon, Longford, Cavan, Galway, Roscommon, Sligo and Kildare. They will perform their duties in the normal way, but will also be available for crime duties that require 'specifically feminine handling'.

To simplify sorting and to help Dublin's 356 postmen deliver letters and parcels to 500,000 homes and businesses on 3,500 streets, on Monday, 16 January 1961, the city is divided into 14 postal districts. Every business and householder has received a card showing them the postal code they are in.

Sunday, 31 December 1961

A new feature is appearing on the city's rooftops. It is the television aerials that have been erected in readiness for Teilifís Éireann's first broadcast. Tonight, the homes of those lucky enough to have rented or bought a television are crowded with families, friends and neighbours.

The broadcast starts with the national anthem. Then President de Valera addresses the nation on the new medium of communication, and warns of its dangers:

Archbishop McQuaid prepares to bless the new television station, Teilifís Éireann, before its first broadcast on 31 December, 1961.

> I find it hard to believe that the person who views the grandeurs of the heavens, or the wonders of life on this marvellous and mysterious world in which the good God has placed us, will not find more pleasure in these than in viewing, for example, some squalid domestic brawl or a noisy street quarrel.

The largest crane in Ireland is handed over to the B&I Line at the North Wall of Dublin Port on Tuesday, 2 January 1962. Until today all cargo had to be unloaded by hand. Now the crane will do the work of dozens of men with no chance of breakage and little of pilferage.

I feel sure that full use will be made of the immense repertory which is now at our disposal. Apart altogether from the wonders of nature, we have the great achievements of man himself – the masterpieces of architecture, engineering, sculpture, painting – and who, on looking at these or on hearing the beautiful composition of the great masters of music, will want to descend to the drab or the mean or the vulgar?

The Metal Bridge is still there.

Something odd has happened. Sentiment towards it has changed. What had once been deemed 'ugly', 'archaic' and 'ignoble' is now being regarded as unique, as beautiful.

In 1946 the *Irish Independent* featured an artistic photograph of the Metal Bridge, its single arch perfectly mirrored in the Liffey waters. Then the *Irish Press* published a photograph of the bridge taken from the deck of a Guinness barge on its way to the Custom House. In 1947, the Dublin Woollen Mills shop started using the bridge in their advertisements, a landmark to guide potential customers to its doors.

A turning point came in 1953 when a serious crack was discovered in the bridge's ironwork. Instead of taking the opportunity to demolish it, getting rid of it once and for all, it was restored, its wooden laths replaced and its metalwork painted. After three-months' work it re-opened.

Remarkably, the bridge which was so often seen as a sign of a backward city is becoming one of Dublin's tourist attractions. Until this year, visitor guides to the city have avoided even mentioning its existence. Not once had any of them invited visitors to walk past it, look down the river at it, let alone cross over it. But for the first time the *1962 Official Guide: This is Dublin* features the bridge. There it is, among the highlights of the best and most beautiful buildings and sites in the city, a picture of what is describes as 'the graceful hump-backed Metal Bridge'.

Monday, 6 May 1963

The city is in the throes of three separate labour disputes. The dockers have been 'out' for two weeks, Radio Éireann journalists for three and the city's bus workers have been on their longest strike in three years.

For the last month, the city's buses have been off the roads. Each day, 80 army trucks bring people to and from work. There have been record sales in ladies' flat shoes, while the city's dance halls and cinemas have been badly hit. However, with the RDS Spring Show on, there are plenty of people in town and for their entertainment, a new show is being put on in the Gate Theatre by promoter John Molloy. The show is called *The Ballad Tour of Ireland*.

Molloy has been at the centre of a wave of interest in ballad singing in the city. He has taken Irish traditional music out of the informal sessions in city venues such as the Fiddlers' Club on Church Street and the Pipers' Club on Thomas Street. In March, he put a 'show' on in the Royal Hibernian Hotel which people had to pay to see. It was so popular, hundreds were turned away. Meanwhile, at Howth, a band led by Ronnie Drew, recently returned from Spain, have been playing to full houses every week.

Newly constructed suburban houses are another sign that incomes are rising and that the Dublin middle classes are growing.

For the first time, it seems possible to make money from playing folk music.

Tonight at the Gate, the audience is brought on a musical tour that begins and ends in Dublin. Among the performers are Ronnie Drew, Barney McKenna, Ciaran Burke, Dolly McMahon, Ian Calder, Paddy Moloney and Luke Kelly. Many in the crowd are familiar with most of them but Luke Kelly is regarded as a 'find'.

Kelly was born in Lattimore Cottages, Sheriff Street, near the Five Lamps. When his house was condemned, he and his family moved to St Laurence O'Toole flats and then, in 1953, to Whitehall, one of the fastest-growing suburbs. But Kelly never settled in Whitehall and left Dublin when he was 17. He went to the Isle of Man, Manchester, Leeds, Birmingham and Newcastle. With little education and no trade, he did various jobs including cleaning windows, railway cars and toilets.

Kelly loved jazz and was a fan of Frank Sinatra, Bing Crosby, Perry Como and Duke Ellington. In Newcastle, he regularly attended jazz clubs, but one afternoon, a friend suggested that he go to a folk session. While he was queueing, he heard a group of English singers give a rendition in perfect harmony of Brendan Behan's 'The Auld Triangle' from *The Quare Fellow*. Kelly was transfixed and since then has dedicated himself to folk music. In addition to the folk scene, he immersed himself among various socialists.

At the Gate, Kelly stands out not only for the quality of his rapier-like voice, but also for the type of song that he sings. They are not the usual ones heard at sessions, but ballads from northern English working-class towns where many Irish emigrants are living. Some Dubliners in the audience identify more with these songs of the English working class than they do with the others.

❖ ❖ ❖ ❖ ❖ ❖ ❖ ❖ ❖ ❖ ❖

Wednesday, 19 June 1963

The collective sigh of relief among the city officials, councillors and the government is almost audible. The crisis is over. And just in time too.

No doubt, some will blame the deaths and destruction on factors that are beyond anyone's control – the cold winter, the hot spell last month, the thunderstorms, or a crumbling city that has simply become too old.

But whatever the cause, for the last two weeks, it has seemed as though the city is on the verge of falling down.

The crisis started around dawn on 2 June when garda motorcyclist John Blessy was driving down Bolton Street and heard what sounded like an explosion. He then watched a cloud of dust billow towards him. At the same time, one of the tenants in number 20 was awakened by a crash. 'I did not know what it was,' he later told reporters, 'but suddenly the whole floor gave way and I found myself, still in bed, falling down to the ground floor.' Among the rubble that minutes before had been number 20, was an elderly couple, Mr and Mrs Leo Maples, both in their eighties, who were smothered and crushed to death.

Following the Bolton Street collapse, hundreds of tenement buildings in the area were inspected for cracks. Several were evacuated because they were deemed uninhabitable. Then the situation settled down for a time. There were no more collapses, no more deaths.

But on 12 June numbers 2, 3 and 4 Fenian Street collapsed.

Miraculously, no occupant was injured. Tragedy seemed to have been averted. But then people realised that two young girls, Linda Byrne and Marie Vardy, who had gone to a shop in the terrace, were missing. As hundreds crowded the street, many crying, gardaí and firemen shovelled through bricks and rubble. After three hours, they reached the girls. But it was too late. They were dead.

Coming so soon after Bolton Street, the Fenian Street collapse caused panic throughout the city's tenements.

The situation became a full-blown emergency. Corporation workmen were on duty day and night answering calls from worried tenement dwellers. In the four days following the Fenian Street collapse, there were 1,550 calls to the Dangerous Buildings Department. As a result, over 800 people were left homeless. Accommodation was found for some in flats in the city centre and new houses just being finished in estates in Finglas. But others with nowhere to go, or who do not want a flat or to go to Finglas, are sleeping in the streets.

The city began to resemble a warzone as gardaí closed off streets and traffic diversions were put in place. Gangs of corporation workmen have been busy around the clock on

A new housing crisis starts as an old tenement house collapses on Bolton Street killing two people.

what has been dubbed 'Operation Prop Up' while those in temporary accommodation have marched on government and corporation offices, demanding action.

In the last two days, meetings have taken place between city officials and government departments to put together a comprehensive emergency plan. The situation is finally under control. And just in time too, because next week the president of the United States, John F. Kennedy, will arrive in Dublin to start a four-day state visit.

❖ ❖ ❖ ❖ ❖ ❖ ❖ ❖ ❖ ❖ ❖

Wednesday, 26 June 1963

At 9.39 a.m., President Kennedy landed at Berlin's Tegel Airport for a day of high politics at the tense interface between East and West, between NATO and the Warsaw Pact, between capitalism and communism.

Earlier this evening, the president left Berlin's Cold War politics behind him. After circling Dublin, Air Force One lands at the airport at 8.04 p.m. The visit to Ireland is going to be a world away from Berlin. Because this is a homecoming. The president has returned to the land of his forefathers. Tomorrow he will address the Dáil and then go elsewhere in the country. But for the next hour, he brings glamour, charm, promise, youth and the prospect of a brighter future to the streets of a changing city.

Dublin is the capital of a country that is in the process of modernising. Since a policy of isolation and protectionism was abandoned in 1958 and the First Programme for Economic Expansion was adopted, Ireland has been opening up to the world.

This evening, the leader of the United States, the most powerful country in the world, has come to Dublin.

The black presidential limousine leaves the airport behind garda cars with armed Special Branch men and a lorry carrying television cameramen and press photographers from around the world. Unlike in Berlin, where trench-coated, sunglass-wearing secret service agents had flanked Kennedy's car, they are consigned to a single following car. Because Dublin is not Berlin.

At first the cavalcade passes mainly open fields until it reaches the new outer suburbs of Santry and Larkhill. By the time it reaches Drumcondra, dense crowds line either side of the route. All the while, the young president stands, smiling, waving. Then, before reaching Bolton Street, the site of one of the recent house collapse tragedies, it turns down Parnell Street.

On O'Connell Street, huge crowds wave American flags bought from street

President Kennedy's cavalcade reaches the quays.

vendors – 'Flags, only six pence each; flags and badges'. The Savoy Cinema's usual billing notice has been replaced with the letters 'Welcome, President Kennedy'. Confetti is thrown from one building in a brief attempt at a Wall Street ticker-tape parade. But this is not New York, this is Dublin.

As the cavalcade makes its way down the country's main street, the president looks up curiously to the vertiginous height of Nelson's Pillar.

At College Green, young women shout from a window, 'Stay with us, Jack!'

On Dame Street a handful of people break through the garda cordon and begin running alongside the presidential car. Suddenly, hundreds more do the same. The secret servicemen are anxious, ready to spring into action. But President Kennedy is not concerned. He has a calm word with his driver. The president smiles and waves. This is Dublin.

❖ ❖ ❖ ❖ ❖ ❖ ❖ ❖ ❖ ❖

Thursday, 7 November 1963

The Adelphi Cinema has hosted many memorable musical evenings: Ella Fitzgerald, Louis Armstrong and Marlene Dietrich have all graced its stage. But there has been nothing like this evening.

At the end of their second performance, The Beatles run out the rear door and straight into the open back doors of an *Evening Herald* delivery van. As John

Lennon, Paul McCartney, George Harrison and Ringo Starr sit on piles of yesterday's newspapers, the doors are slammed shut. Then the van starts making its way slowly through the streets that are packed with young people still screaming for the band. The driver fears what might happen if the crowd knew who he had in the back of his van.

Around them there is still evidence of a small riot that broke out between this evening's shows. When gardaí tried to clear Abbey Street, they were showered with stones and lumps of coal. Young people then broke windows and overturned cars on O'Connell Street.

At the concerts, girls in the audience screamed their way through each song, which meant that most heard little of the music. Nevertheless, the concert's 40 minutes, starting with 'I Saw Her Standing There' and ending with 'Twist and Shout', will live on in the memories of teenagers like Catherine Cahill, who works at Jacob's biscuit factory and whose ticket cost her twice her weekly wage, Frank Grimes and Maggy Collins, who had just come into town to see the crowds outside the theatre and found themselves pushed against a door that gave way and into the concert, and Mags Graham, a 16-year-old who had bluffed her way into the earlier press conference posing as a journalist from the 'National Syndicate of Newspapers' – during the concert McCartney dedicated 'Till There Was You' to Mags.

Now, the important thing is to get the Beatles safely to the back door of the Gresham Hotel where they are staying. But while Lennon, McCartney and Starr will remain in the hotel, George Harrison is going to Drumcondra to spend some time at a cousin's house, where he went on holidays when he was a child.

The Beatles arrive at Dublin airport.

1964–1979

Lurching towards Modernity

Friday, 18 September 1964

The remarkable economic progress of the last few years has led to an increase in service jobs. And this is changing the way the city looks because the city needs more offices, and plenty of them. The office boom that was experienced in other cities in Europe in the 1950s has well and truly arrived in Dublin.

Some companies, organisations and institutions that have been based in Georgian premises in the city centre for years are moving into modern buildings that are being constructed in the suburbs.

The most popular area is Ballsbridge, where new office blocks are rising from among the area's characteristic red-brick houses. One of the first was in 1962, when Irish Life Assurance moved from its Hammam Building offices on O'Connell Street to a modern block on Mespil Road along the Grand Canal – they used the opportunity to replace their punch-card record system with an up-to-date IBM computer.

A goat along the banks of the canal looks at Mespil House on Mespil Road, one of the first offices built in Ballsbridge.

Huge new office buildings in Ballsbridge.

In May, the American Embassy moved from overcrowded conditions at Merrion Square to a remarkable new building. Designed by American architect, John Johansen, who studied at Harvard under Bauhaus founder, Walter Gropius, the circular building draws inspiration from Ireland's ancient round towers, Dublin's Martello towers and in the shape of its windows, the knit stitch of Aran jumpers.

Not far from the embassy is the eight-storey Intercontinental Hotel. Opened last year, it is Ireland's largest hotel with 316 rooms, the popular Embassy Grill, the Martello rooftop restaurant and 'Dublin's most exclusive dine-and-dance spot'.

Another area on the south side that is being developed is on the road to Bray.

One of the first to set up offices on the main road south was the oil company Esso. In 1961, it moved headquarters from O'Connell Street five and a half miles south to a sleek new building on landscaped grounds at Galloping Green. It left the city centre for what are becoming familiar reasons: its staff had been in overcrowded offices, there was no room to expand and, ironically given their business, there were problems related to traffic, noise, pollution and parking. Esso's move was also facilitated by the fact that the majority of its well-paid staff lived in the southern suburbs – those who were not were given grants to help them relocate.

In the same year that Esso moved, Teilifís Éireann opened its new studios,

designed by Michael Scott, on the grounds of Montrose House, Donnybrook. It also erected a 360-foot-tall transmitter imported from Norway.

The television station's site was purchased from St Andrew's School which had previously moved from St Stephen's Green to Ballsbridge but which will use the funds from this sale to go further south again, to Booterstown.

Today, further down the Bray Road from the television studios, the first students are arriving at University College Dublin's new campus on the lands of Belfield House. Campus is the wrong word for the moment, since all that is there is a massive block of concrete, steel and glass that is the college's new science building.

The departure of thousands of UCD students from the city centre is without doubt a loss to its vitality. Some think that the reason the college is leaving the city centre is because of the presence of Trinity College and its Protestant students. But Earlsfort Terrace and other UCD buildings have become intolerably overcrowded. After alternative locations for the university were sought, a 1959 government commission recommended that UCD move.

Today's opening of the science block is just the start. An international competition held for the design of the entire Belfield campus was won by a young man who has never seen Dublin or Belfield, never been to Ireland and, in fact, has never been out of Poland. He is Andrzej Wejchert who laid out the design for Ireland's largest university on the kitchen table of his mother's Warsaw apartment.

Born in Gdansk in 1937, Wejchert studied architecture in the Warsaw Technical High School and graduated just two years before winning the UCD competition. His plan includes various faculty and administrative buildings, a lake, 'sculptural' water tower and, linking them all, 'a pedestrian mall of interesting and irregular shape'.

But all that is yet to come.

Archbishop McQuaid at the turning of the sod ceremony at Belfield for the construction of University College Dublin's new campus.

Saturday, 1 May 1965

In addition to the construction of office buildings in the southern suburbs, the city centre is also being transformed.

Plate glass and brightly lit interiors have replaced traditional shops at Boylan's shoe shop on Camden Street, the Aer Lingus Booking Office on Grafton Street, Kennedy's bakery on Stephen's Street, the Dublin Bakery Company Restaurant on Stephen's Green and the Kayser Bondor lingerie showroom at Wicklow Street. Entire buildings are starting to be replaced by modern ones. Woolworths demolished the four buildings on Grafton Street that it had been using since 1914 and replaced them with a modern shop, while on O'Connell Street, CIÉ has opened its ultra-modern Passenger Bureau. At South Frederick Street, five Georgian buildings were demolished for a New Ireland Assurance office block and at the junction of Earlsfort Terrace and Leeson Street, an eight-storey slab office block has been built for the Irish Sugar Company.

But the most dramatic changes in the centre are taking place between Butt Bridge and O'Connell Bridge.

Today is May Day, the workers' holiday, and the Irish Transport and General Workers' Union is celebrating in fine style by opening its new headquarters at Liberty Hall. Liberty Hall is, by far, the city's tallest building, the tallest in Ireland.

The newly constructed Liberty Hall, Dublin's first 'skyscraper'.

Apart from the usual presence of President de Valera and Archbishop McQuaid for the speech and blessing, there are relations of the late labour leaders Jim Larkin and James Connolly. They must be wondering what those two men would think of the trade union headquarters, erected with union subscriptions, becoming the dominant landmark in the city.

Liberty Hall is 17 storeys high, 197 feet tall. With 30,000 square feet of glass, it is described as an 'inspiring monument', a 'crystal tower'. According to one observer, it is a building which, when set against the typical Dublin sky

O'Connell Bridge House rises from the site of what had been the Ballast Office.

of blue with passing white clouds, has 'a gossamer quality as charming as a Japanese print scene'.

Liberty Hall is not just for union officials. Many of the offices will be rented out, there is a 1,000-seat theatre, a ballroom and a rooftop viewing deck, reached by high-speed lifts, that has panoramic views of the city. From this deck one can see two other buildings in the area nearing completion.

At the corner of D'Olier Street and O'Connell Bridge on the site of what had been Carlisle House, erected by the Wide Streets Commissioners in 1779, rises another monument in concrete, glass and steel. It is the 12-storey, 75,000-square-foot O'Connell Bridge House. If Liberty Hall is the tallest building, O'Connell Bridge House boasts the highest and largest restaurant in Ireland, with 'plenty of room for dancing in soft light under the stars'. The ground floor Carlisle Grill claims to have the country's longest bar.

Behind O'Connell Bridge House, another 12-storey office block is being constructed. Hawkins House is the city's largest building with 122,000 square feet of office space. Among the buildings that were demolished to make way for this ugly behemoth was the Theatre Royal where Bill Haley and the Comets, Judy Garland, Nat King Cole, Danny Kaye and Caruso had all once performed. The theatre had its last emotional night on 30 June 1962.

The scale and height of Liberty Hall, O'Connell Bridge House and Hawkins House have transformed the appearance of the city centre. However, as far as the corporation is concerned, Dublin is not going to become an American-style city. Although these buildings are diminutive compared to those in other cities, the corporation fears an onslaught of 'skyscrapers' and have announced that in future tall buildings would only be permitted in 'exceptional circumstances'.

But the city is not only being changed by the height of buildings. A building project that cannot even be seen from the top of Liberty Hall has caused more controversy than any of the three office giants.

Since 1927, the ESB has had its headquarters on Lower Fitzwilliam Street, between Merrion Square and Fitzwilliam Square. Starting with just two buildings, it now owns 16. For some time it has planned to replace them with a purpose-built office block, claiming the buildings are 'structurally unsound'. An architectural competition was won by the young firm of Samuel Stephenson and Arthur Gibney. Their plan is to replace the 16 terraced buildings with a single modern block of similar height.

The proposals submitted for the office block were twice rejected by Dublin Corporation. But the ESB appealed to the Minister for Local Government Neil Blaney, and with what some regard as cynical timing, he granted full planning permission the day before the long-awaited Planning Bill came into law.

The granting of permission for the destruction of 16 buildings in the middle of Europe's longest unbroken line of Georgian houses, running almost continuously for 1,000 yards from Holles Street to Leeson Street, has prompted serious

Controversy surrounds the Electricity Supply Board's demolition of buildings at Lower Fitzwilliam Street.

opposition. A petition calling for the preservation of the ESB buildings was signed by thousands of people. An *Irish Times* editorial even invited its readers to 'stand outside Holles Street Hospital on a fine summer's evening and look up towards the Dublin Mountains: what would Canaletto have made of that view?'

But now it is irrelevant what Canaletto may or may not have thought, because demolition of the Georgian buildings is to begin later this month.

'To most Dubliners, the fate of the Georgian houses and terraces is a matter of safety and economic viability. With land value rising, can a city like Dublin – fighting for greater prosperity – afford to shore up at great cost houses which would not necessarily make efficient use of land when renovated? Do Dubliners anyway want to ensure the survival of a style which is associated in so many minds with foreign rule: a colonial style which offered elegance at any expense?'

Andrew Causey, *Illustrated London News*, April 1966

Tuesday, 8 March 1966

At 1.32 a.m., an explosion on O'Connell Street cleaves the top two-thirds of Nelson's 134-foot pillar from its base, sending hundreds of tonnes of rubble to the ground. Amazingly, no one is injured – the closest call comes for a taxi driver whose cab is showered with debris.

There is no doubt that the attack is the work of Republicans who could not bear the thought of Nelson's statue lording it over the Republic's capital

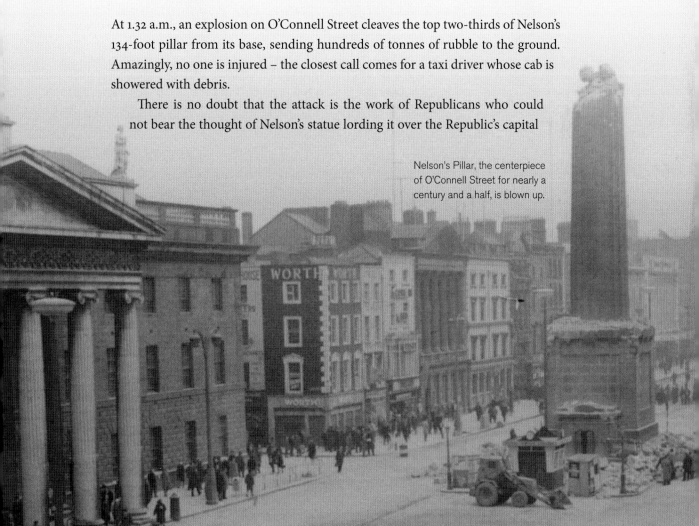

Nelson's Pillar, the centerpiece of O'Connell Street for nearly a century and a half, is blown up.

during next month's celebrations of the fiftieth anniversary of the 1916 Rising. Such sentiment was also behind a recent arson attack on the British Legion offices and a petrol bomb attack on the Ballsbridge home of the British military attaché. And with this abrupt removal of the lithic witness to the city's history for nearly 150 years, the only significant historic British memorials remaining are the much more formidable Wellington monument in the Phoenix Park and the War Memorial Gardens that are now unkempt, overgrown and languishing at Islandbridge.

In April 1963, a new magazine called *Woman's Way* was launched. It was Ireland's first magazine for women and about women.

Although compiled from an office on Grafton Street, it is careful not to focus on Dublin – rarely is the capital referred to by name, it is just called 'the city'. However, from the magazine's content, it is clear that its readership is comprised of women who either live in Dublin or would like to live there.

Woman's Way articles almost never deal with rural issues. There are no features on farming life and little about small-town Ireland. Most of the ads are for Dublin shops including Arnotts, Roches Stores on Henry Street, Dockrell's and Macey's on George's Street, Philips in Clonskeagh, Hector Grey's on Upper Liffey Street, the Happy Ring House on O'Connell Street and Courtelle on Nassau Street.

The articles cover many of the familiar topics of women's magazines such as cosmetics, slimming, hairstyles, beauty tips and recipes. But the magazine also confronts issues affecting the modern Irish woman.

There are articles on planning for parenthood, whether women should work, learning to drive a car, pregnancy and birth, prostitution in Dublin, difficulties facing teenagers, children who are brought up by grannies, uncles and aunts instead of their parents, career guidance for women – from going into advertising, to becoming a solicitor, garda or an occupational therapist – how to cope when an only son marries, women and alcoholism, the contraceptive pill, the rehabilitation of the mentally ill, women in the 1916 Rising and DIY.

But if there is one thing that defines the type of life that the *Woman's Way* reader aspires to, it is their 'house of the month' features. The ultimate in domestic desirability for the *Woman's Way* reader is the semi-detached Dublin suburban home – in Glenageary, Rathfarnham or Sutton – with front and back garden complete with fitted kitchens, sliding doors between sitting rooms and dining rooms so they can entertain guests, and smart new electric fireplaces.

Sunday, 10 April 1966

The nation's attention is on Dublin today, the 50th anniversary of the 1916 Rising. An impressive military parade passes the GPO – the press are in a stand where Nelson's Pillar had so recently stood. There is a 21-gun salute from the grounds of Trinity College. At noon, the thousands on O'Connell Street fall silent as the Proclamation is read out and the Irish flag is hoisted over the GPO.

Almost all of the events associated with the commemorations have been organised by the government and various official bodies.

This afternoon, Kilmainham Gaol Museum is opened as a tribute to the men and women such as Charles Stewart Parnell, Patrick Pearse, Michael Davitt, William Smith O'Brien, Countess Markievicz, Anne Devlin and Robert Emmet who had been imprisoned there. But Kilmainham is also a testament to members of a restoration society who have since 1960 worked voluntarily to restore the gaol which had been allowed to fall into ruin by successive governments.

❖ ❖ ❖ ❖ ❖ ❖ ❖ ❖ ❖ ❖

Thursday, 1 December 1966

There is yet more evidence of Dublin's new-found prosperity in the middle-class suburbs to the south.

Last month, the first 'superstore' in Ireland opened at Cornelscourt, on the Bray Road near Cabinteely. Designed 'to take the drudgery out of shopping and make it a pleasurable outing', it has 9,000 square feet of supermarket space and 10,000 square feet of hardware and household goods. Cornelscourt rivals the only other European centres of its kind, in Hamburg and Frankfurt.

Such were the crowds that day that every one of the 700 car park spaces were full before the superstore opened, and traffic in the area was brought to a standstill. After the opening speeches, people rushed in and pushed their 'shopping trolleys' around pillar-less aisles.

A new H. Williams supermarket opens in Deansgrange.

Less than a month later, Ireland's first 'shopping centre' is opening at Stillorgan, again on the Bray Road. Billed as 'a town within a community', there is parking for 600 cars, while parents can leave their children under the care of 'a trained supervisor in a special day nursery with toys galore'.

At Stillorgan, there are shops along traffic-free outdoor 'malls' that can supply everything one could possibly want: there are supermarkets (Lipton's, Power's, Findlater's, Quinnsworth), butchers (Fenelon's, Cullen's), a delicatessen (À la Francaise), fashion stores (Cassidy's, Bolger's, Topaz, Frewen and Aylward, White House Boutique), cleaners (IMCO, Prescott's, Blue Line), television suppliers (RTV, Irish TV Rentals), chemists (Roches, Murrays), a wine shop (Fosters), a newsagent and bookshop (Henri-Newsagent and the Paperback Centre) and motor accessories (The Motor Shop). As the advertisement reads, 'Buy all you need at Stillorgan!'

A girl surrounded by consumer goods at the opening of Stillorgan 'Shopping Centre', the first in Ireland.

198

'Dublin is a city of quite exceptional character and beauty, with a long history and vibrant cultural tradition. The closely interwoven pattern of eighteenth-century streets and material, once quite a common sight in Europe, can now be found only in Dublin, and the city's architectural heritage becomes rarer and more vulnerable every day ... Thus on the one hand this city has the great inheritance of Georgian domestic architecture of a unique quality and scale, but on the other hand, there is an acute threat that the effects of rapid expansion over the next two decades could be all the more damaging.'

Walter Bor, *Journal of the Town Planning Institute*, Vol. 53, 1967

Monday, 10 April 1967

Dublin is on the verge of the greatest transformation in its history.

When the 1964 Planning Act was passed, it was recognised that an overall plan for the capital was needed. So Professor of Planning at the University of Liverpool, Myles Wright, was engaged to come up with the vision for the city. Today his report *The Dublin Region: Advisory Regional Plan* is published. And everyone wants to know what Dublin's future is going to be.

According to the report, the future layout of Dublin will be determined by three factors.

One is increasing wealth.

Dubliners are already the wealthiest people in Ireland (in 1960 they had the highest per capita income with £259), but the Second Programme for Economic Expansion, continuing the process of modernisation, will bring more service and industrial jobs to the city. And with more jobs comes the second factor affecting the city: an increasing population.

Driven by the economy, Dublin's population is going to grow at a pace unmatched anywhere else. In 1961, it was 708,000. By 1971, it is estimated there will be 817,000 people in the capital and in 1985, more than a million.

For Wright, increasing wealth and more people will inevitably lead to the third factor affecting the city: cars. Many more cars. Wright predicts that by 1985, car ownership will be at least three times current levels. It is a trend he believes he cannot change. As far as he is concerned, public transport in Dublin has failed, while internationally 'no attempt to persuade motorists not to use the cars to the fullest extent that proves practicable has so far met with success.' According to Wright, though arriving late to the era of the family car, 'as sturdy individualists' the Irish will fully embrace the phenomenon of car ownership. By the mid-1970s, the city will be faced with a new source of traffic congestion – 'shopping expeditions by motorist housewives'.

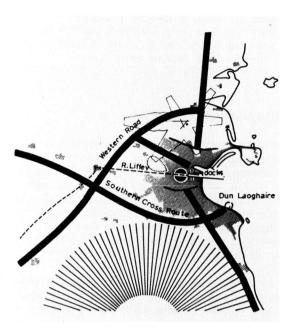

Myles Wright's report proposes a new major road network around the city.

Wright's plans for how to deal with Dublin's increasing wealth, population and cars are dramatic.

Between 1951 and 1961, the city centre's population increased by 3.7 per cent while numbers living in the suburbs increased by 88 per cent. Wright is not only going to accelerate this trend towards suburbanisation, he is proposing the greatest single change in Dublin's layout in its history.

In 20 years' time, 300,000 people are going to live in the west of the city in four new towns built on 20,000 acres of what are now open fields. The west has not been chosen for any particular planning reason, but because to the east of Dublin is the sea, to the south the mountains and to the north, the airport which, in the era of the jet plane, should be surrounded by a three-and-a-half-mile *cordon sanitaire*.

The new towns will be at Blanchardstown/Mulhuddart, with 80,500 people, Lucan, with 76,000, Clondalkin with 63,500 and, the largest, Tallaght, with 116,000. While it is intended that each will have town centres, significant employment and civic amenities, most people will live a distance from these and, if they can afford them, will have to buy cars.

The new towns are not the only changes proposed by Wright. Overlaying this expansion is a new road superstructure to manage the huge increase in cars.

The most important new road will be a highway called the 'Western Road'. Starting at the Belfast Road in the north, it will cut a swathe through countryside, cross the Liffey and link up with the Galway, Limerick and Cork roads. The Western Road will also connect to a new 'Southern Cross Route' which will skirt the Dublin Mountains and encircle the city by joining with Dún Laoghaire and Bray. There will also be a new bridge near to the mouth of the Liffey that will connect the Belfast and Bray roads, as well as a new road to take the port's traffic away from the city centre.

Wright's vision for the city is so dramatic that it is hard for people to envisage how the city will look when his proposals come to fruition.

Thursday, 19 October 1967

Following the building collapses and tenement deaths of 1963, the city's authorities try once more to come to grips with the housing problem. But instead of inner city flats and garden suburbs, they have turned to Le Corbusier for a new concept of how to house the poor.

Ballymun is like nowhere else in Ireland. It is being seen by many as a symbol of progress with every home having two or three bedrooms, hot water, central heating, flushing toilets and BBC and UTV on their televisions. It is described as 'probably the most exciting happening in public building in Ireland for generations. Sleek and elegant, at least from a distance, no doubt the families living in them are happy to be out of the rat-infested slums of the city, which those with the correct aspect will be able to see from their sitting rooms.'

When it is finished, there will be more people living in Ballymun than in Athlone, Kilkenny, Dundalk or Sligo. Last August, people moved into the first of 452 two-storey houses. This week tenants are moving into the first of what will be seven 15-storey tower blocks. It is called 'Patrick Pearse Tower' – the remaining six towers will all be named after the other signatories of the 1916 Proclamation.

Despite the scale of Ballymun, still many more remain on the Corporation's housing list waiting to be rehoused from living conditions that have hardly changed since independence.

The new town at Ballymun is a world away from the slums of the city centre.

On Tuesday, 22 October 1968, a new type of school opens at Haddington Terrace, Dún Laoghaire. Called the Dublin School of English, it is primarily for the purpose of teaching English to foreign au pairs in the city.

'A large minority of Dublin men, approximately a third, were born elsewhere; and they seem to be of a high average social status than their Dublin-born colleagues: the Dublin-born become relatively more numerous as we descend the status hierarchy. Such social and economic success, however, is not enjoyed equally by all migrants to the City. It was noticeable that men born on farms, or otherwise away from population nuclei, do not differ in status significantly from the Dublin-born average ... In considering these phenomena, however, the possibility has to be borne in mind that Dublin aspirants to higher status levels combine social and geographic mobility – that is, that they are now overseas ... Yet it is also clear that the Dublin-born, on the whole, are less educated than migrants to Dublin from other parts of the country; or, in other words, that it is the better-educated of the provincial born who move to the Capital...'

Bertram Hutchinson, *Social Status and Inter-Generational Social Mobility in Dublin*, 1969

A public toilet along the quays.

Monday, 28 April 1969

No Irish novel has caused such excitement before its launch. Tonight in the Bailey pub on Duke Street there is no doubting the success of James Plunkett's first novel, *Strumpet City*. The hardback rights were bought after a bidding war, American rights sold for £42,000 and it is already being translated into German, Swedish, Danish and Dutch. Orders are flowing in and reviewers are falling over themselves to praise it. One describes *Strumpet City* as a novel 'that tugs at the heart without importuning it, that convulses by its wild comicality, and shocks by its unflinching perception of mortal misery'.

Plunkett joins a list of writers who have used Dublin as their literary canvas. Starting in 1907 and ending with the outbreak of the Great War in 1914, it is set around the conflict between the city's labourers and their employers, culminating in the 1913 Lock-out.

Plunkett, a former trade union official, now working in RTÉ, gives us an array of vivid characters including the kind, alcoholic priest Fr Giffley, the parsimonious and overly pious Fr O'Connor, Yearling, the liberal intellectual, the Bradshaws, the kind but complacent landlords, the tramp Rashers Tierney and his hilarious antics and, at the novel's heart, Fitz and his wife Mary who are just trying to get on with their lives in a city where that simple achievement can be something of a miracle.

'It was closing time. The barman in McDaid's was shouting 'Time, gentlemen, please' with automatic insistence that intimidated nobody. Drinks continued to be sipped slowly and sensually, and the barman's end of day ritual was, as usual, an unrealized failure. Yet it would be the barmen who would win in the heel of the hunt, for it was within their power to cut off supplies from behind the counter, forcing us to leave. But that would be later, perhaps fifteen minutes later, and in the meantime there were things to be said ...'

Joseph Cole, 'Night Out in Dublin', *The Dublin Magazine*, Vol. 8, Spring/Summer 1969

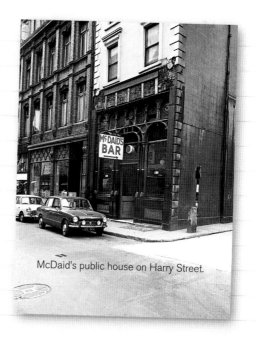

McDaid's public house on Harry Street.

Friday, 24 October 1969

It is turning out to be a great year for literary Dublin as today it is announced that Samuel Beckett has been awarded the Nobel Prize for Literature. He is the first Irish winner since George Bernard Shaw. Beckett is modest and famously wary of the press so instead of revelling in notoriety, he and his wife are in hiding in a Tunis hotel where they have been on holidays. Both are said to be distressed at the news, his wife declares the Nobel announcement a 'catastrophe'.

Chosen by the Nobel Committee 'for his writing, which – in new forms for the novel and drama – in the destitution of modern man acquires its elevation', Beckett is the most international of writers. He has lived in Paris for much of his life, writes mainly in French and looks at the problems of the modern world – he does not address the usual subject matter of Irish writers and his works are far from Plunkett's *Strumpet City*. But he remains unmistakeably Irish and his works are permeated with references to Dublin – including his Foxrock house, the train stations on the old Harcourt Street line, Leopardstown racecourse, the stonemasons of Barnacullia, Dalkey Island, the Pillar, Dún Laoghaire pier and the Dublin Mountains.

❖ ❖ ❖ ❖ ❖ ❖ ❖ ❖ ❖ ❖

Wednesday, 14 January 1970

The first parking metres are introduced onto the city's streets to help solve the traffic and parking problem.

Today is 'M-day', the day that the first of 2,400 parking meters come into operation in Dublin. Installed on streets throughout the city centre to help the business and shopping community by making people move on rather than hoard a parking space for the day, they also mark what could be the beginning of the end for Dublin's unofficial, self-employed, self-appointed parking attendants.

Dividing the city into 'patches', these men have long claimed the city's parking spots as their own, to be given out for a fee with the cars parked under their care.

Among these attendants have been Frankie Farrelly who has been working on St Stephen's Green since 1953 and Charlie Dillon who started with his father parking bikes at Dalymount Park in the 1920s before eventually progressing to O'Connell Street which he has shared with 'Battler' McCann, 'Smokey' Crosby, 'Kit' Crosby and 'Bullhead'.

The peaked cap motor car attendants have not had a set rate, but the metres will charge a shilling an hour. When the time expires, a red flag will pop up on the meter. Avoiding the attendants has been one of the city's unofficial sports, but there will be less chance of escaping the parking meters and their 100 traffic wardens. Motorists caught with a red flag will be fined £1 and might even have their car removed.

❖ ❖ ❖ ❖ ❖ ❖ ❖ ❖ ❖ ❖ ❖

Wednesday, 14 April 1971

'Women's Liberation' is being discussed all over the country. But it is in Dublin where there has been most activity. Apart from 'consciousness' meetings, there have been Women's Liberation protests at the Archbishop's Palace, picketing of the Four Courts demanding equality before the law and some women breaking into the Seanad while its members were voting against the latest contraceptive bill.

Last October, the Irish Women's Liberation Movement was founded by 20 women who felt they were 'the slaves and chattel of men'. Tonight, around a thousand people, the majority women, but also a fair number of men, attend their first ever meeting

At Connolly Station members of the Women's Liberation Movement return from Belfast with contraceptives. It is still against the law to import contraceptives into Ireland.

in the Round Room of the Mansion House. The purpose of tonight's meeting is to inform people of the movement's aims and to encourage others to become involved.

Two hundred pamphlets outlining the civil inequalities faced by women were snapped up. Among the issues highlighted were: unequal pay; the 'marriage bar' which means that when women working in the civil service get married they have to leave their jobs; the discrimination against women sitting on juries; the fact that if a working woman paying full insurance gets sick she only gets half the pay of a man; that the father is the legal guardian of children – he can draw on their post office savings but the mother cannot, he can take children abroad but the mother cannot; that if a woman wants to buy goods on hire purchase she normally requires her husband's permission; and that if a husband leaves his wife she has no say in how the family home is dealt with.

The night is a great success and as they leave, many are already planning to set up their own Women's Liberation branches in Dublin and around the country.

❖ ❖ ❖ ❖ ❖ ❖ ❖ ❖ ❖ ❖ ❖

Friday, 1 October 1971

Earlier this year, Lewis Mumford, one of the world's foremost thinkers on urban matters and the author of *The City in History*, visited Dublin. He was not impressed. He described the Ballymun towers as 'insane', 'the most extravagant way of doing the wrong thing' and a place where children will inevitably become delinquents because they have nowhere to go and nothing to do. He was also scathing about other suburbs of the city, where parents and their children have been condemned to a monotonous, 'mock life' in areas that are not 'neighbourhoods' but mere adjuncts to shopping centres. Ominously, Mumford warned that if Dublin continues to go the way it is going it is in danger of 'eventual destruction'.

A mother and her children on the road reservation at Santry for one of the proposed new motorways.

This month's *Plan Magazine* continues the criticism. It is a tragedy 'that the future development of Dublin will take the course it is taking. The tragedy they are witnessing now will be nothing compared to the tragedy 15 years hence when this unplanned sprawl – Tallaght, Clondalkin, Lucan and Blanchardstown – has really gelled.'

It also attacks the reality of Ballymun which has all the problems associated with similar developments in large cities in Britain and America – there are the financial worries of the poor, lack of employment and community identity. There is isolation and virtually no amenities for more than 10,000 people, except a supermarket and a pub.

Famed for its chip shops, Dublin has also had burger restaurants before. Among the first were the Green Rooster on O'Connell Street and Billy's on Prince's Street, both opened in the 1930s and 1940s by Australian Billy Wills. There are also the Wimpy burgers. But Captain America's Cookhouse located on the first floor of a Grafton Street building is something completely different.

Inspired by the new London chain of burger restaurants called The Great American Disaster, Captain America's is as 'hip' as anything in Dublin. Sitting under murals by artist Jim Fitzpatrick, served by young, attractive waitresses, diners tuck into real burgers with French fries and garnish and for afters, deep-dish apple pie and ice cream served with a hot chocolate sauce. Judging by their first night on Tuesday, 14 December 1971, they have a sensation on their hands.

In February 1973, Thin Lizzy, headed by Philip Lynott, a mixed-race Dubliner from Crumlin, with Brian Downey, also from Crumlin and Eric Bell and Eric Wrixon from Belfast, appear on Top of the Pops to play 'Whiskey in the Jar', which has reached number 6 in the UK chart.

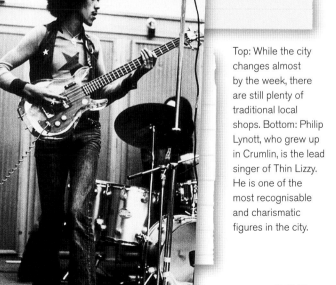

Top: While the city changes almost by the week, there are still plenty of traditional local shops. Bottom: Philip Lynott, who grew up in Crumlin, is the lead singer of Thin Lizzy. He is one of the most recognisable and charismatic figures in the city.

Friday, 17 May 1974

There are no warnings. It is Friday evening, the busiest time of the week in the city centre.

The first thing people notice is the light. Bright, blinding flashes. Then come the dull thuds, the shock waves from explosions. Shattering glass. So much shattering glass. Cars on fire. Death. Smoke. Death. People on fire. Death.

At 5.28 p.m. on Parnell Street, outside Barry's Supermarket, near the junction with Marlborough Street, a bomb goes off in a green Hillman Avenger car that was stolen in Belfast this morning. Ten people die: 21-year-old Marie Butler, from Cappoquin, County Waterford, a temporary shop assistant at Clerys; 80-year-old John Dargle from Ballybough, a veteran of the Great War; Patrick Fay, 47 years old, from Ardee but living in Artane and employed at the GPO; Antonio Magliocco, a 37-year-old from Casalattico in the region of Italy where all the chip shop families in the city come from; Edward John O'Neill, a painter and decorator from Dominick Street, who was a married father of five; Breda Turner from Thurles who worked in the income tax office and was engaged to be married; John and Anna O'Brien and their two children, who were originally from Finglas, but who lived in Gardiner Street.

At 5.30 p.m., Talbot Street, one of the busiest in the city, is packed with shoppers, people leaving work, others making their way to Connolly to catch a train, or to Busáras. A blue Ford Escort, also stolen in Belfast this morning, parked outside Guiney's shop explodes. Suddenly there are body parts on footpaths, on the road, in shop windows.

Twelve people die at Talbot Street: Simone Chetrit, a 30-year-old French woman who came to Dublin to learn English; Josie Bradley, a 21-year-old civil servant from

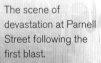

The scene of devastation at Parnell Street following the first blast.

In September 1974, crowds celebrate the Dublin Gaelic football team's first All-Ireland win since 1963.

Offaly; Anne Byrne, 35-year-old wife and mother of two from Raheny; Colette Doherty, married mother of one who was nine months pregnant – her two-year-old daughter is found wandering the streets two hours after the explosion; 35-year-old Breda Grace, originally from Kerry but now living in Portmarnock, was married with one son; May McKenna who worked in Clerys and lived above a shoe shop on Talbot Street; Anne Marren from Sligo who lived in Harold's Cross; Dorothy Morris from Kimmage who worked at the Cadbury's factory; Marie Phelan, a 20-year-old civil servant from Woodstown, County Waterford living in Philipsburgh Avenue; 19-year-old Siobhan Roice, another civil servant, from Wexford; Maureen Shields from Hollyford, County Tipperary; 27-year-old John Walsh from Crumlin. Two others are fatally wounded: 65-year-old Concepta Dempsey, a shop assistant at Guiney's who lived in Drogheda, and 59-year-old Elizabeth Fitzgerald from Phibsborough who was with her husband when the bomb went off – he survived.

At almost the same time as the Talbot Street blast, a third bomb, in a blue Austin 1800 Maxi, again hijacked in Belfast, goes off in South Leinster Street, near the wall of Trinity College. Two die here: 51-year-old Christina O'Loughlin, a French polisher at the Shelbourne Hotel, and 21-year-old Anna Massey from Sallynoggin, who worked at Lisney's and was engaged to be married.

The Troubles have come to Dublin before. On 2 February 1972, the British Embassy at Merrion Square was burned down by an angry crowed after the Bloody Sunday killings in Derry. There were four car bombs between November 1972 and January 1973 that killed three people. But in a matter of minutes, this day has become the worst day of death in the city since Bloody Sunday of 1920.

Tuesday, 17 December 1974

In the last two years, there has been an almost continuous stream of books published about Dublin.

The Economic and Social Research Institute published Kathleen O'Higgins' report on *Marital Desertion in Dublin*. For the first time, the causes of marriage break-ups in the city are examined. One third of women who separated – or were 'deserted' by their husbands – were pregnant when they married. One third said that things were 'wrong' at the time they married. There was a strong link between large numbers of children and marriage breakdown. Violence was not a significant factor, though more than half said drink was. But the main reasons given for marriage break-ups were that the couples did not know each other well enough when they married and the 'disillusion' they experienced when the reality of married life diverged from what they had hoped for.

The Catholic Community Institute of Ireland published a report, *Educational Opportunity in Dublin*, based on a survey of 3,000 Dubliners over the age of 21. It found that, in sociological terms, Irish society was in transition from being a 'gemeinschaftlich', or traditional society, to a 'gesellschaftlich', or modern one. One of the signs was the higher education attainment of the younger generations. Half of the respondents had gone on to at least secondary school, while the parents of four out of five of those questioned had only attended primary school.

Social Status in Dublin: Marriage Mobility and First Employment found, perhaps not surprisingly, that people of the same social and educational class tend to marry each other and that a Dubliner's educational attainment is directly related to his or her father's social status.

UCD's Department of Psychiatry's report *The Inner City of Dublin* focuses on the area between the Liffey and Dorset Street. In less than a decade, this area's population has declined by almost 20 per cent as people have emigrated or moved from the tenements to Ballymun or Wright's new suburbs. Less than half the national average of children are in post-primary education, 38 per cent of men have no skill, and one in every ten women is a widow. It is an area for which there is no plan and the property developers have no interest. Once full of life, it is now 'hostile and lacks variety and amenities which constitute necessary substructures for healthy human development ... this environment must exert intolerable strains on families and make neglect of children, not a chance or a choice, but a fact of life'.

With Dublin in the throes of so much change, there have been a number of publications looking to the future of the city.

The *Architecture Review* brought out a special feature called *The Future for*

Dublin by Laurence Wright and Kenneth Brown. Examining the problems facing Dublin as it modernises, they ask the very topical question, 'Can she become a truly modern capital city without destroying herself?'

Dublin: A Living City was published to make people aware of the level of destruction in the city, the huge profits being made by developers and the prospect that in five years' time, nothing might be left of the old Dublin. One of the worst consequences of this is the loss of the sense of community: 'The essence of a city is its people, living in communities, which have developed from generation to generation, giving character to its own neighbourhood. The city's true life is in the life of such communities. In Dublin, private enterprise is destroying those communities, expelling the inhabitants to the old suburbs and to new reservations outside the city, replacing the citizens and their houses with offices and warehouses empty at night of all life and all activity, making the rich, empty nocturnal city a temptation to criminals and a terror to ordinary people.'

The Essential Dublin by Terry Kelleher is a guide book that makes some interesting observations about the difficulties people experience in trying to achieve the simple task of making a phone call in Dublin:

> In theory at least, making a local telephone call is very simple; when you hear the dial tone, insert a 2p coin or two 1p coins, dial the number required, and when your call is answered press button A, and begin your 3 minutes-worth of conversation. In practice, however, you will require a great deal of luck, patience and usually more than the appropriate 2p. Out of ten attempts to call from a public phone box, you are likely to find four of the booths smashed by vandals, three simply out of order, and one where the coin box has not been emptied, so that either you are unable to fit any money in, or having fitted it, you cannot get a refund if there is no reply to your call. One more call is likely to lead to a crossed line – too late – you have pressed button A and so have lost another 2p. With luck on your side, your fourth attempt may be successful, provided of course that the other person's phone is not out of order …

There is also a whole host of Dublin history books published, as though there has been a sudden need to study Dublin's past before it is completely destroyed, or to highlight what makes Dublin unique just as it is becoming increasingly like other places.

There is *Literary Dublin* by Herbert Kenny, *Changing Dublin: A Portfolio of Drawings* by Michael O'Brien, Liam Martin's *Dublin Shopfronts and Streetscenes*,

Dear Dirty Dublin by G.W. Target, the National Gallery's *Exhibition of Topographical Views of Dublin, Viking and Medieval Dublin: National Museum Excavations 1962– 1973*, and Elgy Gillespie's *The Liberties of Dublin*, which documents the history of one of the city's oldest areas.

The most popular of all the books is today the number one hardback bestseller. It is *Me Jewel and Darlin' Dublin* by Éamonn Mac Thomáis. Described as 'a Dubliner's Dublin', it tells the story of inner-city life, the part of the city that is struggling the most, the part that is disappearing. There is nothing of the suburbs here, no stories from Coolock, Tallaght, Ballyfermot, Cabinteely, Rathfarnham, Blackrock or Stillorgan. As far as Mac Thomáis is concerned, these areas are not the 'real' Dublin.

Me Jewel and Darlin' Dublin tells of the rush for one-penny cinema tickets and the sweets that could be bought for a penny – 12 Rainbow Caramels, 32 Aniseed Balls, 16 Jembo Balls, 2 Peggies or two 'Taffey' apples. There are the street games – 'Follow the Leader' in which children follow a one child and have to do whatever he or she does, such as knocking on doors and running away, leaving those at the end of the line in greatest danger; 'Kick the Can' for those who could not afford a football; and 'Rope the Door' which involves tying a rope to a door, ringing the bell and then playing tug o' war with the person inside. There is the long tradition of city street characters including 'Endymion', who walked the streets in deerstalker hat, knee britches and tunic shirt while carrying a sword, fishing rod and an umbrella, always up on a fine day; the eighteenth-century ballad singer 'Zozimus'; and from the city's current characters 'Bang Bang', otherwise Thomas Dudley from the Liberties, who takes part in Wild West shoot-outs with total strangers on the city streets using a key as a shooter.

There are tours of the city centre and directions to some of the city's hidden places. There is the history of some of the city's commercial premises – the oldest is Rathborne's candle manufacturers at East Wall Road, in business since 1488, Thomas Read's on Parliament Street is one of the oldest cutlers in the world and the Sun and Commercial companies are two of the world's oldest insurance brokers.

There are also the sounds of the city – 'Listen to Dublin,' Mac Thomáis tells the reader. 'Listen to its heart beating, its children laughing and crying. Listen for the Dalymount roar or the cultured cry from Hill Sixteen in Croke Park. Listen to the dealers in the streets, and the jingle sounds of silver and copper coins in the apron pockets. Listen for the footsteps or the odd horse-car go over grey cobblestones, or seagulls screeching over waster bins.' And then there are the smells 'as sweet as honey, or as fragrant as new mown hay – the smell of the fish-and-chipper on a cold winter's night, sometimes they even smell better than they taste'.

Thursday, 30 January 1975

Since 1961, 117 large office blocks have been built in Dublin. They have been paid for by developers' money, but it is the architects who are changing the everyday experience of being in Dublin.

Sam Stephenson is described as Dublin's 'most loved-hated-well-known-busiest architect'. Short, bearded, quietly spoken, at times charming, but doggedly determined, he has found himself, or put himself, in the middle of a number of controversies.

Stephenson was the architect for the controversial ESB offices. In 1971, he was in the thick of a stand-off between conservationists and developers over the demolition of more Georgian buildings at Hume Street/St Stephen's Green.

Stephenson infuriates conservationists with his forthright views on the city's Georgian architecture. At the time of the Fenian Street collapses, he wrote that Georgian buildings 'were never supposed to last more than a lifetime'. During the Hume Street controversy, he said that preservationists should 'stop bleating about all of Georgian Dublin being preserved for posterity – posterity might not want it'.

Stephenson believes that architects are society's 'pathfinders'. And pathfinders should be prepared to meet controversy head-on.

He is fond of comparing himself to James Gandon, the eighteenth-century architect who built the Custom House and Four Courts, but who was vilified by many in his own lifetime. Comparing his own and Gandon's experiences, Stephenson says, 'I don't think there has ever been a public building of value in Dublin that there hasn't been trouble about.'

The occupation of Hume Street buildings trying to stop its demolition to make way for a new office block.

Like many of those doing well out of the city's development, Stephenson is well connected politically. But in other ways Stephenson is not typical of the people demonised by conservationists.

Many claim, with some justification, that the city is being destroyed by people from the country who have no feel for the city, no urban sentiment or sense of civic pride. There is certainly no shortage of those, but Stephenson is a Dubliner, through and through. He proudly boasts that his family have lived in the city for more than two centuries and that his father was the first president of the Old Dublin Society that had been founded to help increase appreciation of the city's history. Stephenson shares the belief of the conservationists that Dublin should be a living city and has used his own money to convert an eighteenth-century mews into his home, while his offices are not in one of the fashionable areas such as Merrion Square or Fitzwilliam Square, but at Bride Street, in the historic Liberties.

Rarely far from controversy, he has, with his latest project, the Central Bank on Dame Street, found himself right in the middle of another one.

The Central Bank had been granted planning permission for an eight-storey building, 120-feet tall. In a remarkable method of construction, two reinforced concrete cores rose from Dame Street to support cantilevered trusses from which the floors were going to be hung, starting with the top floor. But then it was noticed that the building, instead of being 120-feet high, was going to be closer to 150 feet.

The bank's president, T.K. Whitaker, claimed to have known nothing about the extra height. Stephenson said he was not aware of any breach of permission that was granted by the corporation, but the corporation insisted they had only granted permission for a building 120-feet tall and that this had been exceeded. Due to Stephenson's method of construction, taking the top two floors off would cost as much as starting the building from scratch. If one had wanted to present the extra height as a *fait accompli*, one could not have devised a better method of construction.

After a public inquiry was held, the Central Bank lodged another planning application. What was built does not have to come down. The only change is that a pitched copper roof, which would have finished off the building, will not be built. Instead, the heavy trusses from which the building is suspended will be clad in copper and left on view, making the oddest rooftop in the city.

When the building is finished, Stephenson will have made another permanent mark on his city. Perhaps as the years pass, his works will come to be regarded in the same light as Gandon's, masterpieces. However, if Stephenson's aim is for his buildings to be loved and admired as much as Gandon's then people will want to paint his buildings, buy postcards of them or bring visitors to see his works out of a sense of pride.

And only time will tell if that is going to happen.

In 1970, New York advertising executive Bob Fearon was on a shoot in Dublin when he went for a Sunday-morning stroll around the pleasant surroundings of the terraced Georgian townhouses of Fitzwilliam Square. As he did so, he took particular notice of the front doors at the top of short flights of steps.

The panelled doors were painted various hues of red, taupe, white, brown, grey, orange and yellow. Some had delicate carved inlays. Above them were arches of glass fanlights which ranged from the sheer banality of clear glass with a taped-on house number, to others as colourful as peacocks' tails. There were knockers and letter boxes of various designs, boot scrapers, a variety of door casings. Fearon photographed a number of them and when he went back to New York he turned his photos into a collage.

When Joe Malone, North American manager of the Irish Tourist Board, saw the collage, he asked Fearon if he could put it on display in the Board's New York office window for St Patrick's Day. On the day, passers-by were so interested that the Tourist Board bought the rights to the display. Then they produced a poster.

On Thursday, 6 March 1975 the 'Doors of Dublin' poster takes first prize from among 88 entries in a design competition sponsored by the German publishing house Jaeger. In second place is the poster advertising last year's Winter Olympics at Innsbruck and in third is one for the Sydney Opera House.

Sunday, 26 September 1976

The crowd shuffles, shoulder to shoulder, through air thick with the smell of sweat, tinged with the aroma of Guinness and the pungent whiff of dense farts. They funnel down a narrow laneway into the back of the Hill 16 terrace at Croke Park.

In a city in which so many people are no longer living in the area they grew up in, where communities have been broken and fragmented, the Hill is one of the places where they come together and where they can celebrate the fact that they are from Dublin.

Today Heffo's army, named after the manager Kevin Heffernan, are here in force. They are here in expectation. They are here in dread. Because today is the real test. And the people on the Hill know that the rest of the country is watching and wants them to fail.

Because everyone hates Dublin.

Two years ago, Dublin beat Galway to win its first All-Ireland football final since 1963. But every Dublin supporter knows that the Dubs will only be considered a great team, true champions, when they manage to beat Kerry. And the capital has not beaten the Kingdom in a meaningful game since 1934. The hoodoo continued last year when Dublin walked out from the Hogan Stand tunnel as favourites and walked back in vanquished.

The Hill is more like a terrace at an English soccer stadium than anything in another GAA ground. On the Hill, people clap hands in unison, sing songs, wave banners with messages ranging from the obvious such as 'The Jacks are Back' and 'I'd Rather be a Jack than a King' to the more enigmatic 'Bobby [Doyle] Will Bite Your Legs'.

On the Hill there is the usual competition between wits slagging the opposition and the referee, but saving the most vitriolic and amusing for their own team, for their neighbour, their club mate.

The Hill is a great leveller. On the Hill the teacher, banker, bricklayer and drunk is just another face, another pair of arms, another flag.

Matches are preceded by the traditional team parade behind the north side Artane Boys Band. Starting at the Hogan Stand, with its VIPs, the band march to the Canal End terrace, then along the Cusack Stand. All the while cheers rise and fall in a wave. But before they reach the Hill, and the mass of Dublin supporters, they take an abrupt left back towards the Hogan, as if it is too dangerous to venture as far as the Dublin supporters on the Hill.

Today Dublin wins by seven points.

Now Stephen Rooney from the O'Dwyer's club in Balbriggan, Tony Hanahoe and his St Vincent's club mates Brian Mullins, Gay O'Driscoll, Bobby Doyle and Jimmy Keaveney, as well as Bernard Brogan from the Navan Road, Anton O'Toole from Synge Street, Robbie Kelleher from Glasnevin, David Hickey from Raheny, Sean Doherty from the hills of Ballyboden, Paddy Cullen from just down the road at O'Connell's, Tommy Drum from Whitehall, Garda John McCarthy and, everyone's man of the match, Kevin Moran, born in Rialto but living in Walkinstown, can all say to themselves, 'We have beaten Kerry.'

And as the Dublin supporters leave they say to each other, to themselves, 'I can't believe it, we've beaten Kerry. We have beaten Kerry.'

❖ ❖ ❖ ❖ ❖ ❖ ❖ ❖ ❖ ❖

Friday, 29 October 1976

Six months ago, a new magazine called *In Dublin* went on sale for the first time. With a banner motif combining the Ha'Penny Bridge and O'Connell Bridge, it is the city's only magazine aimed at the people in the city. Selling at ten pence, the 1,000 copies printed in the first edition sold out. Now 7,000 are printed every fortnight.

At first, *In Dublin* only provided free listings. If you want to know what there is to do or see in the city, *In Dublin* is the only place to look.

But the magazine now features reviews of concerts and exhibitions as well as articles about the city. In June it had an article on the closures of the Kenilworth Cinema in Harold's Cross and the Classic in Terenure – they are just the latest of nearly 20 suburban cinemas that have closed in the last five years, mainly as a result of the introduction of multiple-screen cinemas in the city centre. Another article called for the introduction of cycling facilities in the city including cycleways and cycle lanes: 'Imagine going in by bicycle – on a bicycle lane! Could happen!'

The cover of the first *In Dublin* magazine.

In a city in which over half the population is under 25 years old, the city's nightlife is of particular interest.

Showbands playing the traditional Dublin ballrooms such as the Olympic, off Camden Street, the Tara Club on D'Olier Street and the National and Ierne on Parnell Square are still holding their own. According to *In Dublin*, 'Bright lights and lively showbands are standard in Dublin ballrooms. If you like to dance and really want to enjoy yourself you will rarely be disappointed.'

In the latest edition, two *In Dublin* writers head out into 'the shadowy unknown night life of this once-fair city'. After arriving too late at Tailors' Hall for the Brendan Balfe satire (admission £1.50, including dinner) they head to Annabel's in the Burlington Hotel in Ballsbridge. According to the article, Annabel's caters for 'the mid-twenty, trendy, and affluent set who can't decide whether they want to be West Europeans or East Americans'. Shirts and ties are preferred to denim jeans, 'glossy lovelies' serve tables, the DJ plays New York's top 25 records and, apparently, it is the place to go if you are looking for 'an elevating fling'.

Then the two head to Zhivago's, behind a Baggot Street supermarket. Run by the very 'with it' Billy Bolton, it is advertised as the place 'where love stories begin'. At the Celebrity Club on Lower Abbey Street, the walls are covered with photos of stars from Buster Keaton to Roger Moore, there is a disco until 12.30 a.m. and a band until

3 a.m. At the Lord John on Sackville Place, Dave Heffernan is the usual DJ and most of the crowd are women and the men are over 45. At Rutland Place there is the more daring Revolution Club. The *In Dublin* scribes do not enter, but content themselves with looking at 'necking couples' using locked warehouses in the laneway as lean-tos.

And after that the pair end the night in traditional style. By going to the Lido café for a single of chips.

On Monday, 16 May 1977, the first McDonald's fast food restaurant in Ireland opens on Grafton Street.

The first punk concert by a band from outside Ireland is held on Friday, 21 October 1977 in the Exam Hall in Trinity College when The Clash play.

In March 1978, Danny Doyle has been at number one for ten weeks with 'The Rare Old Times'. A song written by Pete St John, it tells the story of Sean Dempsey from Pimlico who lives in a changing Dublin with the Pillar gone, the Theatre Royal gone and concrete and glass cages making a city of his town.

On Thursday, 1 June 1978, a new bookshop opens at 10 South King Street, opposite the Gaiety and above Sydney Vard's Fur Remodelling shop. Books Upstairs has been started by two UCD students Enda Doherty and Maurice Earls to 'fill a void in the literary life of the city' and to 'provide for the needs of a changing city'. Featuring publications about cinema, politics, music and feminism, it is a bookshop where the serious is always chosen over the flippant, where bluebells are in the centre of the shop and where browsing is encouraged.

Saturday, 23 September 1978

It is ironic that the modernisation of the city is leading to the discovery of its past.

The Dublin Corporation Civic Offices plan shelved in the 1950s has been resurrected. In 1970, planning permission was granted for three office blocks on the site below Christchurch. And once again Sam Stephenson finds himself in the middle of controversy. But this time, while his functional blocks and the effects they will have on the view of the cathedral are criticised by many, the main controversy comes from what is being found underground.

People had been aware of the city's Viking past, but it is only after excavations in the early 1960s at Dublin Castle and High Street that this past has come to light..

When excavations began at Winetavern Street as part of the preparatory work for the new Civic Offices, there was great excitement about the wealth of material being found. But soon the question of whether or not the Civic Offices should be built at all began to be raised.

In May 1974, excavations began at Wood Quay proper and it soon became apparent that it was the most important Viking site outside Scandinavia. By the spring of 1975, there were 80,000 finds. However, as excavations took place in one area, diggers moved into others. The situation developed into a full-blown controversy as it became clear that if the whole site were to be excavated it would take many years before the offices were built. In 1976, the Friends of Medieval Dublin succeeded in having part of the site designated a national monument. For the last three years, the archaeologists have been racing the diggers.

Today thousands of people are on the streets in the largest cultural demonstration in the history of the state. They walk through the city from the Dáil to Wood Quay in a show of public anger at the destruction of its past. But something that the protesters do not know is that the consent to continue the work and destroy the monument has already been signed by the corporation and the Office of Public Works. The deal is done. The future of Wood Quay is decided. The Civic Offices will be built.

Protesters march against the erection of the Civic Offices on what is now known to be one of the most important Viking sites in Europe.

On Monday, 4 September 1978, 80 children are brought for their first day at school to a terraced Georgian house in Monkstown. Called Dalkey School Project, it is a new departure in how children of the city are taught. Until now, schools have been Catholic or Protestant. But Dalkey School Project is different. It is the first multidenominational primary school to be recognised in the history of the state. It also has both boys and girls and its policy is decided by dialogue between parents and teachers. The Dalkey School Project prototype is one that others are already looking to copy.

Friday, 13 October 1978

Some 2,500 women, many carrying torches, march through the streets under the slogan 'Women Against Violence Against Women'. They are protesting against attacks on women in the city and the fact that they live their lives in fear of sexual abuse.

The marchers call for a raped woman to be treated as the victim, not the accused, in Irish courts. They call for changes in the laws of evidence so that a woman's sexual history is not brought out in court or held against her, and for an end to suspended sentences being handed down to rapists. It is also announced that next month a Rape Crisis Centre will open in Dublin that will provide 24-hour counselling and advice to women who have been attacked.

❖ ❖ ❖ ❖ ❖ ❖ ❖ ❖ ❖ ❖ ❖

Thursday, 23 November 1978

Most young people with access to BBC television turn it on at 7.20 p.m. to watch this week's edition of *Top of the Pops* and the countdown to the number one record. For the last seven weeks, Olivia Newton John and John Travolta have topped the charts with 'Summer Nights', a song about innocent teenage love from this year's hit movie musical *Grease*. But today they are knocked off the number one spot by quite a different song. It is the first 'New Wave' number one and the first ever by an Irish band. It is 'Rat Trap' by Dublin's Boomtown Rats. Before they start, members of the Rats turn to the camera, tear up pictures of John Travolta and yawn. Then they break into 'Rat Trap'.

The Boomtown Rats' first gig was in Bolton Street Institute of Technology in 1976. They were led by Bob Geldof, from Dún Laoghaire. After attending the well-heeled private school Blackrock College, the unconventional Geldof worked for a

time in an abattoir that backed onto the Grand Canal. He then went to Canada where he worked for a progressive newspaper before returning to Dublin in early 1975. After failing to raise money to set up a new publication called *Buy and Sell*, he sold spyholes for doors to people in the new suburbs in the west of the city. Then he got involved with a new band called Nightlife Thugs. While they were finding their way, bashing out tunes, they were offered the gig at Bolton Street.

At the break in the middle of that first gig, Geldof decided a name change was needed. 'Nightlife Thugs' was rubbed off the board beside the stage and 'The Boomtown Rats' written in its stead – at the time Geldof had been reading Woody Guthrie's biography *Bound for Glory* which featured a gang of children called 'the Boomtown Rats'.

The Rats quickly became the most popular band in the city. They are not just known for their lyrics and music but also for laughs – they invite the audience on stage to 'Do the Rat' – enthusiasm, bravado and a lead singer in Geldof with a

big mouth and big head – at one gig 'Geldof is God' was emblazoned on his T-shirt. At another he told the audience they were going to make him rich. And he was right.

The Rats moved to England and in February last year signed with the Ensign record label for £700,000. It is the biggest record deal in the history of pop music. After successful singles including 'Looking After Number One', 'Like Clockwork' and 'She's so Modern' they released 'Rat Trap'. It is the most unlikely of hits. It could hardly be further from *Grease*'s sweet teenage dreams of 1950s Middle America.

'Rat Trap' tells a tale from the darker side of Dublin nightlife based on Geldof's experiences

The Boomtown Rats are the most popular, and outrageous, band to emerge from Dublin's music scene.

A man advertises Freebird, a new independent record shop that has opened on Grafton Street.

The Phoenix Park on the day Pope John Paul II says mass.

at the Grand Canal meat factory. It features Dublin landmarks such as the Five Lamps, at the top of Amiens Street, the gasometer along the Liffey, an Italian café, flats and the meat factory. It is a story of poverty, street fights, urban blight, boredom, fighting parents and Billy and Judy who do not have the sweet teenage dreams of Danny and Sandy from *Grease* but have been caught in a rat trap from which there is no escape.

❖ ❖ ❖ ❖ ❖ ❖ ❖ ❖ ❖ ❖ ❖

Saturday, 29 September 1979

At 10 a.m., in glorious autumn sunshine, the Aer Lingus 747 carrying Pope John Paul II banks low over the Phoenix Park's Fifteen Acres. Over one million people look up and wave. It is the greatest welcome ever extended to a visitor to Ireland.

Two hours later, the Pontiff walks onto the altar on the huge stage.

The crowd burst into spontaneous cheers when he tells them, 'It is with great joy that I received the news that the Irish bishops had asked all the faithful to go to confession as part of a great spiritual preparation for my visit to Ireland. You could not have given me a greater joy or a greater gift.'

The Pope speaks directly to the youth who are present. He warns of the dangers of affluence and 'new trends'.

'Yes, Ireland, that has overcome so many difficult moments in her history, is being challenged in a new way today, for she is not immune from the influence of ideologies and trends which present-day civilisation and progress can carry with them. The very capability of mass media to bring the whole world into your homes produces a new kind of competition with values and trades that up until now have been alien to Irish society. Pervading materialism imposes its dominance on man today in many different forms and with aggressiveness that spares no one …'

1980–1993

A Time of Shadows and Light

Tuesday, 22 January 1980

Against a background of increasing oil prices, rising VAT and income tax rates, never before has the divide between rural and urban Ireland been so pronounced. And it is to those in Dublin that the gap seems widest.

Today, the largest demonstration in the history of the state winds its way, for hours, through the streets of the capital – 300,000 people are protesting against what they believe to be an unfair tax burden borne by those on salaries and wages, those who are part of the 'Pay As You Earn' (PAYE) system, those who mainly live in urban areas.

The protesters are angry about the small amount of tax paid by the self-employed and corporations, but they are most angry about the favourable treatment of Irish farmers. Because while 16 per cent of a PAYE worker's income is taken in tax, only 1 per cent is taken from farmers. Demonstrations are taking place in urban centres throughout the country but the Dublin march is by far the largest. This is not just because it is in the largest city. It is also because nowhere in Ireland is the disparity between the farmer and the income-tax payer most pronounced. In Dublin, there are just 1,000 farmers out of a population of 1 million. The city's residents believe they are paying way above their fair share of tax. So today Dublin gravediggers and journalists, teachers and business owners, civil servants and dockers, shop workers and labourers, even people who work in the tax office are on the streets, united in demanding a more equitable Irish taxation system.

PAYE workers march through the streets against what they regard as an unfair tax system that is biased against urban workers who pay income tax.

Wednesday, 19 March 1980

Nearly three years after the Boomtown Rats signed their record deal and went to London, another Irish band have made the breakthrough. Out of the group of Dublin bands that have included Radiators from Space, The Blades, The Virgin Prunes, Revolver, The Vipers and The Sinners, U2 have just signed with Island Records. Tonight they play their first gig as the next big band to come out of Dublin at Notting Hill, London.

U2 are not the most representative of Dublin bands. They formed three years ago in Clontarf's Mount Temple Comprehensive School, where creativity, open discussion and independent thinking were encouraged. Lead singer Paul Hewson is from Cedarwood Road, Glasnevin and now wants to be known as 'Bono'. Drummer Larry Mullins is from Artane. David Evans, known as 'the Edge', was born in England, as was Adam Clayton. First known as The Larry Mullins Band, then The Feedback, then The Hype, they are now known, enigmatically, as U2.

U2 have not been without their critics – some of their gigs have been interrupted, sometimes stopped, by people jumping on stage and attacking them. Though lacking the street cred of other bands – they do not follow the usual rock 'n' roll stereotypes of drink and drugs and singing about uncool subjects such as spirituality – they

Left: Material relating to some bands popular on Dublin's music scene.
Right: The Radiators from Space.

have built up a growing and loyal following. Last year a series of Sunday afternoon gigs on the stage to the rear of the Dandelion Market on St Stephen's Green and some Thursday nights at McGonagle's cemented their place as the most promising Dublin band in years.

They released their first single in September, an EP featuring 'Stories for Boys', 'Boy/Girl' and 'Out of Control', they supported Talking Heads on a tour of England, they beat off the Rats and Thin Lizzy for a number of *Hot Press* Music Awards, they appeared on *The Late Late Show*, they went on an 11-gig Irish tour, becoming the first Irish band since the Rats to play the National Stadium without having a hit abroad, and next month they start a tour of England. But what most people agree on is that there is nothing derivative about U2. According to the young music journalist Dave Fanning:

> They're an odd breed; they don't boogie, they don't rock steady and you'll never find them in any three-chord wonder, wham-bam-thank-you-mam, ongoing situation. The energy is controlled, the lead vocalist is mad and the drummer could kick-start the 46A. Perfect credentials. Their rock is rambling and spacey, minus keyboards, plus vitality, and frontman Paul Hewson is at once so bewildered and so adept at the task of dishing out the latter that … U2 are guaranteed to leave you breathless.

Although not universally popular, U2 from the northside of the city are the most promising band to emerge from the Dublin music scene since the Boomtown Rats in 1977.

The start of the first Dublin City Marathon. It is one of the first new street events in the city for a number of years.

The biggest selling single in the summer of 1980 is by a band from Bray, just outside Dublin. Bagatelle's 'Summer in Dublin' taps into a fleeting haunting summer in an imperfect city, where the air is thick with the stench of the polluted River Liffey, where drunks give financial advice on buses and where young people suddenly look so much better walking down Grafton Street in glorious sunshine.

'Down the river at four in the morning the abiding sound is of a rope tapping against a flagpole. Nobody's here. For a few hours now the roads lose all purpose but the traffic lights continue to change. There is something eerie about this, almost as though it were their work-to-rule in protest against the anarchy of the night. Down the river no-one can hear you scream. If a few people decided to throw you into the water for their amusement, there would be nothing you could do and nobody would ever know. But somewhere in the distance the other abiding sound of the dead city can be heard: an alarm bell is ringing in someone's property. Thieves are out tonight.'

Colm Tóibín, *In Dublin*, 30 October 1980

After nine years at 'Gaiety Green', the famous Dandelion Market closes on Sunday, 28 December 1980 to make way for some future commercial development. While some of the stallholders who sell second-hand clothes, craft items, bric-a-brac and jewellery will go out of business, others have found a new home in the Victorian South Great George's Street Arcade.

Friday-Saturday, 13-14 February 1981

Tonight tragedy strikes in the Stardust Ballroom on Kilmore Road in Artane. Over 800 people are in attendance at this long-established venue for a Valentine's disco. After the bar has closed at 1 a.m., a dance contest is taking place and, as people crowd around the dance floor on tables and chairs to watch 36 contestants, a fire breaks out.

As Patrick Hernandez's hit 'Born to be Alive' comes to an end, some of the patrons near a section closed off with a pull down blind start to feel warm, as though the central heating has turned up full blast. Soon people smell smoke and the fire is discovered behind the blind. As people continue dancing, others go over to look at what is going on behind the screen – some think a fight has broken out. The alarm is raised. The fire spreads.

Gardai outside the charred remains of the Stardust in Artane the day after the fire.

At 1.42 a.m. a barman dials 999. 'Would you come down to the Stardust Club in Artane as fast as you can,' he says. 'There is a large fire. There are over 800 people in the place. For God's sake quick, it's getting out of control.'

But it is already too late. Within a matter of minutes, 48 young people are dead from fire, from smoke, from the crush to get out and the fact that some exits are partially blocked – some had been made to look locked to deter people from letting in friends and one exit was actually locked.

Dublin is a city reeling from shock and grief as news of the tragedy spreads, and families affected search desperately for missing children.

A march in the support of hunger strikers in the H Blocks in Northern Ireland ends in a riot as marchers try to break through police lines to reach the British Embassy.

A march takes place in Dublin on Saturday, 18 July 1981 to protest against the death of IRA hunger strikers in Northern Ireland. Gardaí decide that the march must be stopped before it reaches the British Embassy. There is rioting and a baton charge – 50 people are injured in the worst political violence in the city for years.

The humble bicycle is making a comeback. In 1961 a cycling survey counted 164,364 bicycles passing various census points. In 1971 a similar survey counted just 32,976 – how quickly Dubliners had changed their transportation habits with increasing wealth and the lure of the car. But with the recession, rising petrol prices and traffic congestion that has reduced the average speed of traffic in the inner city to just 7mph, in 1981 the figure has gone back up to 50,103.

Thursday, 1 October 1981

It is a time of great change for Irish women. Equality legislation, increased social freedom, better education and travel opportunities, have all resulted in a wide range of choices being available for women in the 1980s – which job to aim for, where to live, with whom to live, to marry or not, to live with someone or not, to stay in or leave a bad marriage, whether or not to bring up a child alone. Every year young women from around the country move to Dublin for employment, new experiences and a better social life According to the latest census, there are 30,000 more women in Dublin than men. To help them survive life in the capital, Lorna Hogg has written *A Guide for Single Women in Ireland*.

Hogg provides mainly practical advice. Newcomers to Dublin should buy a large map of the city and order a copy of *In Dublin* and read the *Evening Press* and *Evening Herald* to find out what is going on. There are suggestions as to where to eat and what to do. There is advice on building a wardrobe – because, according to Hogg, learning to dress effectively is 'an absolute priority for the modern woman' – managing money – because 'money is power' – buying a car, buying a house and setting up a business.

While many women successfully navigate single life in Dublin, others are less successful, and for these Hogg outlines the tell-tale symptoms of alcoholism and signs of depression.

She also addresses the issue of relationships. According to Hogg, the biggest difference between the current generation of young women and those of previous generations is that they want a 'sharing' relationship, not one in which women are subservient to men or dependent on them.

But Hogg warns about the infidelities of Dublin's married men. Because not all are what they make themselves out to be. The single woman needs to be on the lookout for men who do not ask to be introduced to their friends and family, who do not ask about their day, who do not take an interest in their lives. She also advises

Mary Dunne from Dun Laoghaire, known to most Dubliners as 'Dancing Mary' or 'Mad Mary', is a familiar figure on O'Connell Street where she dances for the Holy Trinity and the Virgin Mary.

Friday, 8 January 1982 sees the largest snowfall in Dublin in living memory as 25 cm falls.

Maeve Binchy from Dalkey, an *Irish Times* journalist, is the talk of the literary world. Following on from the success of Central Line and Victoria Line, short stories about the seemingly anonymous lives of one's fellow underground traveller, earlier this year her book of connected stories set in the postal district 'Dublin 4' was a number one. Today she sells the rights to her first novel *Light a Penny Candle* for a record IR£52,000.

avoiding what she describes as Dublin's 'ineligible men' which include drunks, the confirmed drug addicts, the violent, the permanent womanisers and the gays and transvestites who marry women or form relationships with girls simply to convince either themselves or society, or both, that they are straight.

❖ ❖ ❖ ❖ ❖ ❖ ❖ ❖ ❖ ❖ ❖

Tuesday, 9 March 1982

Thirty-four-year-old Tony Gregory, TD for Dublin Central, gets up from his seat in Dáil Éireann and begins reading from a piece of paper. He is the only person in the chamber who is not wearing a tie, the only one who speaks with a working-class Dublin accent.

Gregory represents the north inner city, the part of Dublin that has been in continuous decline since independence, that has been without any plan except to get as many people out of it as possible. In the last ten years, Dublin's population has increased quicker than at any time since independence but the numbers living in the inner city have fallen by 30 per cent. It is a place with virtually no private investment, with the worst unemployment rate in the country (three times the national average), where Dubliners are the poorest. It is a place people do not go to unless they have to.

In the weeks since one of the closest general elections in the history of the state, Gregory has been the most expensive man in the country as political rivals Charles Haughey and Garret FitzGerald vied for his vote to become Taoiseach.

Haughey met Gregory on 23 February at 20 Summerhill Parade. It was in

the offices of the North City Centre Community Action Project where the only furnishings were a wooden table, some chairs, a ladder leaning against a wall, and a bare light bulb hanging from the ceiling flex. It was not the most auspicious surroundings to decide the political future of a country.

Gregory presented Haughey with a list of requests. After an hour and a half, the Fianna Fáil leader left. Nothing was signed at the time, but the substance of a deal had been outlined. In a subsequent meeting, Fine Gael leader FitzGerald was much less accommodating.

The paper Gregory has in his hand as he stands in the Dáil is the agreement that was eventually signed by Haughey.

In all, it is estimated that the 'Gregory deal' has secured £60 million worth of investment for the city centre, the largest single investment ever offered by an Irish government for the area.

Tony Gregory, TD, and Taoiseach Charles Haughey, who have agreed the biggest investment package for the inner city in the history of the state.

At 8.15 a.m., on Sunday, 29 August 1982, the Liffey's quays close and 60 corporation workers take hoods off new traffic signals and put them onto what are now the redundant ones, because this morning the flow of traffic along the quays is being reversed in an effort to speed things up by removing as many right turns across the river as possible. Two bridges have also been built to facilitate the change, the Matt Talbot Bridge which opened in 1978 and the Frank Sherwin Bridge, near Heuston Station, which opens today. At 8.30 a.m. traffic is allowed on the roads again but now cars going west are on the south side of the river and those going east are on the north.

Saturday, 19 March 1983

To try and change attitudes in a city that is often hostile to gays and lesbians, 200 people take part in a rights march on Saturday, 25 June 1983 between St. Stephen's Green and the GPO.

Four hundred people march from Liberty Hall to Fairview Park. They are protesting at the savage killing of 31-year-old Declan Flynn from Whitehall, at the lenient sentences handed down to his killers this week and at the violence that is regularly inflicted on the city's gay and lesbian population who exist in the city under the shadow of illegality and condemnation by the Catholic church.

Last September, Flynn had been attacked by five boys who, in the words of one, were out 'to get rid of queers from Fairview Park'. Flynn was kicked, beaten unconscious and died from inhaling his own blood.

Earlier this week, his killers walked free from court having only been given suspended sentences of between one and four years. In stark contrast to their sentences, a Dublin man was recently given 12 months in prison for stealing £20. When one of those convicted of Flynn's killing returned to Fairview, his friends brought him on a victory parade through the streets while singing 'We Are the Champions'.

As the marchers make their way to the park where Flynn was killed the reaction of onlookers varies. Some are bemused, some smirk derisively, others take their leaflets promoting tolerance.

In May 1983, the latest restaurant opens in the increasingly trendy Crown Alley area of Temple Bar. Called the Bad Ass Café, its lunchtime clientele of businessmen, politicians and legal figures tuck into food called 'Too Muchio', 'Almond in the Mood for Love' and 'I Scream You Scream'.

Tuesday, 20 September 1983

Until recently the Dublin drugs scene had consisted of people taking cannabis, hash and LSD as well as morphine and other drugs stolen from doctors' surgeries. No one was prepared for the arrival of heroin. In a matter of a few short years, this addictive and destructive drug extracted from the poppy plant has taken a grip on the city.

The first major heroin consignment arrived in Dublin in June 1979, after the fall of the Shah of Iran. But it was only after the Soviet invasion of Afghanistan in December that heroin started to become widely available.

Now Dublin is one of Europe's heroin capitals, where the emaciated, desperate addict has become a feature of its streets. It is estimated that there are at least 1,500 heroin addicts in the city, with 3,000 more experimenting with the drug, many of whom will soon join the ranks of the addicts.

In April, the first official report into

Magill magazine features an exposé on one of the city's heroin dealers.

what was being witnessed by families, priests, gardaí, community leaders and doctors was published. It showed that a generation is being destroyed by heroin. Concentrating on the north inner city area, the findings were shocking. One in every ten of the 15–24-year-olds in the area is a heroin abuser – the percentage is even higher for girls aged between 15 and 19. Parts of Dublin are as bad as the New York ghettoes were in the early 1970s. While the inner city flats are the worst affected areas, heroin is a significant problem in Dublin 8, the towers and flats of Ballymun and Dún Laoghaire. But no area is immune.

Unsurprisingly, according to the report, most heroin abusers come from the ranks of the long-term unemployed. For these young people, Dublin has become a world they want to escape from. In the words of one addict, when he takes heroin '… reality goes away. You are just nice. You are floating on air … You are in a world of your own.' According to one person involved in the treatment of heroin abusers, 'Heroin is beautiful stuff. You've got to realise that. It's the perfect high. But the cost is enormous – overdose, police, family breakdown, losing friends, turning to crime, physical degeneration, liver diseases, jail, mental hospitals.'

Heroin is not only destroying addicts. It is also decimating communities.

One of the main problems is crime. Needing ever-increasing doses, addicts quickly develop habits costing over £100 a day. As a result, robberies and burglaries in the city have increased dramatically. Since 1979, the number of crimes reported in Dublin has increased from 36,000 to over 60,000. Nothing has affected the city's conviviality more than the heroin epidemic.

Prison is no deterrent. More than half of the addicts interviewed for the report had already been in Mountjoy. There is evidence that heroin is becoming available in prison while within a week of release, most are back on the drug that had landed them in jail.

With a gram of heroin being bought in England for £100 and selling on Dublin's streets for £1,500, drug dealers are becoming very wealthy on misery and death. There are dealers with American gangster-style nicknames such as 'Ma Baker', 'Bugsy' and 'the Dukes' but the majority of the heroin trade is believed to be controlled by three criminal families.

An indication of the rate of growth of the drug has been the dramatic increase in the amount of heroin seized by gardaí. In 1979, the force seized 5 grams. In 1980, it was 105 grams, in 1981 170,000 grams and last year 1.2 kilograms. This year, the city has been flooded with heroin, with well over 2 kilograms already intercepted.

Despite the huge money being made, or perhaps because of it, drug dealers are fighting among themselves for control of the city. On 10 April Gerry Hourigan, a small-time Ballymun dealer with ambitions, became the first person to be killed in a drug turf war. He was gunned down by a man on a motorcycle in the flats complex.

So what is being done to tackle the problem?

Ireland's only day treatment centre is at Jervis Street. Staffed by a doctor and three social workers, it has a small waiting room, four cramped offices, two toilets and a storeroom. The staff face a near hopeless task. In 1979, the daily average number of patients being treated there for heroin abuse was five. Now it is over 230. Every month, 100 new patients – children as young as 13, pregnant women – are presenting themselves. But those coming to Jervis Street are not the majority of heroin abusers. Those who make their way there are the ones who have run out of drugs, who have been told by a judge to go for treatment or else face prison and those who are so sick from the effects of heroin that they simply cannot cope any longer.

There are just 43 full-time members of the Garda Drug Squad, with less than a dozen on duty at any one time. Among these are the 'mockeys', a new undercover unit operating in the inner city. Scruffily dressed, posing as junkies, they have arrested scores of drug dealers. Their biggest catches have been members of the Dunne

People from areas most affected by the heroin epidemic take to the streets in opposition to the drug dealers.

family. In February, an unemployed Henry Dunne, whose Crumlin corporation house has mock-Tudor-style woodwork, a bay window, porch, mock Georgian door, sauna and bar, was sentenced to ten years for heroin dealing. But usually the ones the Gardaí arrest are not the main players; they are the addicts who get heroin in return for every £10 deal they sell, children as young as 13 who are paid £5 a day.

In the face of the heroin onslaught, some communities have been taking matters into their own hands. Last year, the first Concerned Parents Against Drugs groups were set up in Hardwicke Street flats in the inner city and St Teresa's Gardens in the Coombe to drive drug dealers out.

The stark picture painted by the April report prompted the government to set up a 'task force' to try and tackle the heroin problem. Though it has not completed its work, today the government announces a programme to combat drug abuse. It includes amending the Misuse of Drugs Act, introducing a new Criminal Justice Bill, establishing a new treatment centre and setting up drug awareness programmes.

The government's announcement is a start. But there are few who believe that these actions will be in any way sufficient to control the heroin dragon that is being chased by thousands of people in the city.

❖ ❖ ❖ ❖ ❖ ❖ ❖ ❖ ❖ ❖ ❖

January 1984

It is the worst of times in Dublin. The tax marches of 1980 are now just a memory, because people in the city are less concerned with the amount of tax they pay than they are with keeping a job they might be lucky enough to have. For four years, Ireland has been in the grip of economic recession. Nowhere has been hit worse than Dublin.

Since 1980, thousands of Dubliners have lost their jobs. Manufacturing employment has been decimated. Among the longer-standing firms that have closed are the Smyth clothing factory in Balbriggan which had been in business for 200 years – the firm was once so famous for its underwear that the term 'Balbriggan' is in the dictionary for knitted cotton underwear. Dublin Meat Packers in Ballymun and International Meat Producers on Grand Canal Street – where Bob Geldof worked – have closed. Clondalkin Paper Mills shut with the loss of 450 jobs. The Rank bakery and the Mother's Pride bakery on North Portland Street went out of business, as did Lemon's, one of Dublin's oldest sweet companies, and Ever Ready at Portobello Harbour, the last battery manufacturer in the city.

With visitor numbers falling, the tourist trade has been badly hit. The Gresham, the Shelbourne and every other city hotel has had to let staff go, while the Royal Hibernian Hotel, the oldest hotel in Ireland, which opened in 1751, has shut.

It is not only the older firms that have been affected. The Talbot car assembly plant, Beechlawn Knitting Mills in Tallaght, the Bally Manufacturing Company, Data Terminal Electronics, Janell Wear clothing manufacturer in Finglas, Tallaght's Telektron plant, the Plessey Telephone company in Swords and Kilmainham, Weatherglaze in Walkinstown, the European Printing Corporation in Coolock and Roadstone's Inchicore works, have all shut with the loss of thousands of jobs.

Running at 20 per cent, Dublin has the highest unemployment rate in the country. Some areas such as the inner city, Ballyfermot, Cabra, Finglas and parts of Crumlin and Artane have more than 30 per cent unemployed. In Tallaght, the figure is closer to 50 per cent. But it is not just the working-class areas that are suffering. St Vincent de Paul is now under pressure to help the new middle-class unemployed.

❖ ❖ ❖ ❖ ❖ ❖ ❖ ❖ ❖ ❖ ❖

March 1984

Unemployment, crime, emigration, dereliction. There seems to be no end of reasons to leave Dublin. And that is what is happening. For the first time in decades, more people are emigrating from the capital than are moving into it from other parts of Ireland.

Posters for sale at Westmoreland Street.

Despite the depressed conditions, *In Dublin* magazine is far from downbeat about the capital. To celebrate its two-hundredth issue, it publishes a list of 200 reasons that people should stay in Dublin, 200 reasons for Dubliners not to emigrate, 200 reasons not to give up.

From being on a suburban train as it leaves the Dalkey tunnel and the view of Killiney Bay opens out below, to playing rings in Kavanagh's pub in Glasnevin.

From sipping a glass of whiskey in Kehoe's pub on South Anne Street, to going to the corporation's Fruit and Veg Market on Chancery Street.

From the 31 Turner watercolours exhibited in the National Gallery in January's dim light, to the sound of a saxophone or tin whistle echoing in Merchant's Arch by the Ha'Penny Bridge.

From the near-forgotten – except for cider parties – War Memorial Gardens in Islandbridge, to Ricardo's Pool Hall on Camden Street.

From the 'Why Go Bald' sign at the bottom of South Great George's Street, to the reading room of the National Library.

From the brass bands in the tea tent at the Dublin Horse Show, to the half-wild horses of Ballyfermot and Finglas.

From eating fresh cod and a large single from Burdock's on Werburgh Street, to watching the sun set on the Sugarloaf from the Baily Lighthouse on Howth Head.

Because even in this, the worst of times, there are many things to still love in the city, still things that make Dublin unique.

At 7.57 a.m. on Thursday, 19 July 1984 some 20 kilometres below the ground south-west of Caernarvon, Wales, two tectonic plates slip against each other. Moments later, the effects reach Dublin. For between five and ten seconds the city is shaken by an earthquake measuring 5.5 on the Richter scale. It is the largest earthquake to hit the city.

Monday, 23 July 1984

It has been the subject of much carping and begrudging. It has been variously condemned as providing a new way for Dublin people to kill themselves and a 'White Elephant on Tracks'. But on this, its first day of full service, the Dublin Area Rapid Transit system, or DART for short, the critics are conspicuously absent.

From the start it is obvious that the DART is going to be a success.

The new suburban train that runs between Howth and Bray is the most important development in the city's public transport system since the world's third steam railway, the first commuter railway, between Westland Row and Dún Laoghaire was opened almost 150 years ago.

The DART is similar to systems that have been installed in Hong Kong and Newcastle, bringing an end to some of the most obsolete rolling stock in Europe, sickening diesel fumes and a slow, unreliable service. The new green-liveried carriages built in West Germany are powered by 1,500 volts carried along 50 miles of overhead wires supported by 1,700 masts. An air-suspension system ensures a smooth ride, there is upholstered seating, push-button sliding doors, renovated stations, electronic ticket checkers and, most importantly, the promise of a fast, reliable and frequent service.

Last Monday, the first DART left Bray – to everyone's amusement it was five minutes late. But by the end of the day, 35,000 people had used it, 15,000 more than

The DART is the biggest change in the city's public transport system since the ending of the tram service. It is hugely popular in the communities between Bray and Howth.

the old diesel train. Yesterday 45,000 people travelled, more than on any day in the railway's history.

It is apparent that the DART is going to change the pattern of travel in Dublin. But its effect is predicted to go well beyond merely how people will get from A to B. Already it is being estimated that houses along the line have increased in value by between £5,000 and £10,000, while it is thought that the DART's late-night service will lead to a large increase in people partaking of Dublin's nightlife.

In another sign of the deepening economic crisis, on Wednesday, 25 July 1984 Woolworths announces it will be closing all of its Irish shops in October. Having set up its first shop on Grafton Street in 1914 and the second on Henry Street in 1918, the closures mark the end of an era in the city.

Nearly two decades after the Myles Wright report, the first piece of transport infrastructure that it recommended finally opens, on Monday, 22 October 1984. It is the East Link Bridge, at the mouth of the Liffey, built to take some of the city's north–south traffic away from the centre. It is estimated that each day, 22,000 cars will pay the 20-pence toll.

Monday, 8 April 1985

A former military base at Spike Island in Cork Harbour opens as a prison for the third time. The first was during the Famine, the second during the War of Independence and this time it is to help deal with the largest crime wave in the capital since independence.

Dublin is a city stalked by fear. Heroin, social dislocation, poverty, boredom and rampant unemployment have made it a dangerous place.

Every week, a litany of calls are made to Dublin garda stations reporting break-ins, assaults, handbag snatches, drunken youths fighting on the streets, alarms going off at premises, fights on buses, at discos, in pubs, vandalism, stabbings, women being harassed on the streets, armed robberies, rowdy youths annoying residents, youths throwing stones at passers-by, at buses, there are gang fights, buildings set on fire, people wielding knives on the streets, bus crews being attacked. But the crime that epitomises the current state of near-lawlessness is 'joyriding'.

The stealing of high-powered cars has become a feature of Dublin's nightlife.

Everywhere is affected by the car thieves, but the most notorious areas are the inner city, Tallaght, Ballyfermot, Coolock, Finglas and Crumlin. So far this year, it is estimated that more than 300 cars have been stolen in the city. Such is the prevalence of joyriding that taxi drivers are stopping at *green* lights to look out for speeding stolen cars. In February, the latest deaths occurred when three Coolock teenagers driving a stolen BMW crashed head-on into another car at Swords killing the driver of the other car, Dermot Lea, a 38-year-old teacher, as well as one of the joyriders.

Mountjoy Prison, supposedly a symbol of law and order, has become one of lawlessness and disorder. In the last five years, the numbers of people committed to Mountjoy Prison has increased by 60 per cent. The vast majority of its inmates are from Dublin, and most of those are from a few working-class postal districts, some within a short walking distance of the prison. Such are the numbers being sent to Mountjoy that the prison is operating a 'revolving door' system – when someone is committed they are either released immediately, or someone who is in for a less serious crime is let out. To help solve the problem of overcrowding in Mountjoy and to try and deal with the cohort of joyriders, Spike Island is once again called into action.

Burnt-out stolen cars have become a familiar site around the city as joyriding has become a favourite pastime.

Wednesday, 3 April 1985

After three years work, a team of 22 planners has produced 'The Eastern Regional Development Organisation Settlement Strategy 2011'. Few people who are not professionally connected with the future planning of the region may read the report, but it is going to have a huge impact on the future growth of Dublin and the surrounding counties for the next quarter century. The part of the country that is already by far the most urbanised is set to become even more so. According to the strategy, Dublin, Meath, Kildare and Wicklow will become home to 500,000 more people. This will increase the population of the Eastern region from 1.3 million people to 1.8 million.

One of the main social changes will be the increasing participation of women in the workplace because they will have fewer children and therefore more time for work; in addition, more women will earn university degrees and pursue a career. Whether inside or outside marriage, the very notion of the male being the sole 'breadwinner' is coming to end.

According to the strategy, the changes to some communities will be huge. Blanchardstown will grow from 35,000 people to 125,000, Lucan from 15,000 to 105,000, Swords from 20,000 to 100,000, Leixlip/Celbridge/Maynooth from 17,000 to 67,000, Donabate from 6,000 to 56,000, Bray from 25,000 to 48,000, Greystones/Delgany from 25,000 to 47,000 and Balbriggan/Skerries from 20,000 to 40,000.

The sheer scale of the population shift outlined in the strategy is causing alarm. Some people regard it as a disaster for Dublin, with more suburbs, more cars and more new roads, all centred on the capital. People fear the consequences of adding another 500,000 people to a city with high unemployment, widespread crime, poor housing and insufficient transport infrastructure.

❖ ❖ ❖ ❖ ❖ ❖ ❖ ❖ ❖ ❖ ❖

Saturday, 29 June 1985

It began last August in Christchurch, New Zealand, with 15 shows at the Town Hall Auditorium. Since then, U2 have played at 86 venues in Australia, France, Belgium, Holland, England, Scotland, Czechoslovakia, Germany, the United States, Canada, Norway, Sweden, Italy and Switzerland. Tonight the four boys from Dublin's northside are back in town.

Since their last Irish concert in the Phoenix Park two years ago, U2 have become the country's biggest ever musical export. But unlike other bands such as The Boomtown Rats and Thin Lizzy who moved to England when they made it big, U2, despite the world tours and international acclaim, have remained Dublin-based. At each concert on their world tour they remind their fans that they are a Dublin band. And tonight when Bono walks out onto the Croke Park stage he proudly tells the nearly 60,000 that 'The Jacks Are Back!'

The Croke Park gig is their first headline stadium show. Ten thousand have come from Northern Ireland, a thousand from Britain and some have even come from America to see U2 play in front of their home crowd. The area around Croke Park has been thronged with young people all day, leaving the area littered with empty flagons of cider. But all has been peaceful.

U2 start their show with '11 O'Clock Tick Tock' and 90 minutes later end it with '10'. It is a triumphal return for the Dublin band. It is also an evening of hope and optimism for a generation that has had little cause for either in the dole-queue summer of 1985.

❖ ❖ ❖ ❖ ❖ ❖ ❖ ❖ ❖ ❖ ❖

Thursday, 28 November 1985

A book is published called *The Destruction of Dublin* by *Irish Times* journalist Frank McDonald. McDonald clearly loves Dublin. And it is also clear that he is angry

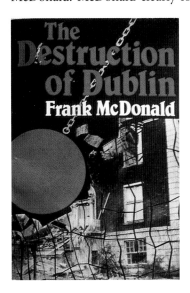

A book by an *Irish Times*' journalist sheds light on the forces that have destroyed many of the city's historic buildings since the early 1960s.

at what has happened to it over more than two decades. At what the developers, the planners and the politicians have done to what was once a beautiful city.

The Destruction of Dublin documents the assault on the city that has been taking place since the early 1960s. Lamenting the losses of fine Georgian buildings and decrying the construction of modern, unsympathetic buildings, he sheds light on the murky links that have existed between the city's politicians and developers. He names names, points the finger and lays the blame for what has happened to Dublin since O'Connell Bridge House, Hawkins House,

Liberty Hall and the ESB offices scarred what had once been an almost uniformly Georgian city. McDonald brings the story right up to date with the construction of Sam Stephenson's Dublin Corporation Civic Offices at Wood Quay. Reading *The Destruction of Dublin* will anger anyone who cares for the city. But McDonald does not excuse its citizens. Because they too are culpable. 'People get the cities they deserve,' McDonald writes. 'And if our capital city has been reduced to a shambles, it is because we never cared enough to save it. Through our own apathy, we acquiesced in the destruction of Dublin. We can't even say that the city was destroyed before our very eyes because, when it comes to our environment, most of us seem to be blind as bats. We simply do not *see* what is going on around us. If half of O'Connell Street were whipped away tomorrow morning, most Dubliners would probably shrug their shoulders and say, 'So what else is new?' Others would bemoan the loss and wonder why, and fewer still would take the trouble to find out.'

❖ ❖ ❖ ❖ ❖ ❖ ❖ ❖ ❖ ❖

Friday–Sunday, 7–9 February 1986

Just how long can a crisis remain a crisis? Because a crisis, by definition, is supposed to be a turning point. If one goes on for long enough, the crisis ends and the situation

Self-contained suburban life is becoming the defining feature of the city. Here a local supermarket serves many of the needs of the people of Kilbarrack.

becomes fact, just the way things are. With the spectre of the population explosion recommended by the ERDO report and the salutary warning of Frank McDonald's *Destruction of Dublin*, the city seems to be on the verge of being beyond saving. But at the Synod Hall of Christchurch Cathedral, there is a conference called 'Dublin in Crisis' being attended by people who do not believe it is too late. But they believe the clock on Dublin's future is at 'five minutes to midnight'.

For three days, the conference discusses many of the city's problems. And there is no shortage. Dozens of streets that have been left derelict by road-widening plans from the 1970s. Among these are the entire quays. The buildings along the feature that has been the almost defining characteristic of the city have been falling apart. There has not been a planning application for any building along the river for years because every building is destined for demolition to make way for new roads on either side of the river. The now not-so-new town of Tallaght has 70,000 residents but its only amenities are a few shops, a few youth clubs, five pubs and a completely inadequate public transport infrastructure – a plan to have a similar rail system to the DART was dropped due to lack of funds. There is chronic air pollution. There is unemployment. There is an unprecedented decline in the birth rate – people seem to be giving up on the city. In the last five years, the population has increased by just 15,000, the lowest increase since the 1950s.

There is little good news.

But perhaps the conference will be seen as a turning point. Because for the first time, there are not just conservationists, community leaders, activists and environmentalists talking to themselves at the Synod Hall. There is a new generation of planners, architects, academics and economists in attendance. But most importantly

246

there are some key decision-makers. There is the Taoiseach, Garret FitzGerald. There is Frank Feely, Dublin City Manager, and his Chief Planner, both of whom have been the focus of much criticism from conservationists. Everyone in the Synod Hall might not agree on everything, but they do agree on the most important thing: they all want to make Dublin a better place. And that might be just enough for a start.

❖ ❖ ❖ ❖ ❖ ❖ ❖ ❖ ❖ ❖ ❖

Friday, 23 May 1986

A new airline called Ryanair has its first flight from Dublin Airport. Its 15-seat turbo prop aeroplane takes off for Luton and finally breaks the end of the monopoly that has been enjoyed by Aer Lingus and British Airways on the Dublin–London route, one of the busiest and most profitable air corridors in the world. The opening of the route was pushed by the European Commissioner with responsibility for competition policy, Peter Sutherland from Foxrock, and was facilitated by the British government's deregulation policy.

Until Ryanair's arrival, the lowest return fare to London had been £209 – this had to be booked a month in advance, could not be cancelled and the traveller had to stay at least one Saturday night. When Ryanair announced its 'supermarket fares' in April they were less than half the existing fare, had no restrictions and under-2s could travel free. Aer Lingus and British Airways immediately dropped their fares to match Ryanair's. Ryanair then reduced theirs by a penny.

With Ryanair planning to introduce flights to Rome, Paris, Brussels and Amsterdam, it is already being predicted that fares will halve. As the small plane heads off to London, air travel to and from Ireland will never be the same again.

❖ ❖ ❖ ❖ ❖ ❖ ❖ ❖ ❖ ❖ ❖

Tuesday, 2 December 1986

Today, Dublin's Lord Mayor, Bertie Ahern, officially opens two three-storey office buildings flanking a domed courtyard with a BP petrol station at Usher's Quay. It may not seem a landmark event but it is the first development that has benefitted from tax breaks designed to bring life back to the city centre.

Last October, seven months after the 'Dublin in Crisis' conference, an Urban Renewal and Finance Act came into effect to try and address the problem of urban decay. It marked a turning point in the official attitude towards older buildings and inner-city renewal.

Under its provisions, property developers will be given significant tax breaks to invest in areas of the city that would otherwise remain derelict. The smallest of the designated areas is Henrietta Street, Dublin's most intact Georgian street. The largest area encompasses Gardiner Street Upper, Gardiner Street Lower, Dorset Street and Beresford Place, the most deprived area in the city. With the corporation dropping the road-widening scheme along the Liffey, both sides of the river have been included. There are also the 27 acres of the Custom House docks. This area is to be developed by a development authority. Finally, in the suburbs, the commercial centre of Tallaght is included in the scheme to encourage the long-awaited building of the town centre.

❖ ❖ ❖ ❖ ❖ ❖ ❖ ❖ ❖ ❖ ❖

Thursday 16 April, 1987

The Commitments is not the first novel to be set among modern working-class suburban Dubliners. In 1984, Dermot Bolger's *Nightshift* was set in a Finglas factory. But this debut novel by Roddy Doyle, a teacher of geography and English at Greendale Community School in Kilbarrack, is different.

Told in the voices of the young working class, with their humour, their curses, their slagging, their lack of confidence, their bravado, *The Commitments* is set in the fictitious north-side working-class suburb of 'Barrytown'. It follows a group of Dublin youths who form a band to stop themselves spending the rest of their lives being 'tossers'. The leader of

the band is Jimmy Rabbitte who does not want to follow the route of other Dublin bands – the ad for auditions explicitly stated that 'rednecks and southsiders need not apply', while anyone influenced by U2 is certainly not welcome.

Once assembled, the band is given a mission by Rabbitte. He believes that Dublin needs soul. And people such as them, from a place like Barrytown, are the very ones to bring it because, according to Rabbitte, if the Irish are the blacks of Europe, Dubliners are the blacks of Ireland and the northsiders are the blacks of Dublin.

❖ ❖ ❖ ❖ ❖ ❖ ❖ ❖ ❖ ❖

Friday, 12 February 1988

As soon as the lights dim in the Savoy Cinema and the opening scenes of *The Courier* flicker onto the screen it is obvious that this is not a typical Irish movie.

For one thing *The Courier* is set in Dublin. This is not *The Quiet Man*. Not *Ryan's Daughter*. It is also not a period piece but set in modern Dublin, the here and the now. This is unusual.

And this Dublin of *The Courier* is not that of tourist brochures. There is no Trinity College, no St Stephen's Green, no Phoenix Park, no Ha'Penny Bridge. Like *The Commitments* in literature, *The Courier* shows Dublin, and Dubliners, as they have never been seen before.

The Courier is made by three Dubliners – Hilary McLoughlin, Frank Deasy and Joe Lee. One of the directors described it as 'a very, very violent film about Dublin, a very violent city'.

While *The Courier* could be set in any western city, from the opening scenes showing the Poolbeg chimneys, the gasometer, the docks, Liberty Hall, streets clogged with traffic and the flats at Ballymun, Dublin is very much a central character.

Following a love story set against an underworld of gangsters, drug dealers and heroin addicts, there is nothing about being Irish, or struggling with Irish identity. The only country accent belongs to a police detective investigating the capital's gangland scene. The only traditional Irish music comes from a pathetic lone busker who plays his accordion to a deserted street. Instead the movie's music comes from Hothouse Flowers, U2, Aslan, Something Happens and Lord John White.

When the credits roll, the lights come up and the people who have watched *The Courier* walk out into the cool night air on O'Connell Street, they all look at the city in a different way.

A view of the Ha'Penny Bridge on the day of the annual UCD and TCD Boat Race gives an example of the ability of Dubliners to ignore authority.

Friday, 17 June 1988

'Dublin's Great in '88'. Or at least so goes the slogan for Dublin's Millennium year. After the successes of 'Galway 500' in 1984 and 'Cork 800' in 1985, Dublin City Manager Frank Feely thought Dublin should get in on the act. The year chosen by the corporation for Dublin's anniversary was more than a little arbitrary. Because there are many more suitable years which could be said to mark the centenary of the birth of the city of Dublin – the Viking settlement of Dyflin dates back to 841 while in 917, a permanent trading post was established on the Liffey. But 988, when High King Mael Cechnaill captured Dublin from the Vikings, was conveniently near. So,

'The other great myth ... was that of 'the true Dub'. The man whose great-great-great grandad had walked the cobbled streets, worked the ancient city trades and probably even – if current historical research on her sideline occupation is to be believed – contracted nefarious social diseases from Molly Malone. A city by its nature is comprised of migrants and the children and grandchildren of migrants. Dublin – like the country it is capital of – has a blessedly bastardised population with each generation producing its own influx of fresh blood and vitality. This folksy nostalgia has created the illusion that somehow the real Dublin is dead, the real Dubliners scattered and dying as some alien city is rising in its place. To me, at least, a real Dubliner is anyone who has been born or has chosen to live there and now regards the city as his or her home, the real Dublin is wherever they stake their claim to that home.'

Dermot Bolger (ed.), *Invisible Cities: The New Dubliners*, 1988

at least officially, Dublin is 1,000 years old this year. But for most people, it makes no difference whether or not it is the right date. Because Dubliners of all backgrounds have not had much to celebrate about their city for many years and now they are embracing their opportunity.

Gulliver, a character from Dubliner Jonathan Swift's *Gulliver's Travels*, makes his way down the Liffey during the Millennium year.

The year began with the Lord Mayor, Carmencita Hederman, hosting a 'Millennium Ball' in the Mansion House, the 'Millennium Anthem' being launched on the New Year's Eve *Late Late Show*, the presentation of specially made silver ingot pendants to the first three Dubliners born in the Millennium year – the very first was 8lb 6oz Sinead Lambe from Clonsilla – 50,000 people availing of free hot whiskeys and half price New Year's Day DART fares, and 160,000 'Millennium milk bottles' being delivered to doorsteps throughout Dublin.

There have been hundreds of Millennium events including exhibitions, the largest of which is the corporation's that showed how much they do for the city – from housing to libraries, community development to roads, water works to public parks. There has been free music, literary pub crawls, an international piano competition, celebrations of Dublin street games, of Dublin writers, there was a Millennium stamp issued and last month a Millennium 50-pence coin was put into circulation. A number of Dubliners have been specially honoured by the Lord Mayor, including actress Maureen Potter who has given decades of enjoyment to theatre-goers, and cyclist Stephen Roche for winning the Tour de France, Giro d'Italia and World Championships in 1987.

Among the physical developments in the city during the year have been the laying of the foundation stone for Ireland's first modern, five-star hotel at Earlsfort Terrace, to be called the Conrad, the refurbishment of Dublin Castle, and the beginning of the construction of the International Financial Services Centre at Custom House Dock. St Stephen's Green Shopping Centre is nearing completion seven years after the Dandelion Market closed, the Viking Adventure Centre, celebrating the early history of the city, opened, Grafton Street has been repaved, the central pedestrian mall of O'Connell Street reinstated, while the city's bridges have been floodlit as though they are works of art.

Today, one of the most eagerly awaited Millennium events is taking place in the middle of O'Connell Street, on what was once the site of Nelson's Pillar. Hoarding is removed to reveal the city's newest piece of public sculpture. It is a gift to the city from businessman Michael Smurfit as tribute to his father, Jefferson Smurfit.

The sculpture is of Anna Livia Plurabelle, a character from James Joyce's *Finnegans Wake*. Reclining in a fountain's flowing water, she is the personification of the River Liffey.

Dubliners might not have been able to have their say in what sculpture would be commissioned for the most important site in the city, but they are having it now. 'Brilliant. Very impressive,' Joseph Ward from Phibsborough tells a reporter. But others are not convinced. Bernadette Moran from Finglas says, 'Oh God – she's ugly. It looks like a body pulled out of the river after 20 years.' Jude Flynn from Rialto

In the 1988 Dublin Corporation Draft Development Plan, the single most important objective is to 'reinforce the core of the city as the commercial, cultural and social centre'. For the first time, it lists interiors of buildings for preservation, while the proposed widening of the roads along the quays has been abandoned and the plans for road widenings and major junctions curtailed.

At 7.30 p.m. on Monday, 18 September 1989 hundreds of thousands of people tune in to the first episode of RTÉ's new soap. Since Tolka Row finished in 1968 Irish soaps have been set in the countryside. There have been The Riordans, Bracken and, most recently, Glenroe. But tonight Fair City, like its Dublin predecessor Tolka Row, is set in another fictional northside suburb. This time it is called Carrigstown.

says, 'She looks like a half-unwrapped mummy from one of those Egyptian tombs.'
Marie Haman from Glasnevin tells a reporter, 'She certainly looks like 'the floozie
in the jacuzzi' … Every hen party and every stag party in Dublin will be throwing
someone in the fountain with her.'

The West Link Bridge crossing the River Liffey at the Strawberry Beds opens on Sunday,
11 March 1990. It is the first section of the 'Western Parkway' proposed by Myles Wright
in 1967. Some 385 metres long, 37 metres high, the height of Liberty Hall and made with
1,500 tonnes of reinforced steel and 11,000 cubic metres of concrete, it is the second
biggest bridge in Ireland, after Derry's Foyle River Bridge.

April 1990

Cranes have returned to the city's skyline in numbers not seen since the 1970s. After years
of economic recession, there are signs that, at last, the economy might be improving.

On the south side, there are new housing estates at Carysfort College in Blackrock
and St Helen's in Booterstown while on the north side, large housing estates are
being built at Ayrfield in Dublin 13 and on the Navan Road. But the parts of the
city showing the greatest activity are in the areas designated for urban renewal. In
the last four years hundreds of millions of pounds have been put into construction
projects in these areas by private developers, by the corporation and by the Custom
House Dock Development Authority.

More than half of all office developments are taking place in the designated areas.
The largest of these is the International Financial Services Centre (IFSC) at Custom
House Dock. Since 1960, just 47 of 389 office developments that were built in the
city have been on the north side. But at Custom House Dock, the single biggest
property project undertaken in Ireland in the twentieth century is in progress.

There is building
activity around the
city for the first
time in many years.
Urban renewal
schemes are being
built in designated
areas in the city,
while the long
awaited commercial
centre of the 'new'
town of Tallaght,
called the Square is
nearing completion.
But the biggest
building site is in
the docks where the
new International
Financial Services
Centre is being built.

It is not just the Liffey views that are attracting such interest but also the 10 per cent corporate tax rate for the insurance, currency, computer software and money management firms that will be based there. So far, the IFSC has attracted leading Irish companies such as Allied Irish Banks and Bank of Ireland but also some of the most important financial services firms including Chase Manhattan, Citibank, Sumitomo Bank (the world's largest), Barings Bank, Nat West, Credit Lyonnaise, Germany's largest insurance firm Colonia, Marsh and McLennan, and Dresdner, Germany's second-largest fund management group. It is estimated that there will be a total of 6,000–7,000 people working there. Few will have voted for Tony Gregory in 1982 and many will be earning salaries many times that of the average Dubliner.

It is not just offices that are being built in the city. The most remarkable change is that thousands of new residential units, mainly apartments, are also under construction. The Liffey quays, which did not see one single planning application between 1975 and 1986, have residential developments at Arran Court, Sarsfield Court, Fisherman's Wharf, Ellis Quay, Merchant's Quay, Ormond Quay and Bridgewater Quay.

There are also significant developments around Christchurch Cathedral including Christchurch Square, Inns Court at Winetavern Street and the City Gate development at Bridge Street. Meanwhile, at Tallaght, Ireland's largest shopping centre called The Square is nearing completion.

❖ ❖ ❖ ❖ ❖ ❖ ❖ ❖ ❖ ❖ ❖

Saturday, 2 June 1990

Sinead O'Connor from Glenageary is one of the biggest-selling musical artists in the world.

Until now, Irish music success in the British charts has been almost exclusively male, with Thin Lizzy, The Boomtown Rats and U2 leading the way. The only female Irish artist to reach the number one slot in the British charts was Dana with the song that won the 1970 Eurovision song contest, 'All Kinds of Everything'. But one of the biggest music sensations of the year is Sinead O'Connor, from Glenageary, who could hardly be more different.

O'Connor is a 22-year-old skinhead with forthright views. Her first album, *The Lion and the Cobra*, which she produced herself, was one of the most unusual albums of the 1980s. Her second album, *I Do Not Want What I Have Not Got*, is selling 400,000 each week worldwide and has been number one in Britain, Switzerland, Australia and Canada. Today marks its sixth week at number one on the American album charts. After U2's *The Joshua Tree*, it is only the second album by an Irish artist to top the American charts.

❖ ❖ ❖ ❖ ❖ ❖ ❖ ❖ ❖ ❖ ❖

Sunday, 1 July 1990

There has never been anything like it before. Never. It all started three weeks ago, on 11 June. Since then something has fundamentally changed.

Over the last three weeks, there has been other news in the city. While the government announced the best employment figures for six years, a study by the University of Reading ranked Dublin as the hundred and first worst city in Europe in terms of unemployment, business vitality and tourism. Open casting took place in the Mansion House for roles in a movie adaptation of Roddy Doyle's novel *The Commitments*. A statue of James Joyce was unveiled at North Earl Street on Bloomsday. The Dublin team reached the Leinster hurling final for the first time since 1964. The leaders of every EU state were in Dublin for a European summit. But none of that was important. None of that compared to Ireland's participation in the soccer World Cup in Italy.

Dublin is the traditional centre of the Irish soccer world. But it is not just those who support the League of Ireland teams, or English ones, who have been interested. The tempo of the city has fallen into line with the World Cup. Pubs, off-licences and fast-food takeaways have never had it so good, while restaurants, theatres and cinemas have struggled. Even The Rolling Stones had to cancel a concert because the distracted population of the city had not been buying tickets.

If someone had just arrived in Dublin on the evening of 11 June and did not know any better, they might have thought that a warning of war had been received because everyone in the city seemed to be in hiding. The streets were practically deserted. But at 9.30 p.m. the eerie silence was broken by tens of thousands, hundreds of thousands of roars from people in friends' houses, in pubs, in clubs, in hotels, or among the 6,000 at the RDS watching four, giant video screens when Kevin Sheedy scored a goal that earned Ireland a draw against England. When the final whistle went 20 minutes later, there were cheers, not for victory, but for avoiding defeat.

As much as the draw with England was celebrated, the draw with Egypt was greeted like defeat. In the third match, Ireland required a draw against the European champions Holland to progress to the knockout stages. With 19 minutes to go and 1-0 down, Niall Quinn from Perrystown, who played for Manortown United as a boy, extended a leg to grab the equaliser. Ireland qualified for the knockout stages to play Romania. There was delirium. People wore stupid, idiotic, wonderful smiles. Never before had the city seen the likes of this. Never had the city witnessed such scenes of joy, good humour, utter delight. Never.

Before the arrival of this Irish soccer team, the main success on the international stage was victories in the Eurovision song contest. But the World Cup has been much more than that. Everyone became absorbed in team news, injury scares, the confrontation between the Irish manager and a journalist, the fortunes of other teams, especially England, and the scramble for tickets.

People have also basked in the reflected glory of the Irish supporters who won plaudits from all quarters as English fans were arrested, deported and baton charged. In the words of one journalist from the French paper *L'Équipe*, 'Oh Lord, give us more of the Irish and we will make a better world for you.'

At the end of a penalty shoot-out with Romania, David O'Leary, who played for Shelbourne FC as a boy, stepped forward to score the decisive kick.

The city erupted again in even greater celebration, more intense euphoria. The scenes were blissful, chaotic. Car horns sounded everywhere. Thousands converged on O'Connell Street. People waved flags and scarves. The Daniel O'Connell statue was draped in orange and green. People danced in the 'Floozie in the Jacuzzi', soaking themselves and anyone passing by. Men grabbed women and kissed them. Strangers hugged. Cars went up and down the main street of the city with half a

The view from the Irish team bus at the beginning of their journey to the civic reception at College Green.

Paul McGrath salutes the thousands gathered at College Green, after a three-hour bus-top journey through the city centre.

dozen people clinging onto their bonnets waving flags. The gardaí watched and smiled. A young man who waited at a bus stop seemed to be outside the mood. He was distant, distracted, as though he had no interest. But then, as if overcome, he suddenly raised his fist and punched the air.

Never had there been such scenes of joy, good humour, utter delight in the city. Never.

Last night saw defeat to Italy in Rome's Olympic Stadium. After nearly three weeks it is almost over.

But not just yet.

Today sees the greatest celebration in the history of the city. Never before have Dubliners been able to celebrate something together, regardless of background, religion or social class. There were no celebrations at the time of the 1916 Rising. When the Armistice was announced in November 1918, Dublin was again divided in its views. When the Treaty brought an end to the War of Independence there was a different type of division. When Michael Collins arrived at Dublin Castle in January 1922, there was not even a ceremony. Nobody celebrated the end of the Civil War. Apart from the students at Trinity, few celebrated the end of the Second World War. The declaration of a Republic in 1949 was nothing compared to this.

The plane carrying the Irish team arrived at Dublin Airport at 6.30 p.m. and was greeted by over 50,000 fans who crowded the old terminal building, crammed official viewing galleries and made the multistorey car park into an unofficial one.

That was just the start.

A seven-mile route which is lined with hundreds of thousands of people brings them to a civic reception at College Green. The gardaí, who are so used to estimating crowds, have no method of counting so many people. But everyone agrees that at least 500,000 people, half the city, are there. It is the greatest gathering in Dublin's history. No one is here out of obligation. After three hours, the team's bus turns down O'Connell Street and wave upon wave of 'Olé Olé Olé' and 'Que Sera Sera' echo against the walls of the GPO, of Clerys, of Easons. It is the same when it finally reaches College Green and the speeches are made.

Then the three weeks are over. But things will never be the same again. Never.

❖ ❖ ❖ ❖ ❖ ❖ ❖ ❖ ❖ ❖ ❖

Saturday, 1 September 1990

Apart from Reykjavik, Iceland, Dublin is the most north-westerly capital in Europe. As such, its prevailing weather comes in on south-west winds. This might bring cool, damp air but it also brings the freshest, cleanest of air from the expanse of the North Atlantic. When the wind comes from the east, bringing air from Europe's industrial heartland, the pollution levels in the city go up significantly. But when a strong high-pressure system, with hardly any wind, settles over the city in winter an 'air inversion' traps Dublin's own pollution. It is then that things become particularly bad.

Since the conversion of the Poolbeg power station to gas in 1978, the main causes of Dublin's pollution are car exhaust fumes and smoke that is burnt in the city's traditional open coal fires. Each year, 30,000 tonnes of coal are burned in fireplaces. For every tonne burned, 50 kilograms of smoke, of pollution, is produced. When there is air inversion, Dublin is shrouded in Dickensian-like pea soup smog. Visibility is sometimes reduced to less than 50 metres. The smog creeps into buildings. Cyclists wear masks. Pedestrians breathe through scarves. Pollution levels frequently exceed twice the European Commission limits. Last winter, during one 17-day period, the EC limits were exceeded on no less than 13 occasions – the worst-affected areas are Crumlin and Ballyfermot which sometimes have pollution levels four times EC limits.

The smog affects everyone, but it has been a serious issue for those who have respiratory problems. On some nights, more than 100 people are rushed to Dublin's hospitals with breathing difficulties. But all that is about to change.

Following formal warnings from the EC, action is finally being taken. From today, the sale of 'smokey' bituminous coal in Dublin is banned. There has been no count of the number of deaths in the city from smog over the decades, but some believe that the ban will save hundreds of lives each year.

Thursday, 19 December 1991

In the Millennium year, it was announced that Dublin, following Athens, Florence, Amsterdam, Berlin and Glasgow, would have the honour of being the European Capital of Culture in 1991.

This honour was given in recognition of the renaissance that it seemed to be experiencing including the launch of the International Financial Services Centre, the revitalisation of derelict sites, the restoration of the Royal Hospital Kilmainham and the National Concert Hall, the Royal Shakespeare Company and the Peking Opera appearing at the Dublin Theatre Festival, the founding of the Dublin Film Festival in 1985 and, finally, the many achievements of the Millennium year and the enthusiasm with which Dubliners took to it.

As Dublin's year as European Capital of Culture comes to an end, people are taking stock of what has been achieved. Most believe it to have been a disappointment. Planning for the year began late, it was also short of money – Dublin's budget of £4 million was a fraction of Glasgow's £40 million – and it only got started in March. Ninety per cent of Dubliners were aware of it, but only 5 per cent can identify a specific cultural event that took place. Less than one in eight thought that the city's image had been improved during the year. Unlike the Millennium when there were events of all scales, the City of Culture programme was regarded as elitist and aimed at the middle and upper classes. Some believe that *The Commitments* movie premiered in October is going to have a longer-lasting impact on the city's cultural landscape.

Despite the criticism, the year has not been without its achievements, although many of them would have happened regardless of the title of Capital of Culture. The Custom House was restored, the new Irish Museum of Modern Art was opened in the Royal Hospital Kilmainham and the Dublin Writers' Museum on Parnell Square came into being. Perhaps the greatest and most lasting achievement will prove to be Taoiseach Charles Haughey's flagship project for the Year of Culture, the designation of Temple Bar as a 'cultural quarter'.

From the 1970s, the area between Dame Street and the Liffey, under the shadow of the giant Central Bank, was earmarked as the location for a central bus depot. Since then, CIÉ has purchased 60 per cent of the buildings in the area, renting them out on low, short-term rents until they would develop the site. As a result, the area managed to retain its eighteenth-century character as well as developing a 'Left Bank' atmosphere by being populated with artists' studios, cafés, second-hand and vintage clothes shops, second-hand bookshops, Fat Freddy's pizza restaurant, the Bad Ass Café, recording studios and the Auld Dubliner and Temple Bar pubs. In 1986, the Temple Bar Study Group had called for the abandonment of the CIÉ project. Then

Thom McGinty has become one of the most familiar and loved Dublin street characters since arriving here from his native Scotland in 1977. He started off at the Dandelion Market with a painted face and old clothes, sitting absolutely still behind a sign that read 'In love with country but unable to gain employment – please give generously, thank you'. When the market closed McGinty got work with the Diceman games shop on Grafton Street. Today most people still know the street performer as 'the Diceman'. Here he celebrates St Valentine's Day in his own unique way.

the corporation's recent development plan designated 77 buildings as listed for protection, which put the whole bus depot project in doubt. Last year, Fáilte Ireland recommended that Temple Bar be pedestrianised and turned into a major tourism quarter while Haughey insisted that he would stop any moves by CIÉ to damage the area.

In July, the Temple Bar Renewal Act was passed which gives the most generous tax breaks yet to developers who want to rejuvenate the area. Crucially, for the first time, tax breaks for the restoration of old buildings is at the same level as for the construction of new ones. Development will be carried out under the supervision of the Temple Bar Renewal Company under the guidance of a Framework Plan created by Group 91 architects. There will be £20 million of European funds invested, the development of pedestrian walkways and a new square called Meetinghouse Square with 'a public performance space' and open-air stage, while Temple Bar Square will have a 'carnival space for young people and tourists'. An area that was once destined to be a bus depot will instead play a key part in making Dublin once again a living city.

'You still see things in Dublin that make you pause; two young men riding two to the one bicycle, one pedalling for dear life driving the double weight, the other perched on the saddle whistling nonchalantly, languid as though on a chaise longue, his legs trailing along the cobbles.'

Polly Devlin, Dublin, 1993

It's April 1993 and the latest unemployment figures are out. Dublin's unemployment rate is 17 per cent. The only area in the country with a higher rate is the north-west. There are record numbers of unemployed in the city, 96,127, about half of whom have been out of work for three years or more. Despite the changes that have been taking place, people can be forgiven for wondering if things will ever really change.

1994–2008

Celtic Tiger Capital

Monday, 14 February 1994

Dubliners, especially young Dubliners, are changing the ways in which they enjoy themselves.

A city of tea-drinkers is being converted to coffee. Until recently the 'mug of black' or 'mug of white' in a Bewley's café had been the height of coffee sophistication. But with new tastes, greater foreign travel by Dubliners, more European visitors to Dublin and young people wanting to live a 'continental lifestyle' people are increasingly asking for Americanos, espressos, cappuccinos and lattes from trained 'baristas'. Among the first coffee houses to open were Café Java, Costa Coffee and Café Rio. Now new ones are opening almost every month.

The new cafés are not the only change.

Until now, Dublin pubs have been places apart. In O'Donoghue's, The Stag's Head, The Flowing Tide and Mulligan's, drinkers are cocooned, ensconced away from the outside world behind frosted glass, drawn curtains, pulled blinds and high windows. And these pubs are where people drink pints or shots.

But in the last three years, a number of pubs have opened that have more in common with continental establishments than with their Dublin counterparts.

The first was Café en Seine. Located in the former hall of St Anne's Church on Dawson Street, £500,000 was spent on refurbishing its 1,300 square metres in the style of a Parisian brasserie with chandeliers, distressed metal, gilt mouldings,

Café en Seine is one of the new pubs that have opened in the city that is far different to the traditional Dublin pub.

mirrors and frescoes. Café en Seine is the most fashionable pub in the city where even getting to the bar from the entrance requires a walk down a catwalk-like aisle. The mainly French staff serve croissants and a choice of pastries, the usual beers, but also wine, champagne and various types of coffee – their cappuccinos are regarded as among the finest in Dublin.

Other pubs have opened, inspired not by anything in Paris, but Amsterdam. Among these are Hogan's and The Globe on South Great George's Street and Thomas Read's on Dame Street. In these pubs there is a young, intellectual clientéle who sit at huge picture windows facing onto the streets.

Until recently, there have been few things to do in Dublin after midnight apart from going to Leeson Street basement nightclubs with disco music, overpriced wine and easy pick-ups; to the Pink Elephant, long-standing home of the glitterati; Lillie's Bordello, a club off Grafton Street for the mature, rich, wealthy and influential; Midnight at the Olympia, The Rock Garden, Bad Bob's and Drumcondra's Tá Sé Mahogany Gaspipes for late-night music; Jason's in Ranelagh or The Pierrot in Dún Laoghaire for a game of snooker; or renting a video from Late Night Movies.

In the last two years, this has changed dramatically with the opening of new, late-night clubs. Many are run by young people who have spent time abroad.

The POD (short for Place of Dance) was opened in April 1993 by John Reynolds who previously worked in London's Ministry of Sound. With Barcelona-inspired décor, it is in the arches of the former Harcourt Street railway station. It is not just Dublin's hottest nightspot, the POD has been voted the second-best club in Europe. It is a favourite spot for visiting celebrities to hang out, including Marianne Faithfull, Naomi Campbell and Bono, while last year when Mick Jagger was in Dublin recording *Voodoo Lounge* with the Rolling Stones, he celebrated

Ads for new clubs from D-side magazine.

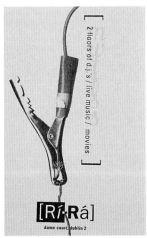

his birthday at the POD. Each night hopefuls run the gauntlet of its bouncers. But here the rules are different. Shirts and ties are taboo: POD is a place to dress down, but well.

To many people's surprise, Dublin has become one of the coolest destinations in the world.

A younger crowd goes to Rí Rá, in the basement of the Central Hotel, for funk and ragga. There is Funk Off in The Waterfront, the Temple of Sound on Ormonde Quay, for the serious dancers, the monthly Zoo Circus in the Setanta Centre, the gay club Shaft on Ely Place that also attracts a straight crowd, Velure in the Gaiety Theatre, and Club M and Club USI in Temple Bar.

Most Dubliners are not part of this new club scene. Some are not even aware of it. But it is largely because of these clubs and the nightlife in Temple Bar that articles in *Elle* magazine, the *Observer*, *The Sunday Times* and a host of other publications have dubbed Dublin the 'coolest' city in the world.

And tonight another club is opening to add to this reputation. Called The Kitchen, it is in the basement of the U2-owned Clarence Hotel which was recently voted the world's 'hippest hotel'.

❖ ❖ ❖ ❖ ❖ ❖ ❖ ❖ ❖ ❖ ❖

Saturday, 30 April 1994

Along with the achievements of the national soccer team, the Eurovision Song Contest remains one of the few international competitions in which Ireland has

The country is entranced as Riverdance is performed at the Point Depot at the interval of the 1994 Eurovision Song Contest.

been able to compete. Ireland's first Eurovision win came in 1970, when Dana sang 'All Kinds of Everything', and since then there have been victories in 1980, 1986 and each of the last two years.

Winning brings rewards to the artist, but it also provides an opportunity to host the following year's contest and showcase the country to 300 million potential European visitors. Last year's Eurovision, broadcast from Millstreet, County Cork, was interspersed almost exclusively with rustic scenes of green fields, sheep, horses, country houses and pristine coastline. A more traditional view of Ireland could hardly have been presented.

In stark contrast, tonight's Eurovision in the Point Depot, in the Docklands, starts with scenes taken from Dublin's city centre of drummers and dancers and torch-carrying figures running across the now iconic Ha'Penny Bridge. There is the Central Bank, Liberty Hall, a Viking longboat on the Liffey, a graffiti-covered railway underpass, fireworks. There are figures in the shape of James Joyce reading Roddy Doyle, Oscar Wilde throwing flowers into the River Liffey, Bob Geldof playing the saxophone solo from 'Rat Trap'. There is Sinead O'Connor. There is Brendan Behan.

During the introductions to many of the night's songs, the Dublin theme continues with footage of the Bad Ass Café, the Irish Film Centre and other places in Temple Bar, the National Concert Hall, the Gate Theatre, the docks, the Joyce Tower, the Ha'Penny Bridge, Grafton Street – Dublin's 'Boulevard Saint-Germain' – buskers, restaurants, Bewley's, Croke Park, Georgian squares, the East Link Bridge, Trinity's Berkeley Library and Henry Moore sculpture and a nightlife that rivals Barcelona.

The message from this Eurovision is clear: Dublin is a modern, vibrant, creative European capital.

But all of that is nothing compared to the interval performance. Though 'Riverdance' has Irish traditional music and dance, people have never seen anything like it before. The music is captivating, the style of dance is mixed with ballet, flamenco and tap and the two main dancers, Irish-Americans Jean Butler and Michael Flatley, are sensual and confident. After a breathtaking finale, the audience in the Point roars its approval. There is a spontaneous standing ovation.

At the end of the broadcast, it is the seven minutes of 'Riverdance' that many people are talking about, rather than the fact that there has been yet another Irish win, this time with Paul Harrington and Charlie McGettigan singing 'Rock 'n' Roll Kids'.

❖ ❖ ❖ ❖ ❖ ❖ ❖ ❖ ❖ ❖ ❖

Wednesday, 31 August 1994

Eight months ago, the British and Irish governments announced in the 'Downing Street Declaration' that they had agreed future decision-making for Northern Ireland. That paved the way for today's declaration by the Irish Republican Army of a 'cessation of hostilities'. After over two decades of conflict, death and destruction there is at last the prospect of peace in Ireland. Although it has been many years since Dublin was directly affected by the Troubles, there is no doubt that it has put many visitors off, especially those from Britain. That all changes now.

On the same day as this announcement, an economic report on Ireland is published by Morgan Stanley in their *Euroletter*. Not since the 1960s has an economic report on Ireland made such pleasant reading. Dublin might be the capital of the second smallest economy in Europe but according to the report it is also the capital of the fastest-growing economy. In fact, there are few countries with better economic prospects. The report even proposes that Ireland is the 'Celtic Tiger', the equivalent of the four Asian economic Tigers of South Korea, Singapore, Hong Kong and Taiwan. With its rate of economic growth accelerating and few reasons why it will not continue, one can only wonder as to how such a change in economic fortunes will affect the city in the coming years.

In 1994, there is the most fundamental change since 1930 in how the city is managed as Dublin Corporation becomes Dublin City Council and the rest of the county of Dublin is divided into the new administrative areas of South Dublin, Fingal in the north (the name coming from Fine Gall, referring to the Vikings that had settled there in medieval times) and Dún Laoghaire-Rathdown (named after the old borough and the historic half barony of Rathdown).

Thursday, 29 December 1994

The year's cultural sensation has undoubtedly been 'Riverdance'. Following the Eurovision, 'Riverdance' was released as a single, topping the Irish charts for a record 18 weeks – it is now the best-selling Irish single of all time. 'Riverdance' has almost redefined what it means to be Irish for many people: if people from Ireland can do something as incredible as that, then they can do anything.

Tonight another new Irish musical phenomenon takes to the stage at the Point.

Until now, Dublin bands such as Thin Lizzy, The Boomtown Rats, The Blades, U2, In Tua Nua, A House, An Emotional Fish and Hothouse Flowers have followed the well-worn route of working hard, writing songs, building a following and doing gigs in small venues in front of people who might never have heard of them.

But this band is different. Boyzone are made up of five young men from Dublin's north side – Shane Lynch, Ronan Keating, Stephen Gately, Mikey Graham and

Dublin's Boyzone – Ireland's first 'pop band'.

Keith Duffy. Picked from open auditions for their singing and dancing and good looks, they are Ireland's first 'pop band'.

Boyzone reached number two on the Irish charts in June with a cover of the Detroit Spinners' 'Working My Way Back to You' – they were only kept off the top by 'Riverdance'. This week they are number four in the British charts with another cover, this time of the old Osmonds' hit, 'Love Me for a Reason'.

Tonight they play their first concert, not in the Baggot Inn or some student bar, but in the Point where there are thousands of screaming girls, a few cringing fathers and many more mothers who are joining in the singing and dancing.

At the end of the concert, parents patiently wait as their daughters stand in long queues to buy the band's merchandise.

Dublin Airport is set for a record year in 1994. Eight years ago when Ryanair's first plane took off, 2.9 million passengers passed through the airport. Since then, numbers have more than doubled to seven million, with the Irish capital connected to Amsterdam, Atlanta, Barcelona, Birmingham, Bristol, Brussels, Cardiff, Chicago, Copenhagen, Dusseldorf, East Midlands, Edinburgh, Frankfort, Glasgow, the Isle of Man, Jersey, Leeds/Bradford, Leningrad, Lisbon, Liverpool, London, Madrid, Malaga, Manchester, Milan, Munich, Newcastle, Paris, Rome, Shannon and Zurich. And this year, for the first time since transatlantic travel was introduced to Ireland in 1958, flights between Dublin and Boston and New York no longer have to stop at Shannon Airport – a stop designed to direct visitors to the West of Ireland. Since then, the number of North Americans arriving in Dublin has nearly doubled.

There are two main topics of conversation in Dublin in the summer of 1995.

One is the weather. It is the warmest on record in the city, the driest since 1887, the sunniest since 1899. For over 40 days, it only rains three times – and then only at night.

The other talking point is that of a film being shot in Dublin. Never before has the city been taken over by a movie. But this is no ordinary movie. This is Neil Jordan's Michael Collins, the first time the life of the man many attribute to winning the War of Independence will be portrayed in film. Thousands volunteer as extras and 80 places around the city are used as locations including Kilmainham Gaol, Merrion Square, the Four Courts, a recreated O'Connell Street complete with a GPO that has been built at Grangegorman, Grafton Street, the Mansion House, Dame Street, Trinity College, Dublin Castle and Dún Laoghaire's East Pier.

Dublin must be the only European capital in which radio traffic reports warn motorists of loose horses on the city's main thoroughfares. But in Dublin, there are thousands of young boys who treat the city streets as if they are the Wild West. In a 'tradition' believed to have started in Ballymun, there are now 3,000 horses owned by 'urban cowboys'. According to an article in *In Dublin*, '… you'll find them in the most incongruous of places: along the green margins of busy motorways, tethered on Corporation wasteland or in the stamp-sized gardens of cramped housing estates.

Drive through any typical Tallaght or Clondalkin estate and you'll see dozens of them ambling around, or being ridden at speed by bullet-headed boys across roads and parklands. They are so out of place in this concrete maze that the whole thing seems vaguely surreal, comical and totally lawless.'

Friday, 24 November 1995

As the capital and the largest city in Ireland, Dublin has always been at the liberal end of the country's moral spectrum – with some parts of south Dublin being the most liberal of all. However, for much of the period since independence, Irish life has been dominated by a largely conservative, rural society. But that is changing.

In 1990, Mary Robinson became the first woman elected president of Ireland. Born in Mayo, she attended Mount Anville Secondary School in Dublin before studying law at Trinity. She then became a barrister, was elected a councillor for Dublin Corporation and a senator, and became a Professor of Law. She championed

Mary Robinson takes office as the President of Ireland. Ireland's first female president was elected with the help of a substantial Dublin vote.

various causes including saving Wood Quay, women's liberation, the ending of the ban on contraceptives and decriminalising homosexuality.

This most unlikely presidential candidate won the election with the help of the Dublin vote. Eight of Dublin's 11 constituencies gave her the highest number of first preferences, as did the neighbouring counties of Kildare and Wicklow.

Today the country has voted in the second divorce referendum. When the issue was first put to the electorate in 1986, it was resoundingly defeated by a margin of two to one. At the time, the only constituencies to support it were five in Dublin.

Nine years later, the Dissolution of Marriage Referendum is passed. But only just. In the closest referendum result in the history of the state, less than 10,000 votes decide the issue.

Dublin's votes have made the difference.

Of the 30 constituencies outside of the capital, 25 voted against divorce. However, every Dublin one voted in favour, with 'Yes' votes of between 58 per cent and 68 per cent.

❖ ❖ ❖ ❖ ❖ ❖ ❖ ❖ ❖ ❖ ❖

Wednesday, 26 June 1996

A new kind of murder is being committed in Dublin. In the last 12 months, newspaper headlines have been dominated by cold-blooded shootings that are all linked to the trade in illegal drugs.

The scene of the shooting of journalist Veronica Guerin by Dublin criminals.

The first gangland killings might have taken place in 1983 but that initial generation of drug dealers gave way to much more brutal and ruthless gangs. In the last year, the rate of killings is unprecedented. Led by men with nicknames such as 'the Penguin', 'the Monk', 'the Boxer' and 'the Psycho', they have been killing each other over territory, for deals gone wrong and now in revenge for previous killings. Many have been carried out with the calm dispassion of the contract killer. Most have taken place in working-class suburbs.

In June of last year, David Weafer was shot four times with a shotgun in his Finglas home. A week later, Fran Preston was gunned down in Moyclare Manor, Baldoyle, by a lone gunman on a bicycle. In August when Gerrard Connolly answered a knock at the front door of his Ballyfermot house, he was shot twice in the chest. November was particularly violent with Catherine Brennan and Eddie McCabe both shot in the head with a 9-millimetre handgun at point-blank range in Tallaght. Less than 24 hours later, a man called to the Finglas home of Christy Delaney and shot him in the head three times. Then Eric Shortall was shot dead near his Ballyfermot home. This year the litany continues.

In March, Gerry Lee was shot twice in the chest by a lone masked gunman in Coolock while he was celebrating his birthday. On 1 April, John Redden was having a drink in the Blue Lion pub, Parnell Street, when a man approached him, took off a false beard and killed him with a single shot. In April, John Kelly was shot in the neck and upper body with a semi-automatic pistol by a man who entered his Clondalkin home.

The attitude of many people to these murders has been ambivalent: if the criminals want to kill each other, let them, the more the better. But committing murder with near impunity has made the gangs more brazen. And today a line is crossed.

At around 1 p.m. Veronica Guerin, a well-known crime journalist with the *Sunday Independent*, who has made many enemies among the city's drug gangs, stops her car at a notoriously busy junction on the Naas dual carriageway. As she waits for the lights to change, a powerful motorbike pull up on the driver's side of the car. The pillion passenger pulls out a handgun and shoots Guerin five times. She dies instantly.

The benefits of economic growth are not being evenly spread among the people in the city. In 1996, in places such as Blackrock, Clonskeagh, Foxrock and Churchtown, there is an unemployment rate of less than 4 per cent, but in areas such as Cherry Orchard, Priorswood, Fettercairn it is between 48 and 59 per cent.

In July 1996, the first Quality Bus Corridor is opened on the Lucan Road. With a dedicated bus lane 12.1 kilometres long, it is hoped that shorter journey times and the sight of buses whizzing past will encourage drivers to give up their cars for public transport.

Saturday, 2 November 1996

When the estate agent for the new 'Riverstown' development on Porterstown Road in Castleknock arrives for work there is a sight he has never seen before. Thirty-five couples have spent the night queuing outside the sales office to buy one of the 64 three- and four-bedroom houses that are on sale. It is another sign of the dramatic changes that have been taking place in Dublin's property market.

Until two years ago, most of new houses and apartments sold were in the areas designated for tax breaks in the city centre. Especially popular were those in Temple Bar, around Christchurch Cathedral and along the Liffey, but there were even new developments in what had been the long-neglected area of Mountjoy Square. For the first time since the 1930s, the population of the inner city is increasing. But it is not just that.

Houses are being sold all around the city. Last year saw an increase of 12 per cent in Dublin house prices, and to nearly everyone's surprise, they are rising even faster this year. By the end of the year, they will have increased by another 18 per cent.

This is a situation that is being driven by powerful forces.

The economic prosperity of the 1960s created a 'baby boom' in Ireland and the generation that was born then is now coming of age and looking for their own houses. Interest rates are at their lowest in 30 years. There are more jobs, and incomes are rising – employment in the financial services area, particularly the IFSC, has considerably increased the number of people in Dublin with high incomes. Now rising prices have become another reason as young people fear that if they do not buy now they will not be able to get 'on the property ladder'.

At first, sales outside of the designated areas were mainly at the top end of the market. Last year, £23 million worth of Ballsbridge apartments were sold off the plans while large suburban houses have been breaking records – Lis na Carrig in Foxrock was sold for a new record of £2 million and Ayesha Castle in Killiney is now on the market for what will be another new record of £2.5 million.

But all prices in the city are rising fast with the average house price £10,000 more than last year.

And so this morning, the estate agent arrives in Castleknock to the queue of house-buyers. In two hours, all of the Riverstown houses are sold. Not only that. Another 40 are sold which not only have not been built – the developer does not even have planning permission for them yet.

At the end of 1996, people are looking back on an extraordinary year.

Gucci and Prada opened in Brown Thomas, fully landscaped gardens were being bought for up to £10,000, the sale of wide-screen TVs boomed. Total retail space in the city increased by 25 per cent – the main addition was Jervis Shopping Centre. The sales of 3-series BMWs rocketed by 22 per cent and there are 12-month waiting lists for the new sporty Mercedes SLK. In the run-up to Christmas, £800 million was spent in Dublin shops, double that of five years ago.

Monday, 22 December 1997

Traffic congestion is now a more important issue than crime in the city.

It is estimated that traffic is costing Dublin's economy £500 million per year, such is the waste of money caused by people sitting in what is often being referred to not as traffic, but gridlock. With only 100 metres of cycleways in the city centre and virtually no subsidy of the running costs of Dublin Bus, 5,000 new cars are being added to the city's streets every single month. With more people working and more people buying cars 'morning rush hour', once between 8 a.m. and 9 a.m., now lasts for the two hours between 7.30 a.m. and 9.30 a.m..

But today, two of the loves of Dubliners, shopping and their cars, meet in a perfect storm.

There is a quiet start as people take the day off before Christmas. But thousands use the opportunity to shop. Traffic begins from 11 a.m. and by late afternoon there is what many regard as Dublin's worst traffic jam. Buses take two hours to travel from Dundrum to the city centre. Every car park in the city is full and queues of cars wait to get in while others try to get out. At Mercer Street, one person takes three hours to get from the fourth floor to the exit. Others take two hours to get from car park entrances to an empty space.

❖ ❖ ❖ ❖ ❖ ❖ ❖ ❖ ❖ ❖

February 1998

Dublin City Council wants to revive the fortunes of the city's main street. Some believe the decline of O'Connell Street started with the blowing up of Nelson's Pillar, which deprived it, and the city, of a focal point. But there is no shortage of reasons for what was once the most important street in the city, even the country, becoming a place for people to pass through, generally as quickly as possible.

There was the rise of suburban shopping centres, the concentration, for decades, of new developments on the south side of the city, the falling population around O'Connell Street with those remaining having serious social problems including unemployment of nearly 80 per cent, poor education, poverty, crime and drugs. Recently, O'Connell Street has been bypassed by the improvements that have been taking place in civic life. Far from there being an 'urban renaissance', the decline has continued. Key businesses such as the tourist office and the Carlton Cinema have closed, with the only new shops selling cheap goods and fast food.

Despite more gardaí on duty, the street does not feel safe. But it is not just crime. Over three-quarters of a century after the first Abercrombie plan proposed reducing traffic to turn O'Connell Street into a thoroughfare suitable for a pleasant stroll, it still has the most traffic of any street in the city as well as the highest number of accidents.

To revive the fortunes of this once-proud street, Dublin City Council have formulated, after much public consultation, an Integrated Area Plan (IAP). Because they believe that the street is not without hope: 'The street's buildings are largely still intact, though mainly concealed behind the garish shopfronts. And for most Irish people O'Connell Street is the heart of Dublin City. Its scale, symmetry, history, elements of architectural grandeur and central location endow it with a sense of place and civic importance which has embedded itself deeply in the psyche of the Irish people.'

Taking inspiration from various European cities, the IAP proposes a way forward for Dublin's Unter den Linden or Champs-Elysées. It proposes reducing traffic, widening footpaths, planting more trees and installing a 'Millennium Project', an art piece, on the site of the original Nelson's column to replace the unloved and much-maligned Anna Livia fountain, still better known to the people of the city as the 'Floozie in the Jacuzzi'.

'The city's emergence from provincialism is, however, only part of the truth, as Dubliners will be quick to tell you. With the continuing drift of population from the land to the capital, Dublin is bulging at the seams, which, of course, brings its problems ... The spirit of Dublin has its contradictions, too, with youthful enterprise set against a traditionalism that won't relinquish its grip for many years yet ... However, the collision of the old order and the forward-looking younger generation is an essential part of the appeal of their extrovert and dynamic society.'

Rough Guide to Dublin, 1998

Tuesday, 30 June 1998

The St Stephen's Green office of Lisney's estate agents is packed for the latest episode in what has become the Dublin property drama.

In the last two and a half years, the average price of a new house in the city has nearly doubled from £83,000 to £162,000. This relentless rise in prices is changing the social geography of the city, with young Dubliners unable to afford a house in the areas that they grew up in and buying in parts of the city in which their parents would never have dreamed of living, or moving as far away as Arklow, Carlow, Gorey, Mullingar and Dundalk to begin life as commuters.

Until today, the most expensive house in Dublin was 'Mount Eagle' in Killiney, which sold for £3 million. But recently all the talk has been about who will buy 1 Sorrento Terrace, Dalkey, a nineteenth-century end-of-terrace house with 1.5 acres of garden and stunning views of Dalkey Island and Killiney Bay. Everyone assumes it will be someone rich and famous. Someone to join the likes of Bono and the Edge from U2, Enya, Lisa Stansfield and Van Morrison and Formula One owner Eddie Jordan and driver Eddie Irvine in the city's most exclusive area. Will it be Michael Flatley of 'Riverdance'? Ryanair's Michael O'Leary? Or maybe American actor Jack Nicholson, who was in Dublin recently? Tom Cruise? Or movie directors the Coen brothers who have been renting in the area?

The bidding at Lisney's opens at £1.25 million, but after ten minutes, the house has sold for a staggering £5.9 million. Despite the speculation, the house is bought by someone most people have never heard of. It is Terry Coleman, who left Ireland in 1979 and made his money in the car alarm business in the UK.

Nearly three decades after the introduction of parking metres, city centre parking continues to be a problem. One-third of cars are parked illegally and of those ticketed just a third pay up. A new weapon against the city's drivers comes into operation on Monday, 10 August 1998 as the city council starts clamping the wheels of illegally parked cars. These clamps will only be removed when a fee of £65 is paid. There will be no escape.

With cheap airline tickets and Dublin's urban regeneration, visitors are coming in record numbers. In 1990, 1,254,000 tourists visited Dublin. In 1998, they will exceed 3 million. Dublin is now the third most popular short break European city after Paris and London.

To meet demand, the number of hotel rooms in the city increased from 4,500 to 6,300 between 1991 and 1997. This year is a record year with a new hotel opening nearly every two weeks. Among these are the Camden Court on Camden Street, the Great Southern at Dublin Airport, the Schoolhouse on Northumberland Road, the Fitzwilliam on St Stephen's Green, Clontarf Castle, the Ibis in Clondalkin, the Plaza in Tallaght, the Radisson in Booterstown, the Trinity Arch on Dame Street and Walton's on Gardiner Row. And there are more being planned or under construction including the five-star Westin Hotel at College Green and what will be the most luxurious and expensive hotel in the city, the 250-room Four Seasons being built on RDS lands at Merrion Road.

Wednesday, 17 March 1999

Today there is a break with tradition in the St Patrick's Day parade. And it is not just that there is no rain, sleet or hail on the warmest national holiday since 1971.

What started as a military parade to show the strength of the young State became an industrial parade to promote employment. With an improving economy and greater ambition it was decided three years ago that a parade of floats for ATA Security, Dunnes Stores, Massey's Undertakers, interspersed with the occasional glamour of American marching bands, was no longer fitting.

This year the vision has been fully realised. There is not just a parade but a St Patrick's Festival. It started on Saturday when 200,000 people packed the quays to watch the largest fireworks display that has ever been seen in Europe – £400,000 worth of fireworks were let off in 30 minutes. Since then there has been a street carnival in Temple Bar, a Cuban carnival and the Galway theatrical group Macnas, and the Catalan group Els Comediants bringing Homer's *Odyssey* to the streets of Dublin.

But the parade remains the centrepiece. Each year it has changed and each year more and more people have gone to watch it – in 1996 there were 350,000, today there are 500,000. This year's theme is 'Saints and Scholars'. But there is hardly a St Patrick in sight in this vibrant, irreverent, even anarchic, parade. Now what had once been the most glamorous part of the parade, the American marching bands, seems traditional, quaint, a throwback to a different era. Today there are scenes unimaginable a few years ago. There are nuns in suspenders, bishops juggling fire and priests playing guitars. When the debauched and drunken 'Father Jack' from the *Father Ted* series makes an appearance a voice over the loudspeaker announces, 'Drink. Girls. Feck.' And the crowd roars back 'Hooray'.

As part of the new St. Patrick's Day celebrations, there is the largest fireworks display in Europe in front of the Customs House.

Thursday, 18 March 1999

Today a new feature in *The Irish Times* property section begins called 'Take Your Pick'. Each week an Irish property will be featured with four others from around the world that can be bought for the same price.

Today there is a three-bedroom apartment in Charlotte Quay, 'the most talked about development in Dublin', which can be bought for £250,000 – parking spaces an additional £15,000 – and then what can be bought for the same price around the world including a two-bedroom apartment in the city of London, on the doorstep of St Paul's Cathedral, a five-bedroom house in Magnolia Grove, Clearwater, 30 minutes' drive from Orlando's Disney World, or a three-bedroom country house in Provence in the south of France, complete with library and sweeping views.

❖ ❖ ❖ ❖ ❖ ❖ ❖ ❖ ❖ ❖ ❖

Wednesday, 26 April 2000

One consequence of people becoming less and less fearful of figures of authority is that uncomfortable truths are coming to light.

Three years ago, a television programme called *Dear Daughter* featured inmates from the Sisters of Charity in Inchicore. Among them was Christine Buckley, a girl who had been known as 'Number 89', whose memories of systematic humiliation, abuse and beatings moved the nation. Last year a documentary series *States of Fear* gave further evidence of how vulnerable children were treated in various religious institutions.

Last May, the Taoiseach, Bertie Ahern, told the Dáil, 'On behalf of the State and of all citizens of the State, the Government wishes to make a sincere and long-overdue apology to the victims of childhood abuse for our collective failure to intervene, to detect their pain, to come to their rescue.' An investigation he promised begins its work today.

The Commission of Inquiry into Child Abuse will investigate allegations of abuse of children in Irish institutions since 1936. Among the Dublin institutions that will be investigated are the Artane Industrial School – by far the largest in the country – the Carriglea Industrial School, the Marlborough House detention centre and Goldenbridge Industrial School. In these institutions, thousands of boys were confined for a variety of reasons, and sometimes against the will of their family, including poverty, homelessness, orphanhood, improper guardianship, poor school attendance, larceny or other crimes.

Amidst increasing wealth, conspicuous consumption, rising disposable incomes undreamt of by previous Dubliners, homelessness remains a problem. There are nearly 3,000 homeless people in the capital. Each night over 300 sleep on its streets.

In January 2000, *Sunday Tribune* sports journalist Paul Howard drives around the bookshops of Dublin in his Nissan Micra. His boot is full of books. It is his first foray into fiction. It started two years ago while he was doing a feature on one of the city's private rugby schools and came across a type of boy he had not encountered before, completely unlike those he grew up with in Ballybrack. These boys had expectations and a sense of entitlement. They did not walk with head down like he did. But it was not just that they were in privileged, private schools. Soon Howard's articles became less about rugby and more about the lifestyle changes taking place in the city fuelled by new wealth and cheap and plentiful credit – this is the age when banks are pre-approving people for £20,000 loans they never applied for or even thought of.

Late last year, Howard turned his articles into a book. With no publisher interested, he published it himself. It is called The Miseducation of Ross O'Carroll Kelly and starts with a scene in Eddie Rocket's in the birthplace of Irish suburban consumerism, the Stillorgan shopping centre. The boys and girls talk in sentences that end in question marks, even if they are not questions, there is an extraordinary use of the word 'like', and they are defined by what they wear and what they consume. There is drink, there is promiscuity. There has never been a book like it before.

When he arrives at the Hughes and Hughes shop in the Stephen's Green Centre hoping for a big re-order, the bookseller tells him that he has not sold one book. But he does tell Howard something interesting. On Saturdays fifth- and sixth-year boys and college undergraduates crowd around the book, reading bits out to each other, parts they recognise in themselves, parts they see in others, saying to each other, 'That's just so, like, Tiernan.'

The children of the Celtic Tiger have more money and more freedom than previous generations. But it is not all good news. Teenage drinking has become a widespread problem. On Junior Cert results nights, city streets are packed with drunken children, young people are enticed to pubs and nightclubs with drinks promotions for alcopops and cut-price vodka and Red Bulls. Going out is no longer something that is done one night a week, it is three or four. On Wednesday, 30 August 2000 at Anabel's disco in the Burlington, there is the usual scene of people hanging around outside before going into the club. There is drunkenness. There is rowdiness. There is a fight and 18-year-old Brian Murphy from Clonskeagh is kicked to death.

For the first time more, than 100,000 cars are sold in Dublin in one year. The car with the coveted licence plate 00-D-100000 is a Hyundai Santa Fe sold by a Rathmines car dealer on Thursday, 26 October 2000.

November 2000

Ten years after being rated one of the worst cities in Europe for a variety of reasons, Dublin now, most surprisingly, heads the list of those with the greatest potential for economic growth. And according to a Department of the Environment report, the city that was once the capital of an agricultural country is now the dominant factor in Ireland's economic and social landscape: Dublin is the 'nerve centre and control focus of virtually all facets of Irish life – business, commerce, finance, government, industry, culture and arts'.

As the capital of an English-speaking EU country, it has been the focus for the vast majority of the recent foreign direct investment into Ireland. Now there are nearly 800 foreign-owned companies in Dublin, among which are Intel, IBM, Gateway, Motorola, Ericsson, 3 Com, Lotus, NEC, Creative Labs and Compaq. Dublin has all of the country's financial institutions, the majority of major companies that are listed on the Irish stock exchange, and 88 per cent of social, cultural and political organisations. It is also the largest, and most rapidly growing, centre of trade and tourism. At the same time, it still retains the traditional features of a capital city including being the home to every government department, every embassy, nearly every civil service body and 81 state-sponsored bodies.

A new magazine, *The Dubliner* – started by Trevor White, recently returned from New York, and edited by Emily Hourican, who grew up in Brussels – is launched on Tuesday, 30 January 2001 at City Hall. Jean Butler from Riverdance, supermodel Sophie Dahl, food writer Domini Kemp and artist Pauline Bewick are all in attendance, and patrons are treated to fish and chips from Burdock's. *The Dubliner* is a magazine for a city with new confidence, new wealth, a city that 'looks set to become one of the great cities of the 21st century'.

Over 16 years ago, *In Dublin* produced a list of reasons not to leave Dublin. But *The Dubliner* does not have to do that, because these days far more people want to live in the city than leave. They publish a list of 'the best 100 things' about Dublin among which are the best aromatherapist, the Blue Eriu on South William Street; the best personal trainer, Niamh Kenny whose one-to-one training involves yoga, kae-bo, weights, diet and nutrition; best deep tissue massage, Muread Hughes whose 'torture includes pummelling her elbows into your back'; best entertainer for kids' parties, Tigay, who does puppets, origami, treasure hunts, jewellery-making and line dancing; Best lunchtime ogling is on Grafton Street, 'the official thoroughfare of the boom is a Mecca to the kind of Irishwoman who has become much better looking because of our recent affluence: gym, chic clothes, year-round tan, pricey make-up and downright sassy confidence'.

Sunday, 8 September 2002

Dublin city has changed more in the last ten years than at any time since the Wide Streets Commissioners laid out the city's eighteenth-century streets. New 'landmark' buildings are appearing at a dizzying rate. Among the most recent additions to the city's skyscape is the Helix Theatre in Dublin City University, the Usher Library in Trinity College, the Millennium Wing of the National Gallery, Fingal Count Council offices in Swords, the huge office development at George's Quay Plaza, the Microsoft Atrium Building in Sandyford, the redevelopment of the old Smithfield market area, and the Citibank Headquarters on the North Wall, the largest single office building in the city. But the largest of all the building projects is the new stadium at Croke Park.

Started more than 15 years ago, before the Celtic Tiger was even a cub, Dublin now has the third-largest stadium in Europe, one of the most impressive building projects in the history of the state. Today it comes of age as the seats of the final stand, the Hogan, are filled for the first time for the Kilkenny–Clare All-Ireland hurling final. As the amateur players of Ireland's national game parade behind the Artane Band the 76,000 people create a wall of noise dispelling any fears that the new stadium would lack atmosphere. In a city that is quick to criticise and that is often bewildered by the pace of change, Croke Park stands out as something that has been delivered on time, within budget, to such a high standard and is universally popular.

Croke Park comes of age for the Kilkenny–Clare All-Ireland hurling final in September 2002.

❖ ❖ ❖ ❖ ❖ ❖ ❖ ❖ ❖ ❖

Tuesday, 21 January 2003

Thousands of people are on O'Connell Street to watch the last piece being put in place on Ireland's largest public sculpture.

The selection committee for the sculpture was unanimous in its choice of the 'Monument of Light', by London architect Ian Ritchie. At 120 metres, it is twice the height of Liberty Hall, seven times the GPO. Three metres wide at the base, it tapers to a small piece of optical glass 15 centimetres across through which a powerful light will shine. The selection committee described it as 'beautiful', 'simple', 'elegant'.

During three years of delays, the sculpture lost its initial name of 'Monument of Light' and become known as the 'Spire'.

The last section of the largest piece of public sculpture in Ireland, the Spire – nicknamed 'the Spike' – is hoisted into place. The Spire is part of the City Council's efforts to regenerate O'Connell Street.

At least officially.

Because over the last four weeks while it has risen section by section, Dublin wags have been trying to come up with a nickname – among recent sculptures to have been renamed by an irreverent public is the one of James Joyce with walking cane that is 'the prick with the stick', Molly Malone is the 'tart with the cart' and two women shoppers resting near the Ha'Penny Bridge 'the hags with bags'.

Among the ones put forward for the Spire is 'the North Pole' – because it is on the north side and looks like a pole – and 'the Stiletto in the Ghetto'. But the most common name is the Spike. However, the name is not an affectionate one. It is one that comes from the affront some have taken at the sculpture which resembles a giant needle used by the city's heroin addicts.

Nobody knows quite what the meaning of the sculpture is. For some its sheer abstractness, its meaninglessness, is its greatest attribute. The sculpture is not rooted in anything Irish, not constrained by the past, and for as long as it stands, it will be seen as a marker of where the city stood in the early years of the third millennium, one of the most remarkable times in its history.

'To anyone who remembers London in the mid-1980s, the similarities are uncanny. There is the same sense of a city possessed by tremendous economic forces. The rules and regulations drawn up for the measured control of development in quieter times can no longer be made fit. The forces of movement have seized the initiative and, on every side, there are indications that it is not time to pause, rather to spring onto the back of the Celtic Tiger and ride, ride, ride.'

Martin Pawley, *The Irish Times*, Thursday, 15 July 1999

On Wednesday, 30 June 2004, the first Luas tram runs between Sandyford and St Stephen's Green mostly along the route of the Harcourt Street railway that was closed over 40 years ago.

Saturday, 10 July 2004

Hundreds of former residents of Ballymun's Patrick Pearse tower block stand, some with cameras at the ready, some with tears in their eyes, as a huge 40-metre crane gets to work. After nearly 40 years, the final days of the most radical and unsuccessful attempts to solve the Dublin housing problem are in sight. Pearse Tower is the first part of Ballymun to be demolished. In five years, the 1960s experiment will be gone.

Last night, a 'demolition wake' was held. Oil lamps glowed from the windows of the Thomas MacDonagh Tower in tribute, songs were sung, stories told and poems read.

A crowd looks on as the demolition of the first of the Ballymun towers begins.

In five years' time, it is intended that there will be 6,000 new homes that will not only rehouse all of the existing Ballymun residents, but thousands of others as well. And unlike the original, it is planned that the new Ballymun will have all the amenities a community needs including shops, a leisure centre, childcare facilities, 11 parks, neighbourhood centres, play-grounds, public art, a swimming pool and civic plaza.

❖ ❖ ❖ ❖ ❖ ❖ ❖ ❖ ❖ ❖ ❖

Wednesday, 6 October 2004

The internet search company Google opens its first office outside of the United States in Dublin, from where it will process internet searches generated in Europe, Africa and Asia.

Google has opted for a building on Barrow Street. Instead of choosing one of the suburban commercial industrial estates, it has set up in an old industrial area within walking distance of the city centre – it is where the gasworks and meat factory of the Boomtown Rats song 'Rat Trap' once were. The arrival of Google confirms Dublin's status as a centre of technology. Joining the likes of Yahoo, eBay, IBM/Lotus, Microsoft, Oracle, Sun Microsystems, Netscape and Informix, Google brings more than jobs to Dublin. It also brings what is already being called the 'Google effect': if Dublin is good enough for Google, cool enough for Google, then other companies will follow.

Cranes dominate the skyline during the Celtic Tiger.

Thursday, 3 March 2005

In another sign of Dublin's spending boom Ireland's largest shopping centre, 'Dundrum Town Centre', opens in south Dublin. With shops such as the House of Fraser, Bershka, Esprit, Mango, Next, Morgan, Coast, East, French Connection, Jane Norman, Massimo Dutti, Tommy Hilfiger and BT2, it caters especially for women. Today they queue in their hundreds, waiting for the official ceremony to end and the doors to open. And in what has become a city of consumers, even the multi-denominational blessing pays homage to the new pastime: 'God of Beauty, may we see in the magnificence of this centre a reflection of your beauty, variety, brightness and colour; may it fill us with wonder, and may it raise our hearts and spirits to you.'

Dundrum Town Centre, the largest shopping centre in Ireland, opens; it is another sign of the boom in consumer spending.

❖ ❖ ❖ ❖ ❖ ❖ ❖ ❖ ❖ ❖ ❖

Thursday, 30 June 2005

After 17 years of construction, and nearly four decades after it was first proposed in the Myles Wright report, the 11-kilometre-long South Eastern Motorway, the last section of the M50 motorway around the city, opens. The final cost of this section is €570 million, or €60 million per kilometre. That it is nine times the cost per

The Port Tunnel nears completion. It will bring Dublin Port traffic straight to and from the M50. It is the last piece of transport infrastructure that was recommended in the 1960s Myles Wright Report.

kilometre of the first section at Blanchardstown, a sign of not only the prosperous area it passes through, but also the remarkable increase in land prices – €300 million went on purchasing some of the country's most expensive parcels of land.

Although the M50 has just been completed, it is already out of date. What many had thought were fantastic predictions in the 1960s by Myles Wright of car ownership have long been surpassed.

With 100,000 cars queuing every day at the West Link toll bridge over the Liffey, the M50 motorway is being called Europe's biggest car park. There are already plans being drawn up to add an extra lane and free-flow junctions as well as buying out the toll bridge operator. If the M50 has become a symbol of just how fast the city has grown and how its infrastructure has lagged behind its development, it is now hard to think how the city could continue to function had it not been built.

❖ ❖ ❖ ❖ ❖ ❖ ❖ ❖ ❖ ❖ ❖

Tuesday, 28 March 2006

After a continuous stream of allegations of sexual abuse by members of Dublin's clergy going back decades, the government appoints the Dublin Archdiocese Commission to investigate a sample of the allegations. If the reports are anywhere near the truth, then this report will forever change the way in which people look at the church.

Sunday, 23 April 2006

The latest census shows the historic transformations that are taking place in Dublin's population.

Over the last ten years, it has grown by 12 per cent. Almost 130,000 more people are living in the city than a decade ago, with by far the greatest increases in Fingal and the lowest in Dún Laoghaire-Rathdown. However, dramatic as this may be, due to a shortage of housing and changes in the economic fortunes of other counties, Dublin's rate of population increase is one of the lowest in the country – it is only greater than Kerry, Limerick, South Tipperary, Mayo, Sligo and Monaghan.

For the first time in the history of the state, the number of people born in and living in Dublin has fallen. In 1996, there were 810,000 people living in Dublin who were born in the city. This year it is 796,000. But one does not have to look far to see where they have gone. Over the same period, the numbers of Dubliners living in the surrounding counties of Kildare, Meath and Wicklow – where homes are cheaper – has increased from 87,000 to 130,000.

There are now 200,000 people living in the city who are originally from outside Ireland. Traditionally the foreign-born have been mainly from the UK and the United States. But now 136,000 are from other countries, up from just 21,000 in 1996. The number of people from Asia has increased from 4,000 to 32,000, Africans from 3,000 to 20,000, and other EU countries up from 15,000 to 33,000. The largest increase for individual countries has been for two of the states that were admitted to the EU in 2004. There are now 7,000 Lithuanians in Dublin and 20,000 Poles.

Never has the population of Dublin changed so much in character as it has in the last ten years.

On Saturday, 1 July 2006 in the War Memorial Gardens in Islandbridge there is the first ever large-scale official commemoration for those Irishmen who died in the First World War.

Dublin City Libraries launches its One City One Book initiative on Wednesday, 17 May 2006 in an effort to get as many people in Dublin to read a book related to the city. The first is Flann O'Brien's *At Swim-Two-Birds*, first published in 1939.

At last the rise in house prices comes to an end in 2006. The price of an average new house in Dublin is €390,000 and a second-hand house €549,000. But as the heat goes out of the market, people are increasingly worried about the huge amount of debt they have as a result of buying property.

In the autumn of 2006, two events inspired by similar ones in Europe are launched to celebrate Dublin's civic and cultural life. In September, 40 buildings around the city, from apartments in Temple Bar to the viewing platform on the roof of Liberty Hall, from the Civic Offices on Wood Quay to Busáras, are opened to the public as part of an Open House programme that showcases the best of the city's architecture. In October, 15 years after the opening of Temple Bar, there is the first Culture Night that includes not only Temple Bar but many other cultural attractions such as the Irish Museum of Modern Art in the Royal Hospital, the National Gallery and the National Museum. All stay open until 9 p.m. with some even offering visitors a glass of wine.

Saturday, 24 February 2007

It is as though everything needs to be new in the city. With the redevelopment of Croke Park, the IRFU and FAI decided to redevelop their international headquarters at Lansdowne Road. In an historic compromise, the GAA overturned years of opposition to co-operation with other games and voted to allow its rival associations to play their games at Croke Park. And in doing so, the scene is set for another defining moment in the modernisation of Irish society.

Two weeks ago the first rugby match at Croke Park was played – Ireland lost to France. Tonight England are the visitors and this match transcends sport. It is an occasion that is freighted with history. Millions watch on TV as a stadium of 82,000 people comes to an impeccable silence for the strains of 'God Save the Queen'. It is the first time that the English national anthem has been played in Croke Park. The home of Gaelic games. The place where 14 innocent civilians were shot dead by crown forces in 1920. Among them was Michael Hogan after whom the main stand of the stadium is named.

❖ ❖ ❖ ❖ ❖ ❖ ❖ ❖ ❖ ❖ ❖

Tuesday, 16 October 2007

Dublin is a city that now looks back with considerable pride on its literary past. Apart from the One City One Book initiative and the annual Bloomsday celebrations throughout the city from Sandycove's Joyce Tower to the Joyce Centre at North Great

George's Street, there are now three bridges dedicated to the city's past. The James Joyce Bridge was opened in 2003, the Sean O'Casey Bridge in 2005 and construction has started on the Samuel Beckett Bridge at a location that was first proposed for a bridge in Abercrombie's 1922 plan.

But as illustrious as the past has been, it is in recent years that Dublin's writers have achieved their greatest commercial and literary success.

It started in 1993 when Roddy Doyle won the Booker Prize for *Paddy Clarke Ha Ha Ha*. Since then, Dublin writers have been to the fore of Irish and international literature. Paul Howard's Ross O'Carroll Kelly series, a satire on the Celtic Tiger, including *The Orange Mocha-Chip Frappuccino Years, The Curious Incident of the Dog in the Nightdress* and *Should Have Got Off at Sydney Parade*, have been among the most popular books in Ireland. John Boyne, former employee of Waterstone's on Dawson Street, became an international best-seller with the parable of the Holocaust *The Boy in the Striped Pyjamas*. There has been the phenomenal success of Cecilia Ahern's novel *P.S. I Love You* which she followed with another best-seller *Where Rainbows End*. Sebastian Barry's *A Long Long Way*, unusually about a Dubliner who fights in the Great War, was shortlisted for the Booker Prize, and is this year's One City One Book. Joseph O'Connor's *Star of the Sea*, about a voyage of a 'coffin ship' to America, was a number one best-seller in Britain. Since Marian Keyes' first book *Watermelon* was published in 1995, she has written best-seller after best-seller and has sold 15 million books so far. Dalkey's Maeve Binchy has had almost continuous success since her debut novel *Light a Penny Candle* in 1982 and with 40 million books sold is the country's most successful writer – her recent work *Tara Road* was an Oprah Winfrey Book Club Selection in the United States. Colum McCann has chosen subject matter that is not usually the stuff of Irish literature: *Dancer* is about Rudolf Nureyev and *Zoli* tells the story of an East European Roma gypsy. Earlier this year, market gardener Derek Landy signed a seven-book deal for his *Skulduggery Pleasant* children's book series.

Anne Enright is the latest Dublin author to achieve international recognition.

And tonight Dublin author Anne Enright is in London where she is awarded the 2007 Booker Prize for *The Gathering*, the story of a family that comes together for the funeral of an alcoholic son and brother who has committed suicide and where the past re-surfaces including revelations of hidden child abuse.

For the first time in a decade, there is unease about Ireland's economic prospects. For months the economy has been faltering. In a city where there are over 60,000 people employed in construction and where so many people's wealth, and debt, are linked to the property sector, rising mortgage interest rates and property prices falling for the first time in 15 years are causing the greatest concern. There are nearly 1,500 fewer houses built in Dublin in 2007 than in 2005, while for the first time since 1994, house prices have fallen during the year – new houses fell from €419,000 to €402,000 while second-hand prices fell even more, from €518,000 to €463,000. Despite all of this, however, record numbers of shoppers fly out of Dublin for New York to do some Christmas shopping.

In 2007, Sean is the most popular name in Dublin for a baby boy. But that comes as no surprise. In each of the last ten years, Sean has been the most common boy's name in the city, except for 2001 when it was Adam. There has been a little more variety with the girls. In 1998 and 1999, it was Chloe. In 2000 and 2001, it was Sarah. In 2003, 2004 and 2005, it was Emma. And last year and this year it has been Sophie.

Monday, 21 January 2008

The world's stock exchanges are in free fall. Less than a year after the Irish Stock Exchange reached its record level, €4 billion is wiped off the value of its shares in one day. One trader tells a reporter, 'It's a complete meltdown, everybody just wants cash.' It has all the characteristics of a classic crash.

The recession is clear to be seen. In the first three months of 2008, there are fewer people shopping, with numbers on Grafton Street down 9 per cent and Henry Street 12 per cent, compared with the last five years.

As the era of the Celtic Tiger comes to an end with banking scandals and huge debt, Sam Stephenson's Central Bank on Dame Street has become a symbol of the broken Irish finanacial system.

Wednesday, 7 May 2008

With Ireland in recession for the first time since 1983 and unemployment in Dublin up by more than 20 per cent, Glenageary writer Joseph O'Connor begins a series of musings on RTÉ Radio 1's evening programme *Drivetime*. Tonight's diary looks at what has become apparent to everyone – the Celtic Tiger has come to an end. It begins:

> Economic lady luck is after giving us the flick,
> She's broken it off
> We're financially heartsick.
> Worst of all she swears to the skies above
> She still loves us as a friend,
> She's just not in love.
> Misty watercolour memories of the way we were
> She said, Let's always be friends,
> It's not us, it's her.
> She just needs some space
> It's a trial separation
> From the sweet happy times
> Of economic generation.

Was it just a passing thing, a fabulous fling
We all went mad and indulged in the bling
Of a love too intense,
As sweet as nectar
But too heavily based on the property sector.

❖ ❖ ❖ ❖ ❖ ❖ ❖ ❖ ❖ ❖ ❖

Tuesday, 20 May 2008

Ireland has not won the Eurovision since 1996, two years after 'Riverdance' stole the show. For many it is no longer a competition that is taken seriously. Our identity is no longer defined by the Eurovision.

This year, in a popular vote, Ireland's entry is not even a person. It is Dustin the Turkey, a puppet with a working-class Dublin accent.

Dustin first appeared on television in 1989 and since then has had a varied career. Appearing on some of the most popular children's programmes, he has run his own mock election campaigns, while his name has been put on numerous election ballot papers – all being deemed 'spoiled' by returning officers.

The Eurovision is not Dustin's first musical foray. He has had six number ones in Ireland. Among these was a version of 'Rat Trap' that he sang with Bob Geldof in which he tells the former singer of the Rats that his recent songs are 'brutal' while asking him, 'as a friend', if he had a mirror in his house.

Tonight in Belgrade Dustin sings his song 'Irelande Douze Pointe' (with deliberate

A poultry puppet with a Dublin accent called Dustin the Turkey is voted by Irish viewers to represent the country at the Eurovision Song Contest. He fails to qualify from the semi-finals.

294

incorrect spelling) – after the maximum score that can be given to a song by each country. Sitting in a shopping trolley, disguised as a disc jockey's turntable and surrounded by scantily clad dancers wearing green, white and orange feathers, he sings his song in which he apologises for 'Riverdance' and name checks every Eastern European country in the hope of getting their vote. When he is finished his song, he is both booed and cheered by the Belgrade crowd. He then asks if he has won. While Irish people thought he was the favourite, tonight in a popular vote among Europeans Dustin does not even qualify for the final.

❖ ❖ ❖ ❖ ❖ ❖ ❖ ❖ ❖ ❖ ❖

Sunday, 21 December 2008

It is a few days before Christmas. It is the shortest day of the year. The time when some people look to longer, brighter days, the stretch in the evening. But it is hard for people to be optimistic. It is the end of the worst year in Dublin economically since the 1980s. Many wonder if that is where the city is going back to. Was the last decade, and more, just a madness? Because it is as though a tap has been turned off.

Unemployment in the country is now 8.6 per cent and during the year, unemployment in Dublin increased by more than 50 per cent. And this is a new kind of unemployment. It is middle-class unemployment including solicitors, architects, accountants as well as those in the building trade and who work in shops and restaurants. This year, instead of shopping trips to New York there are previously unheard of pre-Christmas sales across the city as retail has declined by an estimated 25 per cent during the year.

Most concerning for people is that Dublin house prices have fallen by about 15 per cent in 2008 alone. In fact, Dublin's fall is the largest in the world this year. Those who bought a house since 2005 are already in negative equity and are now saddled with what they had only recently seen as a generous and welcome 100 per cent mortgage that got them on the property ladder.

When the government stepped in 12 weeks ago by guaranteeing deposits of up to €100,000 they thought they had saved the Irish banking system.

Today sees one of the largest financial institutions effectively nationalised. Its story is in many ways that of the Celtic Tiger.

In 1964, the City of Dublin Bank was founded in the capital. It was one of a number of financial institutions to emerge at the time. One by one these were swallowed up by the larger institutions but the City of Dublin Bank survived. Then in 1986, a subsidiary of the main bank, called Anglo Irish Bank and run from a single office by Shankill chartered accountant Sean Fitzpatrick, effectively subsumed its parent company. In 1997, Anglo's share price was less than €1 but the bank, under Fitzpatrick, rode the Celtic Tiger. Aggressively lending money for property, it returned huge profits and huge returns for its investors. By 2007, its shares were worth over €17 and the company was valued at a staggering €13 billion. But with the collapse of the property market, insufficient funds and dodgy deals done behind the scenes, today the government had to step in and take over the bank.

So this day, which is supposed to be one of hope, instead shows that the situation is likely to continue to get worse. In fact no one can yet see the bottom. There is no soft landing. In the mid-1990s, a new Dublin emerged from dereliction, poverty and economic recession. But after a period of rejuvenation, rebuilding and previously unimaginable growth, it is over. One of the most remarkable periods in the history of the city is at an end. But the story, as all stories do, will continue. And so, on this the shortest day of the year, there is anger over what has happened and uncertainty, fear and anxiety over what is to come in the next chapter in the history of Dublin.

Endnotes

To assist the reader when referring to publications that may be difficult to source, I have included the National Library of Ireland (NLI) call number, if available. Many of the accounts included in this publication are taken from general contemporaneous newspaper articles. These are not individually referenced unless an article forms the bulk of an entry or is extensively quoted. Please note that where a number of articles inform the entry but are combined with other source material, the endnote starts, 'See also'. Where there are no contemporaneous newspaper reports the endnote starts, 'See'.

Chapter 1

Monday, 16 January 1922
This entry is on the day when Dublin Castle was 'handed over' to the leaders of the new Irish State. In reality, the situation was far more complicated than this. This was a transitional period, with the British administration and military remaining in Ireland until the end of 1922. However, symbolically it was of great importance.

Thursday, 2 February 1922
See Sylvia Beach, *Shakespeare and Company*, University of Nebraska, 1991. The quotes from letters are taken from Gordon Bowker, *James Joyce: A Biography*, Weidenfeld and Nicolson, 2011 and from Richard Ellman (ed.), *The Selected Letters of James Joyce*, Viking Compass, 1975.

Sunday, 12 February 1922
See diary of writer and political activist Rosamond Jacob, NLI, MS. 32582. Her diary gives interesting first-hand accounts of Dublin in the early 1920s.

Pillar Boxes
See *Irish Independent*, 16 March 1922 p. 5, col. 3.

Friday, 14 April 1922
See Ernie O'Malley, *The Singing Flame*, Anvil Books, 1978, p. 90.

Monday, 26 June to Thursday, 6 July 1922
This account is largely taken from newspaper accounts of the time which often give the experience of the public as opposed to the fighters. The only comprehensive account of the fighting in Dublin during the Civil War is in Liz Gillis's *The Fall of Dublin: Military History of the Civil War*, Mercier Press, 2011. The *Souvenir Album of the Dublin Fighting, 1922*, NLI, MS. 33,460 G/3 Acc. 4712, was most useful. Ernie O'Malley's *The Singing Flame* is an excellent account of the battle from the author's perspective and includes details of his conversation with Eoin O'Duffy. The account of a John Francis Homan, principal of East Wall Wharf Boys' School and member of the St John Ambulance Brigade, is in NLI, MS. 727. Ernie O'Malley, NLI, MS. 10,973/1 has brief, first-hand notes of the fighting on the morning of 3 July by Captain Dalton of the National Army. C.S. Andrews, *Dublin Made Me*, Mercier, 1979, is a useful account by one of the combatants. The quote which finishes the fighting scenes, written under the pen name 'Nichevo', was in fact by Bertie Smyllie, subsequent legendary editor of *The Irish Times*, in that paper on 6 July, p. 3, col. 5. See also Nevil Macready, *Annals of an Active Life*, Vol. 2, Hutchinson & Co., 1924, pp. 652–6; and, NAI, Dept of the Taoiseach, Files S1322 and S1326.

Friday, 15 December 1922
The Town Plan for Dublin competition provides fascinating potential future visions of the city. See *Report of the Adjudicators on the Competitive Designs for Town Plan of Dublin*, Civics Institute of Ireland, 1916, NLI, Ir 9141, p. 56; *Competitive Designs for Town Plan of Dublin*, NLI, Ir 9141, p. 56; and *Dublin of the Future: The New Town Plan Being the Scheme Awarded the First Prize in the International Competition by Patrick Abercrombie, Sydney Kelly and Arthur Kelly*, University Press of Liverpool and Hodder & Stoughton, 1922, NLI, 94133 d 21. See also University College Dublin Archive for two of the unsuccessful reports in *Dublin Town Planning Competition 1914*, http://digital.ucd.ie/view/ucdlib:33058.

Sunday, 17 December 1922
For Macready's departure see Macready, op. cit., p. 674.

Chapter 2

Monday, 29 January 1923
For an account of the GPO controversy, see NAI, Dept of the Taoiseach, File S1966.

Saturday, 20 October 1923
See review of exhibition, *Irish Times*, Saturday, 20 October 1923, p. 6, col. 7.

W.B. Yeats
For the response of Yeats on hearing of the prize, see Roy Foster, *W.B. Yeats: A Life, Volume II: The Arch Poet 1915-1939*, Oxford University Press, 2003, p. 245.

Monday, 5 May 1924
For the name changes proposed see Minutes of the Municipal Council of the City of Dublin 1921 Vol 2, 461; 1922 35, 173, 201, 202 and 596; 1923 278, 296, 297 and 368; 1923 111 and 308; 1924 278, 296, 297 and 368, Dublin City Council Pearse Street Library.

Saturday, 2 August 1924
See *Tailteann Games Souvenir Programme 1924, August 2–17*, Aonach Tailteann, 1924, NLI, Ir 397 t 1.

Tuesday, 7 October 1924
For the process by which Leinster House was decided upon as the seat of the national parliament, see NAI, Dept of the Taoiseach, File S1809.

Tuesday, 11 November 1924
For the background to this episode, see also NAI, Dept of the Taoiseach File S3370A.

Four Courts Restoration
See NAI, Dept of the Taoiseach, File S4290.

Thursday Night, Friday Morning, 12–13 March 1925
See also NAI, Department of Justice, File 90/8/50, which contains the *Report with Appendices on the Inter-Departmental Committee of Inquiry Regarding Venereal Disease*; and Terry Fagan and the North Inner City Folklore Group, *Monto: Madams, Murder and Black Coddle. The story of Dublin's notorious red-light district as told by the people who lived there*, 2000.

Monday, 27 April 1925
See 'The Wonders of Dublin', by Maurice Cloonan, in the *Irish Independent*, 27 April 1925, p. 5, col. 3.

Telephone Kiosk
Dublin Corporation Minutes 1925, Vol. 2, No. 96, p. 32, and photograph in the *Irish Independent*, 2 May 1925, p. 3.

Monday, 22 June 1925
See *Irish Times*, 23 June 1925, p. 5, col. 3.

Monday, 6 July 1925
There are numerous newspaper articles in 1925 on cars, safety and the condition of the roads. For road deaths in 1924 and the increase in the number of cars since 1914 see *Irish Independent*, 18 August 1925, p. 7, col. 4. The figures showing the number of registered cars for 1923–5 come from *The Irish Motor Trader*, 11 March 1926, NLI, p 842. For first bus, see *Irish Independent*, Tuesday, 7 July 1925, p. 6, col. 6. For traffic surveys see *Irish Independent*, Thursday, 24 January 1925, p. 7, col. 6 and Thursday, 26 November 1925, p. 8, col. 2.

Tuesday, 15 December 1925
See *Dublin Civic Survey: Report Prepared by Horace T. O'Rourke and the Dublin Civic Survey Committee for the Civics Institute of Ireland*, University Press of Liverpool, 1925, NLI, Ir 94133 d 6.

Thursday, 11 February 1926
The account given here comes largely from Robert G. Lowery (ed.), *A Whirlwind in Dublin: The Plough and the Star Riots*, Greenwood Press, 1984, pp. 21–36.

Sunday, 18 April 1926
The Irish census reports provide fascinating insights into the city at regular intervals in its post-independence

history. They are available on the Central Statistics Office website, www.cso.ie/en/census/censusvolumes
1926to1991/historicalreports/

Thursday, 9 December 1926
See Tim Carey, *Hanged for Murder: Irish State Executions*, The Collins Press, 2013, pp. 76–88.

Wednesday, 25 May 1927
See *Irish Independent*, 27 May 1927, p. 6, col. 7.

Dublin Civic Week
See *Civic Week Programme, 17–25 September 1927*, Civic Week Committee, 1927, NLI, 2b 1291.

Saturday, 30 June 1928
See also Fred W. Hotson, *The Bremen*, Canav Books, 1988, NLI, Ir 387 h 6; *Bremen 1928: The First East–West Non-stop Transatlantic Flight, Baldonnel–Greenly*, South Dublin County Council, 2004 [?], NLI, 5A 2752; and James P. Fitzmaurice, *Bremen Silver Jubilee: The Story of the First East–West Transatlantic Flight*, Parkside Press, 1953 [?], NLI, p 1861.

Medical Inspection of Schoolchildren
See Mary M. O'Leary, *A Survey of the Health of the Dublin School Child*, the Irish Journal of Medical Science, Sixth Series, 1931, pp. 155–60.

Friday, 19 October 1928
See *The Gate Theatre Studio (In Association with the Gate Theatre Studio, London)*, NLI, MS. 33,038.

Thursday, 11 July 1929
See NAI, Dept of the Taoiseach, File S1966, op. cit.

Friday, 29 November 1929
See also the *Souvenir Programme, Opening Ceremony, Savoy Cinema, Dublin, 1929*, NLI, Ir 308, p 1. For information regarding the film *Ireland* see NAI, Dept of the Taoiseach, File S5983/34. The journalist's account is from the *Irish Independent*, Friday, 29 November, 1929, p. 7, col. 4.

Chapter 3

Tuesday, 14 October 1930
For the background to these significant changes in how the city is governed, see Greater Dublin Commission of Inquiry, Stationery Office, 1926, NLI, OPIE R / 32.

Thursday, 30 October 1930
See NAI, Dept of Justice 247/4/A, B, C and D and Dept of Justice 90/8/50. Many people now regard the suppression of the Carrigan Report as one of the defining events of independent Ireland. See James M. Smith, 'The Politics of Sexual Knowledge: The Origins of Ireland's Containment Culture and the Carrigan Report (1931)', *Journal of the History of Sexuality*, Vol. 13, No. 2, April 2004, pp. 208–33, University of Texas Press.

Monday, 17 November 1930
See also *Irish Hospital Sweepstakes on the Manchester Handicap, 1930, Programme of Draw, 17 November 1930*, NLI, Ir 362 m 2.

Sunday, 5 July 1931
See also *Irish Builder*, 23 April 1932, p. 376 and 13 August 1932, p. 735.

Tuesday, 14 July 1931
The housing issue in the 1930s received a large amount of media interest. For the key period 1931–4, see *Irish Builder*, 31 January 1931, p. 99 (this was one of the first comprehensive articles on the issue); 23 May 1931, p. 461; 18 July 1931, p. 631; 29 August 1931, p. 754; 21 November 1931, pp. 1001–2; 30 January 1932, pp. 97 and 110; 20 May 1933, p. 419; 21 April 1934, pp. 309–39 (this provides a particularly comprehensive overview); 20 May 1933, p. 419; 30 June 1934, p. 549; 28 July 1934, p. 621; 15 December 1934, p. 1072. See also Sean Rothery, *The New Architecture, 1900–1940*, Lilliput Press, 1991 for an excellent overview of Irish modern architecture, including housing, over the period. The quote from the Dublin Corporation housing report is taken from Cathal O'Connell, *The State and Housing in Ireland: Ideology, Policy and Practice*, Nova Science Publishers, 2007, pp. 27–8. For a review of the disappointment of the house construction programme in the 1930s, see

Report on Slum Clearance in Dublin, Citizen's Housing Council, 1938, NLI, Ir 339 c 11; *Committee of Inquiry into Dublin Housing set up in March 1939*, NAI, Dept of the Taoiseach, File S13511; and *Dublin Housing Inquiry: City Manager's Observations 1939-1943*, 1946, NLI, Ir 914133 d 12. See also entry for Wednesday, 21 October 1936.

Opening of the Four Courts
See NAI, Dept of the Taoiseach, File S4290.

Sunday, 26 June 1932
See also *31st Eucharistic Congress Dublin, The Book of the Congress*, Vol. 1, Eucharistic Congress Committee, 1932, NLI, Ir 2820941 e 3; and Rory O'Dwyer, *The Eucharistic Congress, Dublin 1932*, Nonsuch, 2009.

Thursday, 1 December 1932
See entry for 30 October 1930 above.

Wednesday, 29 March 1933
See also Brian Hanley, 'The Storming of Connolly House', *History Ireland*, Vol. 7 (2), Summer 1999, pp. 5–7.

Monday, 19 June 1933
For the story of the Hugh Lane Gallery and the controversial paintings, see *Municipal Gallery of Modern Art* (1933), NLI, Ir 70841 m 4 and *Statement of the Claim for the Return to Dublin of the 39 Lane Bequest Pictures now at the Tate Gallery, London*, by John J. Reynolds, Curator, Municipal Gallery of Modern Art and Civic Museum, Dublin, 1932. The story of the Lane pictures continues up until this day. In 1959, there was an agreement by which half the pictures would be displayed in Dublin every five years. In 1993, this agreement was adapted so that 31 of the 39 paintings would stay in Ireland. The remaining eight were divided into two groups, so that four would be lent for six years at a time to Dublin. In 2008, the Hugh Lane negotiated with the National Gallery London for the return of the entire Bequest for a period of three months, the first time they were reunited with the rest of Hugh Lane's collection since 1913.

The Blueshirts
See also Maurice Manning, *The Blueshirts*, Gill & Macmillan, 1971, pp. 75–87.

Sunday, 26 November 1933
Judge Woolsey's decision on *Ulysses* is regarded as a landmark one in the general relationship between literature and the law.

Flight to Dublin
See Henry Vollum Morton, *The Magic of Ireland*, Eyre Methuen, 1949, p. 13, NLI, Ir 9141 m 51.

Oliver St John Gogarty
See *As I Was Going Down Sackville Street*, Rich and Cowan, 1937, pp. 39–40, NLI, Ir 92 g 45.

Friday, 27 August 1937
See also *Dublin Corporation Minutes 1937, p. 236, Report 416*.

Monday, 3 January 1938
See also *A Motorist's, Cyclist's and Pedestrian's Guide to Restrictions and Procedures under Dublin's New Parking and Traffic Bye-Laws*, issued by the Traffic and Safety First Association of Ireland, 1939, NLI, p 1866.

Monday, 11 April 1938
Dublin Historical Record, Vol. 1, No. 1, March 1938, published by the Old Dublin Society.

Thursday, 7 July 1938
For the Marine Lake see *Irish Builder*, 14 February 1931, p. 144; 26 September 1931, 10 October 1931, pp. 829 and 877, 14 December 1935, p. 1143. For the Dún Laoghaire development see *Irish Builder*, 29 August 1935, p. 735. For the proposal to have Dublin Airport at Merrion Strand see Desmond McAteer, 'Suggested Airport for Dublin', *Studies: An Irish Quarterly Review*, Vol. 24, No. 93, 1935, pp. 73–84.

Sunday, 18 June 1939
See *Irish Times*, 19 June 1939, p. 8, col. 1, and *Air Raid Precautions Issued by the St John Ambulance Brigade*, Irish Stationery Office, 1939, NLI, p 1293.

Sunday, 3 September 1939
For the *Irish Times* article see Monday, 4 September 1939, p. 5, col. 7.

Chapter 4

Friday, 19 January 1940
See also Hugh Oram, *Dublin Airport: The History*, Aer Rianta, 1990.

Monday, 3 June 1940
For the *Irish Times* caricatures, see 'Drawing the Crowd' on Saturdays between 25 November 1939 and 13 July 1940. Although it is often written that *Dublin Culture* was first published in *The Irish Times*, a search of the newspaper during Reeve's time in Dublin was unsuccessful. There was much interest in the piece when the exhibition opened, suggesting it was the first time it was seen by the public.

Tuesday, 10 December 1940
See Patrick Abercrombie, Sydney A. Kelly and Manning Robertson, *Town Planning Report: Sketch Development Plan*, Corporation of Dublin, 1941, NLI, Ir 94133 a 2. While much of this report was not implemented, it did provide the basis for a number of subsequent decisions. In particular, a number of roads in the city owe their origin to the sketch plan, including widening Cooke Street, turning Christchurch Place into a major junction (both to provide easier access to and from Crumlin), a route connecting Fosters Avenue in Mount Merrion to the Naas Road via Dundrum and Templeogue, the extension of Griffith Avenue and a new road to Dún Laoghaire starting from the Big Tree in Loughlinstown via Sallynoggin.

Wednesday, 15 January 1941
See Carola Giedion-Welcker (ed.), *In Memoriam James Joyce*, Fretz & Wasmuth, c. 1941, NLI, 5B 372.

Monday, 10 February 1941
See National Archives, DFA/4/246/131, Air Raid Precaution Scheme: Evacuation of Dublin and Dún Laoghaire, Dept of the Taoiseach, Files S11986 A/1 and A/2, Dept of Defence, File 90/70/5, Air Raid Protection Scheme, Evacuation of Non-Essential Population, 90/70/6 Evacuation Volunteers.

Saturday, 31 May 1941
See also Kevin C. Kearns, *The Bombing of Dublin's North Strand, 1941: The Untold Story*, Gill & Macmillan, 2009. For details regarding the aerial defences of Dublin see Military Archives EDP/01/15/21.

Denis Ireland
See Denis Ireland, 'Scenes from Irish Life 1941–46', *The Dubliner*, No. 5, September–October 1962, p. 30.

Friday, 15 May 1942
The information on the various bicycle thefts is taken from newspaper articles between January and May 1942. See *Irish Press*, 9 April 1943, p. 1, col. 1 for figures for bicycle theft in the city. See also 'Crime in Dublin (2)', *The Bell*, Vol. 5, No. 4, January 1943, pp. 301–7.

Friday, 26 February 1943
Erwin Schrödinger subsequently published the three lectures as *What Is Life? The physical aspect of the living cell, based on lectures delivered under the auspices of the Institute of Trinity College, Dublin*, Cambridge University Press, 1944, NLI, 5701 s 3. There is some argument as to the significance of these talks on the scientific world. But generally there is acceptance that they opened up the possibility to physicists that they could address the question 'What is life?'. Both James Watson and Francis Crick, who discovered the DNA double helix, credit Schrödinger's lectures as presenting an early theoretical description of how the storage of genetic material might work. See also Sir William McRae, *Éamon de Valera, Erwin Schrödinger and the Dublin Institute*, in C.W. Kilmister (ed.), *Schrödinger: Centenary Celebration of a Polymath*, Cambridge University Press, 1987, pp. 119–35, NLI, 92 SC h 53.

Thursday, 9 September 1943
See also *Irish Exhibition of Living Art*, Dublin, 1943, NLI, 15A 4855.

Monday, 28 May 1945
See C.J. McSweeney (Medical Superintendent, Cork Street Hospital), *Flashback on Fevers in Dublin 1934–47*, Monument Press, 1949; J.C. Cherry, 'The Control of Venereal Diseases in Ireland', *Irish Journal of Medical Science*, 6th Series, No. 210, June 1943, pp. 161–70; and *Tuberculosis Exhibition, Mansion House, Dublin, 28 May to 9 June 1945*, Irish Red Cross, Anti-Tuberculosis Section, Dublin, 1945, NLI, Ir 610 p 9.

Unemployed Life

See *What To Do: A Survey of the Unemployment Problem*, Dublin, 1945, the Mount Street Club, p. 86, NLI, Ir 3318 m 3.

Military Exhibition and Tattoo

See *Military Tattoo and Exhibition: at the RDS Showgrounds, Ballsbridge*, August 25th to September 8th, 1945, Official Programme, Parkside Press, 1945, NLI, 4A 2217; and *Illustrated Book of the Military Tattoo and Exhibition, R.D.S. Grounds, Ballsbridge, Dublin, August 27th–September 8th, 1945*, Parkside Press, 1945, NLI, Ir 355941 m 13. For excellent treatment of the significance of the tattoo, see John Fitzpatrick Deane, *All Dressed Up: Modern Irish Historical Pageantry*, Syracuse University Press, 2014.

'On Raglan Road'

Patrick Kavanagh's poem 'On Raglan Road' was originally published as 'When Dark-Haired Miriam Ran Away'. There are a small number of differences between it and what became 'On Raglan Road' but the main one is that line 7 was originally 'Synthetic sighs and fish-dim eyes and all death's loud display' but later became the much different 'The Queen of Hearts still making tarts and I not making hay'.

Monday, 7 April 1947

See also *Irish Press* article is by Anna Kelly: 27 February 1947, p. 3, col 1. For an overview of this meteorological phenomenon, see Kevin C. Kearns, *Ireland's Arctic Siege*, Gill & Macmillan, 2011.

Thursday, 17 April 1947

See G. Ivan Morris, *In Dublin's Fair City*, Home & Van Thal, 1947, pp. 34–7, NLI, Ir 914133 m 10.

Friday, 1 October 1948

See also *Irish Builder*, 16 October 1948, p. 836.

Sunday, 10 July 1949

This is a paraphrased account of Denis Johnston's description of the journey on one of the last trams, 'The Dublin Trams', in the *Dublin Historical Record*, Vol. 12, No. 4, 1951, pp. 99–113.

Chapter 5

Tuesday, 18 December 1951

See Patrick Burke, 'Juno and the Playwrights', in *Dublin and Dubliners: The Drama of Dublin. Essays in the History and Literature of Dublin City*, ed. James Kelly and Uáitéar Mac Gearailt, Helicon, 1990, pp. 218–28, NLI, Ir 94133 d 46.

Saturday, 4 April 1953

See also *An Tóstal Official Souvenir Handbook, 5–26 April 1953*, National Tourist Publicity Organisation, NLI, 4B 625.

Dublin Unemployed Association

See Statement on Unemployment, NLI, ILB 300 p 10 [Item 4] and *Torch: Organ of the Unemployed Association*, Nos 1, 2, 4 and 6, NLI, Ir 05 i 37.

Monday, 19 October 1953

See Paul Clerkin, '50 Years of Busáras', *History Ireland*, Vol. 11, No. 2, Summer 2003; 'Patrick Scott on Michael Scott and Busáras', http://archiseek.com/2014/patrick-scott-on-michael-scott-busaras/, based on an interview in his home in 1995; and, *Áras Mhic Dhiarmada: Offices for the Department of Social Welfare and a Bus Station for Córas Iompair Éireann at Store Street*, Dublin, 1954, NLI, LO 11867.

Wednesday, 16 June 1954

See also Patricia Hutchins, *James Joyce's Dublin*, Grey Walls Press, 1950; John Ryan, *Remembering How We Stood: Bohemian Dublin at the Mid-century*, Lilliput, 1987, NLI, Ir 92 r 89; and 'An Irishman's Diary', *Irish Times*, 17 June 1954 p. 5 col. 7.

Friday, 28 October 1955

See Alan Simpson, *Beckett and Behan, and a Theatre in Dublin*, Routledge & Kegan Paul, 1962, NLI, Ir 391941 s 6.

Friday, 25 November 1955

For buses, see *Dublin District Timetable May–June 1953, Córas Iompair Éireann*, NLI, 3A 3566; and Patrick Joseph Flanagan, *Dublin's Buses*, Transport Research Associates, 1968, p. 38. For cinemas see George Kearns and Patrick Maguire, *A to Z of all Old Dublin Cinemas*, NLI, 7B 649; Jim Keenan, *Dublin Cinemas: A Pictorial Selection*, Picture House Publications, 2005; and Marc Zimmerman, *The History of Dublin Cinemas*, Nonsuch, 2007. For construction of churches, see Dublin diocesan website, http://www.dublindiocese.ie/.

Wednesday, 31 October 1956

See Ray Kavanagh, *Mamie Cadden: Backstreet Abortionist*, Mercier Press, 2005.

Wednesday, 9 January 1957

For the Wood Quay controversy, see Dublin Corporation reports 1955, Report 132, pp. 512–29, Dublin City Council, Pearse Street Library.

Thursday, 23 May 1957

See Gerard Whelan with Carolyn Swift, *Spiked: Church–State Intrigue and* The Rose Tattoo, New Island, 2002. This gives a fascinating insight into the background to the arrest. In the context of the history of the city, the main point to be drawn is that it was not Archbishop McQuaid who called for the arrest of Simpson, but people who believed he would be furious once the play was transferred to the much higher-profile Gate Theatre.

Sunday, 26 January 1958

See Erika Hanna, *Modern Dublin: Urban Change and the Irish Past, 1952–1973*, Oxford University Press, 2013, pp. 70–3.

Sunday, 14 June 1959

Although it does not relate to this particular day, some of the details of this entry on the hottest day of the year are from Olivia Robertson, *Dublin Phoenix*, Jonathan Cape, 1957, pp. 122–8, NLI, Ir 914133 r 5.

November 1959

See also Reports of the Commissioner of the Garda Síochána for the years 1953–9 NLI, OPIE J / 61.

Ha'Penny Bridge

See *1962 Official Guide: This Is Dublin*, The Green Guide Series.

Monday, 6 May 1963

See Des Geraghty, *Luke Kelly: A Memoir*, Basement Press, 1994, NLI, Ir 92 k 107.

Wednesday, 19 June 1963 Apart from the extensive newspaper coverage which very much captures the atmosphere of the time of the collapses, see NAI, Dept of the Taoiseach, File 17486/63, Local Inquiry at City Hall, 24 June 1963 to 5 July 1963.

Chapter 6

Friday, 18 September 1964

For purchase of Belfield by UCD, see The National University of Ireland, *Summary of Progress for the Seven Years 1932–39*, p. 32, NLI, Ir 04 p 16. For UCD moving to Belfield see *University College Dublin and the Future*, NLI, p 2263; *Memorandum from a research group of Tuairim, Dublin Branch, on the report of the Commission on Accommodation Needs of the Constituent Colleges of the National University of Ireland, with special reference to the proposal to transfer University College, Dublin, to a new site*, Tuairim Research Group, December 1959, NLI, Ir 37841 t 38; and University College, Dublin, *University College Dublin and Its Building Plans*, Browne & Nolan, 1959, NLI, p 2297. For the development of the campus see University College, Dublin, *University College Dublin: The Past, The Present, The Plans*, 1976 NLI, Ir 37841 u 18.

Saturday, 1 May 1965

See the magazine *Architecture Survey* for 1959–64 for the variety of new buildings being erected in the city. For background to the developments in the city, see Frank McDonald's seminal work charting much of what happened architecturally in Dublin between the 1960s and 1980s, *The Destruction of Dublin*, Gill & Macmillan, 1985, NLI, LO 3093. For *Irish Times* editorial on the proposed new ESB offices, see *Irish Times*, 12 January 1962, p. 7, col. 2.

Woman's Way

See *Woman's Way*, Dublin, Smurfit Communications, particularly for the years 1963–6, NLI, Ir 05 w 6.

Monday, 10 April 1967

See also Myles Wright, *The Dublin Region: Preliminary Report*, Stationery Office, 1965, NLI, OPIE K / 85; and Myles Wright, *The Dublin Region: Advisory Regional Plan and Final Report*, Stationery Office, 1967, NLI, OPIE K / 85/1–2. For Dublin's per capita income see Michael Ross, *Personal Incomes by County*, in ESRI Paper No. 49, November 1969, NLI, Ir 338 e 4.

Thursday, 19 October 1967

See also *The Ballymun Experience: A Case History of a Community Problem*, Pobal Teoranta, 1971, NLI, 4A 1429; and Ballymun Estate Tenants' Association, *Satellite*, July 1967, NLI, Ir 05 s15.

Wednesday, 14 January 1970

For peaked cap motor attendants, see Kevin C. Kearns, *Dublin Street Life and Lore: An Oral History*, Glendale, 1991, pp. 53–6.

Friday, 1 October 1971

For Lewis Mumford see *Sunday Independent*, 4 July, 1971, p. 19, col. 1; and article in *Plan Magazine*, Vol. 3, No. 1, October 1971, p. 5.

Tuesday, 17 December 1974

See Kathleen O'Higgins, *Marital Desertion in Dublin: An Exploratory Study*, ESRI, 1974, NLI, Ir 338 e 17; Micheál Mac Gréil *Educational Opportunity in Dublin 1972-3*, Catholic Community Institute of Ireland, 1974, quote p. 7, NLI, Ir 370 m 17; *Social Status in Dublin: Marriage, Mobility and First Employment*, ESRI Report, January 1973, No. 67, NLI, Ir 338 e 14; University College Dublin Department of Psychiatry, Community Development Division, *The Inner City of Dublin: Preliminary Report*, 1974, NLI, Ir 300 p 43; Lance Wright and Kenneth Browne, assisted by Peter Jones, *A Future for Dublin*, Architectural Press, 1975 (first appeared in a special issue of *The Architectural Review*, November 1974), NLI, Ir 720 p 10; *Dublin – A Living City*; An exhibition with nightly discussions at Molesworth Hall from Monday 20th November [to] Saturday 25th November 1972, Living City Group, 1972, NLI Ir 9141 p. 56. Terry Kelleher is author of *The Essential Dublin*, Gill & Macmillan, 1972, NLI, Ir 914133 k 6; and Éamonn Mac Thomáis, *Me Jewel and Darlin' Dublin*, O'Brien Press, 1974, NLI, Ir 914133 m 11.

Thursday, 30 January 1975

See also Patrick Malone, *Office Development in Dublin 1960-1990*, 1990, NLI, Ir 720 p 31(2); Frank McDonald, *The Destruction of Dublin*, op. cit.; 'Central Bank Controversy', *Plan*, Vol. 5, No. 14, December 1973/January 1974, pp. 14–15. See interviews with Sam Stephenson in the *Irish Press*, 24 April 1974, p. 3, col. 5 and *Irish Independent*, 31 January, 1975, p. 8, col. 3.

Friday, 29 October 1976

See *In Dublin*, 14–27 May 1976, p. 8; 25 June–8 July 1976; and 29 October–11 November 1976, p. 16, NLI, Ir 94133 i 2.

Saturday, 23 September 1978

See also *Wood Quay*, Friends of Medieval Dublin, 1978, NLI, 4B 1809; and Thomas F. Heffernan, *Wood Quay: The Clash over Dublin's Viking Past*, University of Texas Press, 1988, NLI, Ir 7941 h 14.

Friday, 13 October 1978

See also *Women Against Violence Against Women*, Dublin Rape Crisis Group, 1978, NLI, Ir 3991 p 25.

Thursday, 23 November 1978

See Bob Geldof, *Is That It?*, Pan Macmillan, 2005, pp. 80–132; and *In Dublin*, 18 February–3 March, 1977, NLI, Ir 94133 i 2.

Chapter 7

Wednesday, 19 March 1980

See also Patrick Brocklebank and Sinéad Moloney, *Where the Streets Have Two Names: U2 and the Dublin Music Scene, 1978–1981*, Liberties Press, 2014; *Hot Press* articles, 8–22 March 1979, p. 11; 14–28 September 1979, p. 5; 16–26 October 1979, p. 18; and 12–26 October 1979, p. 11.

Friday–Saturday, 13–14 February 1981
See also *Report of the Tribunal of Inquiry on the Fire at the Stardust, Artane, Dublin on the 14th February, 1981*, The Stationery Office, 1982, NLI, OPIE K / 129; and *Report of the Independent Examination of the Stardust Victims Committee's Case for a Reopened Inquiry into the Stardust Fire Disaster*, which can be downloaded at www.justice.ie/en/JELR/REPORT.doc/Files/REPORT.doc

Thursday, 1 October 1981
See Lorna Hogg, *A Handbook for Single Women in Ireland*, Mercier Press, 1981, NLI, 3996 h 31.

Tuesday, 9 March 1982
The description of the scene at Summerhill Parade is from an article by Colm Tóibín in *In Dublin*, 5–18 March 1982, pp. 14–18.

Tuesday, 20 September 1983
One of the earliest articles on the heroin epidemic is by Mary Raftery in *In Dublin*, 14–27 May 1982, pp. 18–24. For the first major report on Dublin's drug problem, see Geoffrey Dean, John Bradshaw and Paul Lavelle, *Drug Misuse in Ireland, 1982–1983: Investigation in a North Central Dublin Area and in Galway, Sligo and Cork*, Medico-Social Research Board, 1983. See Annual Reports on Crime, An Garda Síochána, 1978–1983, NLI, 1K 1418. For Gerry Hourigan's killing see Paul Williams, *Badfellas*, Penguin Ireland, 2011, p. 177.

January 1984
See also Andrew MacLaran (ed.), *Crisis in Dublin*, Trinity College Papers in Geography, 1991, especially P.J. Drudy, 'Demographic and Economic Change in Dublin in Recent Decades', pp. 17–25.

Monday, 23 July 1984
See also *Dublin Suburban Electrification News*, No. 1, Summer 1981, Córas Iompair Éireann.

Wednesday, 3 April 1985
See also *Eastern Regional Settlement Strategy, 2011, Main Report*, Eastern Regional Development Organisation, 1985, NLI, Ir 350 e 14.

Friday–Sunday, 7–9 February 1986
See also Deirdre Kelly, Dublin Crisis Conference Committee*, Dublin Crisis Conference (Report), 7–9 February 1986, at the Synod Hall, Christchurch Place,* Published on behalf of the conference organisers by Deirdre Kelly [et al.], 1986.

July 1987
See Roddy Doyle, *The Commitments*, King Farouk, 1987, NLI, LO 5527.

Friday, 12 February 1988
See also *Sunday Independent*, 31 January 1988, p. 17, col. 1; *Irish Independent*, 6 February 1988, p. 6, col. 1; *Irish Press*, 10 February 1988, p. 9, col. 1.

Friday, 17 June 1988
See also *Millennium Book*, Dublin Corporation, 1988, NLI, 3B 1970; and Dublin Millennium Press Cuttings, Dublin City Council Library at Pearse Street, Dublin Millennium Box 941.83.

April 1990
For a very good overview of the city and its recent developments, see Andrew MacLaran, *Dublin: The Shaping of a Capital*, Belhaven Press, 1993.

Saturday, 1 September 1990
See Frank Convery, *Air Pollution in Dublin: Some Policy Options*, Resource and Environmental Policy Centre, 1985, NLI, Ir 333 w 17.

Thursday, 19 December 1991
See also *Culture in Dublin in 1991: An* In Dublin *Guide*, NLI, Ir 914133 p 14(2); *Dublin 1991 Events*, Bord Fáilte, NLI, Ir 300 p 155 (7); *Dublin Cultural Capital 1991 Journal*, Aviary, 1991, NLI, 1A 1016.

Chapter 8

Monday, 14 February 1994

See also 'Dublin After Midnight', *In Dublin*, 28 April–11 May 1993; 'Temple Bar Supplement', *In Dublin*, 4–17 August 1993. There are particularly good articles about the new café and coffee trend: see *Irish Independent*, 25 September 1993, p. 29, col. 1; *Sunday Independent*, 23 July 1995, p. 18, col. 1; *Irish Independent*, 25 July 1995, 'Dubliners' supplement, p. 6, col. 1; *Irish Independent*, 2 December 1995, 'Weekender', p. 5, col. 1.

Wednesday, 31 August 1994

The report that is reputed to have coined the phrase 'Celtic Tiger' is Kevin Gardiner, *The Irish Economy: A Celtic Tiger?* Morgan Stanley Euroletter, 31 August 1994.

Dublin Airport

See 1985–6 Winter Timetable Dublin Airport and 1994 Winter Timetable Dublin Airport, Aer Rianta, NLI, Ir 3877 a 2.

Urban Cowboys

See *In Dublin*, 22 June—5 July 1995, p. 8.

Poverty and Economic Growth

See Tony Fahey and James Williams, 'The Spatial Distribution of Disadvantage in Ireland', in Brian Nolan, Philip J. O'Connell and Christopher T. Whelan, *Bust or Boom? The Irish Experience of Growth and Inequality*, IPA, 2000, NLI, Ir 383 b 2.

February 1998

Integrated Area Plan for O'Connell Street, February 1998, Dublin Corporation, NLI, 9B 2187.

Wednesday, 17 March 1999

See also *Irish Times*, Saturday, 16 March, p. 11, col. 1

Paul Howard

Based on personal communication with Paul Howard and 'The Miseducation of Ross O'Carroll Kelly, as told to Paul Howard', *Sunday Tribune*, 2000, NLI, 14A 1906.

November 2000

See *The Role of Dublin in Europe*, a report prepared for the Spatial Planning Unit, Dept of the Environment and Local Government, November 2000; Declan Martin, *Dublin: Fast Growth City. An Economic Profile*, Dublin Chamber of Commerce, 2000, NLI, 1B 1291; Pamela Newenham (ed.), *Silicon Docks: The Rise of Dublin as a Global Tech Hub*, NLI, 16A 1843; and *State of European Cities Report*, EU Regional Policy, April 2007.

The Dubliner: 'The Best 100 Things'

See *The Dubliner*, No. 6, July/August 2001, pp. 44–64, NLI, 1K 142.

Sunday, 8 September 2002

See also Tim Carey, *Croke Park: A History*, The Collins Press, 2004, p. 171.

2007 Names

See *Irish Babies Names* reports, Central Statistics Office.

Wednesday, 7 May 2008

See Joseph O'Connor, 'Bye Bye Celtic Tiger', *The Drivetime Diaries*, RTÉ, Audio CD, 1 October 2010.

Acknowledgements

I was writing this book in my head for years. Since sometime in late 1980s when I was standing outside O'Donoghue's pub on Merrion Row, smoking a cigarette and drinking a pint one summer Sunday afternoon. A middle-aged couple of tourists – well-dressed, tanned – asked me for directions. We got talking and when I asked where else they were going they replied County Clare. Then I heard myself saying something that I did not believe, but was saying anyway, because that's what I had heard other people say. 'Ah, that's the real Ireland.'

For me, this exchange epitomised the contradictions that existed, and still do to an extent, about Dublin's place in Irish society, about the meaning of Dublin. It is something that goes beyond the usual tension between an international city and what was, until relatively recently, a largely rural country, or between a capital and other places. And it is something that has changed dramatically over the years, as Dublin has occupied an increasingly important place in both the Irish psyche as well as how others think about Ireland.

I always felt that there was a good book still to be written about the modern city. There is no shortage of excellent autobiographies by Dubliners and many fine local histories and specialist publications. But nothing captured the evolution of the capital, its increasing importance, its characteristics and the traits that define it.

And so, one day as I was walking across the square in front of the Museum of Contemporary Art in Barcelona, one of my favourite urban spaces, watching skateboarders do their thing, I decided to write this book. Whether it has done what I intended to do is not for me to judge.

While writing books is necessarily a solitary pursuit, this could not have been done alone. Firstly, I would like to thank my mother for giving me my first introduction to the city – in many ways this book would never have been written without her. I have relied almost exclusively on printed and published material contained in Dublin's archives and libraries. In particular thanks and gratitude is owed to the National Library of Ireland, one of the most pleasant places to work, one whose collection is invaluable and whose staff are always patient and courteous. Without the Library and its collection this book, and countless others, could not have been written. Deep gratitude is also due to the National Archives, Dublin City Council's excellent Pearse Street Library, the Irish Architectural Archive and the Library of Trinity College Dublin.

I would like to thank all at Hachette Ireland, in particular Breda Purdue, Joanna Smyth and especially publisher Ciara Considine, for their professionalism, good humour, patience, sheer enthusiasm and absolute commitment to this project. Lucy Hogan gave immense help with far-reaching picture research. I am indebted to my agent Sallyanne Sweeney of Mulcahy Associates for her continuous advice and encouragement. A sincere thanks is also due to Dublin City Council and in particular Owen Keegan, Chief Executive, for supporting this project.

Special thanks to Bert Wright, Clíodhna Ni Anluain and Gerry Clabby for reading early drafts and offering very helpful advice. Thanks also to John Williams for finding me the famous report on the Celtic Tiger from 1994; Fergus Fahey for directing me to the photograph of the bicycles parked on O'Connell Street during World War II; Paul O'Kane, Director of Public Affairs for the Dublin Airport Authority; Paul Howard, Joseph O'Connor, Joe Duffy and Jim Fitzpatrick.

Finally, to all those people who have helped me enjoy and appreciate living in this city, thanks!

Tim Carey
August 2016

Permissions Acknowledgements

The author and publisher would like to thank the following for permission to use inside images/text in *Dublin Since 1922*:

Text

'Bye Bye Celtic Tiger' by Joseph O'Connor (p.293-294), by kind permission of the author; 'On Raglan Road' by Patrick Kavanagh (p.143), reprinted from *Collected Poems*, Antoinette Quinn ed., (Allen Lane, 2004), by kind permission of the Trustees of the Estate of the late Katherine B. Kavanagh, through the Jonathan Williams Literary Agency; *Invisible Cities: The New Dubliners*, Dermot Bolger ed. (p.250), by kind permission of Dermot Bolger.

Images

© Alamy: 124/Nigel J Clarke, 132 (bottom)/Photo Researchers, Inc. © The Artist's Estate, Private collection, image courtesy of Whyte's: 100. © Brian Foley, Freebird Records, Dublin: 221 (bottom). © Brian Seed: ix. © Dublin City Library and Archive: 16, 28, 31, 88, 106, 128, 170, 201, 209, 239, 246, 250, 251. © Estate of Evelyn Hofer: vi, x-xi, 187. © Fáilte Ireland Tourism Collection, image courtesy of Dublin City Library and Archive: ii. With permission of Frank McDonald: 244. © Gestalde fietsen voor het hoofdpostkantoor in Dublin, photo: Willem van de Poll, National Archives of the Netherlands/Fotocollectie Van de Poll, licence CC-BY: 132 (top), 136. © Getty Images: 2, 40, 76, 116, 152, 188, 224, 262/Design Pics/The Irish Image collection (lamppost), 9/Mondadori Portfolio, 62/ullstein bild, 95/Keystone, 115/Paul Popper/Popperfoto, 126/J.Merriman, 127, 137/David E. Scherman, 148/Tony Linck, 149/Larry Burrows,171/Daniel Farson, 176/Three Lions, 193, 195, 272/Independent News and Media, 207(bottom)/Michael Putland, 215/Paul M O'Connell, 223, 253/Tom Stoddart Archive, 227/Virginia Turbett, 254/Paul Natkin, 263/Terry Williams, 265/Alain Le Garsmeur, 270/NUTAN, 280(top)/Pallava Bagla, 291/Fran Veale, 294/Dimitar Dilkoff. © Historic England: 53, 110, 118, 166. © In Dublin magazine: 217. © Inpho.ie: 256, 257. © Ilpo Musto/Rex/Shutterstock: 268. © Irish Architectural Archive: 1, 22, 73, 192/Hugh Doran Collection. Image courtesy of Irish Architectural Archive: 42. © Irish Capuchin Archives: 18, 21, 32, 83, 113, 144, 160, 185. © irishphotoarchive.ie: 142, 151, 153, 157, 158, 165, 173 (bottom), 178, 179, 183, 186, 191, 198 (both images), 203, 204, 208, 222. © *Irish Press* (images courtesy of the National Library of Ireland): 102. © *Irish Times*: 119, 154,159, 162, 172, 205, 206, 228 (top), 260, 261, 274, 277, 284, 285 (bottom), 287, 293. © Library of Congress: 65/Street traders in Dublin, Ireland, c, 1927, image retrieved from the Library of Congress, https://www.loc.gov/item/2002707911 (Accessed May 23, 2016.), 90/Library of Congress, Prints & Photographs Division, NYWT&S Collection, reproduction number, LC-USZ62-124346. © Longreach – Jonathan McDonnell: 278. © Magnum Photos: 175/Elliott Erwitt, 231/Martin Parr, 242/Martine Franck. © Marvin Koner Archive: 168. © Maurice Craig Collection, Irish Architectural Archive: 135 (bottom). © Maxwell Photography: 233. Photo © National Gallery of Ireland: 41, 43. © National Library of Ireland: v, xii, 3, 6, 19, 24, 25, 26, 27, 29, 36-37, 38, 39, 45, 46, 47, 48, 49, 50, 52, 55, 58, 59, 64(bottom), 67, 68, 70 (bottom), 74, 77, 87 (bottom), 96, 99, 120, 121, 122, 131, 141, 150, 164, 174, 181, 189, 190, 194, 200, 202, 229, 235. © National Library of Ireland & Irish Independent: 70 (top), 72, 79, 85, 86(all images), 87(top), 89, 94, 104. © The Old Dublin Collection: 117 (image courtesy of Robert Allen Photography). © Paul Daly: 296. With permission of Paul Howard and David Gorman: 280 (bottom). With permission of Roddy Doyle: 248. © RollingNews.ie: 230. © Rose Comiskey: 234, 245. © RTÉ Archives: 163, 180, 213, 221(top), 225, 228 (bottom), 236, 238, 240, 252, 266, 271. © Sarah 777 and licensed for reuse under the Creative Commons Attribution-ShareAlike 2.0 Licence: 286. © Sean McClean and licensed for reuse under the Creative Commons Attribution-Share Alike 2.5 Generic Licence: 288. Images courtesy Special Collections and UCD Digital Library: 34, 35. Courtesy Special Collections, UC Santa Cruz, Branson DeCou Archive: 98 (both images). © Sportsfile: 283/Brendan Moran. With permission of Stephen Averill: 226 (both images). © stockcam/iStock (notepaper image). ©Thaddeus Breen/History Ireland magazine: 219. © The Dubliner, image courtesy of Trevor White/The Little Museum of Dublin: 282. © William Murphy and licensed for reuse under the Creative Commons Attribution-ShareAlike 2.0 Licence: 285 (top).

The author and publisher have endeavoured to contact all copyright holders. If any images used in this book have been reproduced without permission, we would like to rectify this in future editions and encourage owners of copyright not acknowledged to contact us at info@hbgi.ie.